DATE DUE

MAR - 7 1995	
APR 1 8 1995	
FEB - 7 1997	
MAR 2 1 1997	
APR - 4 1997	
APR 2 8 1997	
MAR 2 6 1999	
FEB 2 8 2000	
MAR 1 3 2000	
MAR 1 2 2001	
APR - 5 200	
MAR 2 5 2002	

BRODART   Cat. No. 23-221

THE
CHANGING ORDER
IN
NORTHEAST ASIA
AND THE
KOREAN PENINSULA

THE
CHANGING ORDER
IN
NORTHEAST ASIA
AND THE
KOREAN PENINSULA

Edited by

Manwoo Lee and
Richard W. Mansbach

THE INSTITUTE FOR FAR EASTERN STUDIES
KYUNGNAM UNIVERSITY
SEOUL, KOREA

DISTRIBUTED BY WESTVIEW PRESS
BOULDER•SAN FRANCISCO•OXFORD

**The Changing Order in Northeast Asia
and the Korean Peninsula**

Copyright ©1993 by IFES, Kyungnam University

Published for the IFES, Kyungnam University, 28-42
Samchung-dong, Chongro-ku, Seoul 110-230, Korea.

Printed in Seoul, Korea
by Seoul Computer Press

Distributed by Westview Press,
5500 Central Avenue, Boulder,
Colorado 80301, U.S.A.

ISBN: 0-8133-8795-7

ACKNOWLEDGMENTS

This project could never have come to fruition without the help of many people. Critical to the success of the project was the support of the Institute for Far Eastern Studies of Kyungnam University and the Korea Press Center, which sponsored the Seoul conference. We would like to thank them for their support and patience in bringing this project to a successful conclusion. Su-Hoon Lee gave his time and skills to organizing and coordinating the conference in an excellent manner. Victor Cha gave unstintingly of his time in the initial stages of corresponding with all the participants. Dave Kang, a Ph.D. candidate at U.C. Berkeley, was a great help in compiling the papers and turning them into a book. Through both his writing and his ideas, Kang offered insightful comments, criticisms, and suggestions about both the content and structure of the book. Lorraine Richey was of incalculable help in editing this book, and she deserves thanks not only for finding our numerous mistakes, but also for having the patience to correct us again and again.

Contents

Preface

The Changing Order in Northeast Asia and the Korean Peninsula grew out of a conference held in Seoul, Korea on October 29-30, 1992. This international conference, which brought together scholars and intellectuals from the United States, China, Japan, Russia, and Korea, was funded by the Korea Press Center and the Ministry of Information and organized by the Institute for Far Eastern Studies, Kyungnam University. The conference marked the highpoint of IFES's celebration of its twentieth anniversary, and as such it served as a means of reaffirming the Institute's commitment to making scholarly contributions in East Asian and international affairs research, to fostering world peace, and in promoting Korean unification.

The goal of the conference was to bring together scholars with an abiding interest and deep commitment to this region to engage in constructive dialogue about the new order in Northeast Asia, particularly the effect that Japan's ascent as an economic superpower will have on the structure of that world order, and, more specifically, how events on the Korean peninsula will affect and be affected by the changes in the region.

The issues discussed in this conference are the very issues that will confront the countries of Northeast Asia as they seek prosperity and security within this highly competitive, rapidly changing, regional context. The U.S. role in Asia, Japan's evolving economic, political, and, of most concern, military role in the region, the future of the North Korean regime and its status as a possible nuclear power, and the potential for Korean unification stand out as major topics for the conference, and they are reflected in the papers that constitute the major portion of this book.

This volume offers no reassuring consensus, but what it does present is some of the first really serious analyses of the key issues that the region will face and the alternatives available to the players in the regional game.

Manwoo Lee and
Richard W. Mansbach

CHAPTER 1

INTRODUCTION

Manwoo Lee and Richard W. Mansbach

International politics has undergone extraordinary change in the last few years. The end of the Cold War has irrevocably altered the nature of both political and economic relationships throughout the world. Although the fall of the Berlin Wall and the unification of Germany in Europe were the most visible symbols of the late 1980s, in an oblique way the end of the Cold War has affected every other region as well. Northeast Asia in particular has begun to grapple with the problems of adapting to a world in which the looming problem is no longer superpower confrontation. Even as the disintegration of communism is hailed as a great achievement for the West, this triumph has not come cheaply, nor has victory solved once and for all the critical problems of international politics.

The Cold War era, for all its tension, produced something of a division of labor among actors, with individual countries assigned well-defined roles to play. The U.S. and former Soviet Union faced each other as adversaries. Japan and Korea were the front-line of a defense against communism, and the U.S. troops in the Philippines, Korea, and Japan were there to keep the region stable both from internal and external threats. China, the balancer, could ally with the U.S. against any growth in Soviet power and ambition. The loyalties and alliances and relationships were clear and changed only slowly, if at all. In such a context, smaller powers, even though they chafed under their superpower's influence, nonetheless understood clearly their role in world politics. With bipolar confrontation came imposed stability and mutually understood, if not entirely accepted, roles.

Change has been so dramatic that, even though the seeds of the future were planted in the past, the old rules no longer apply in Northeast Asia. The U.S., China, Japan, Russia, and the two Koreas are all trying to make sense of what has taken place and what it augers for them, and are seeking to forge new rules and a new order. Northeast Asia, the most dynamic economic region and one of the most militarized regions in the world, faces the choice of creating peaceful economic and political alliances, or of sinking back into the quagmire of conflict that has been the norm for the last century. Not surprisingly, scholars concerned with Northeast Asia have attempted both to respond to and analyze the changes that are occurring. The chapters in this book are a result of a conference held in Seoul, Korea, October 29-30, 1992 in which scholars from China, Russia, Korea, Japan, and the U.S. met to evaluate the changing nature of security and economic relations in Northeast Asia.

The chapters in this book focus on the two major themes of international relations, and economic and security issues. Additionally, most of the papers look in some degree at the U.S., Japan, and North Korea. These papers are timely not only for their substantive content, but also for their use of the current literature and scholarship in the field. Although many points are addressed in this book, five key themes have emerged: the role of the U.S. in Asia, the implications of Japanese economic muscle and potential for rearmament, the problem of economic dependence, interdependence and rapidly merging economies, and the issue of Korean unification.

The Themes

As the Cold War wound down, analysts began asking whether liberalism had, in fact, won the day in international politics. Certainly Marxism was Western liberalism's most prominent opponent, but many other possibilities still exist. For example, ethnic tribalism has pulled apart Yugoslavia and Czechoslovakia and remains a significant barrier to conflict resolution in Iraq, Afghanistan, and many parts of Africa. Realizing that many intractable problems remain in the world, the U.S. has been cautious about expanding its military and political role into these areas.

One of the most important issues that this book deals with is the U.S. role in Asia. The papers converge around two questions, although their conclusions differ. First, will the U.S. remain the only superpower in the future? Second, what role can and should the U.S. play in Asia? Cold war positions, both liberal and conservative, focused on either the U.S. as imperialist or as defender of freedom. The

U.S. will play neither of those roles in the future. Instead, the U.S. must decide exactly what it would like its role in Asia to be, whether that role is to deter the North Koreans from invasion, to calm historically volatile relations between China and Japan, or to retain influence in the region, no matter what the specific problem. Finally, what price will the U.S. be willing to pay in order to remain an influential actor?

The scholars in this book differ in their conclusions about the potential role of the United States. Although none argues that the U.S. will continue to be the only superpower in the world, they disagree on the extent to which the U.S. can play a role in Asia. Some, like Melvin Gurtov, take a cautious approach, arguing that the limits of U.S. power are clear and that other nations should prepare to help themselves, because the U.S. will inevitably reduce its myriad international commitments. Although not isolating itself as it did in the nineteen-thirties, the U.S. simply does not have the resources or will to play the role of international policeman around the world. This does not mean that U.S. power will simply disappear. As Charles Doran argues, the U.S., with its NAFTA market, can remain a powerful actor in Asia.

A second concern raised in a number of papers is the traditional role of military security, in particular the focus on Japanese rearmament. How will the Japanese view their own security problem, and how will they deal with it? Can the other Asian countries, so recently rid of the specter of Japanese aggrandizement, overcome their historical fear? The question of Japanese rearmament is important, both theoretically and substantively, and leads to two important questions. First, under what conditions will an economic superpower attempt to fill a security vacuum? Although scholars have debated this question regarding Germany, theoretical work involving Asia is still in the nascent stages.[1] Given Japan's past reliance on and success with international economic relations, why would Japan see military power as a better avenue toward national security? A second question is whether the smaller states in Asia should fear Japanese rearmament. History explains why the nations in Northeast Asia are particularly sensitive about possible Japanese rearmament and its potential consequences. Of course, the raison d'être for this book is the unprecedented change in global politics, and these papers are acutely aware that reliance on history and performance may be a poor guide to the future. Particularly with regard to security matters, Japan's situation is different now than ever before.

A third major theme that arises from the papers is the serious need to consider more carefully the precise definition of what constitutes a "dependent" relationship between two countries. Although the Marxist variant of "dependency theory" has fallen into disuse, the concept remains intuitively plausible as a way of understanding international relations.[2] The problem with this concept is that a "dependent"

---

1. For example, see John Mearsheimer," Back to the Future: Instability in Europe after the Cold War," *International Security* 15:1 (Summer 1990).

2. The classic work on dependency is Raul Prebisch, *The Economic Development of Latin America and Its Principal Problems* (New York: United Nations, 1950). For an excellent critique, see Alice Amsden, "The State and Taiwan's Economic Development," in Peter B. Evans, Dieter Reuschemeyer, and Theda Skocpol, eds., *Bringing the State Back In* (Cambridge: Cambridge University Press, 1985).

or exploitative relationship is difficult to identify with any confidence.

For example, several of the scholars assume that Japan and Korea are locked in a dependent relationship, with Japan gaining more of the benefit than Korea. Hence the focus by various authors on technology transfer and other economic "aid" which, they argue, Japan *must* give to Korea to equalize this relationship. However, if we look at growth rates over the past thirty years, Korea has grown as quickly as Japan, with the bulk of technology having come from either Japan or the U.S. This being the case, there are two possible explanations: first, that without Japanese technological "interference" Korea would have grown even faster, or, second, that even "dependent" relations with Japan were better than any alternative relationship.

As the dynamic economies of Asia become increasingly open, scholars will have to pay explicit attention to exactly when a relationship is exploitative, and under what conditions. For example, Young-Kwan Yoon, relying heavily on recent discussions in the international political economy literature, claims that the gains from exchange are secondary to the distribution of those gains.[3] Suh argues that in promoting economic cooperation South Korea should only pursue trading arrangements in which the greater proportion of benefits does not accrue to the other party. Although the assumption that states are concerned about relative gains may be true, the

---

3. See Robert Powell, "Absolute and Relative Gains in International Relations Theory," *American Political Science Review* 85:4 (December 1991), and Duncan Snidal, "Relative Gains and the Pattern of International Cooperation," *American Political Science Review* 85:3 (September 1991).

Figure 1: Cooperation and Discord

State B

	Cooperate	Defect
Cooperate	A₁, A₂	B₁, B₂
State A		
Defect	C₁, C₂	D₁, D₂

yardstick that states will use to determine whether to cooperate is *not* merely the relative gains from exchange. Rather, states seek to maximize across all possible outcomes, and they will cooperate only so long as the relative gains from cooperation outweigh the relative gains from defection.

A simple example (*Figure 1*) makes the point. According to Suh, states are concerned about the relative gains of cooperation: A_1-A_2. If State A is preoccupied by relative gains, it must not maximize against its own possibilities ($A_1>D_1$?), but rather be concerned with who gains more ($A_2>A_1$?). However, even if $A_2>A_1$, State A may still decide to cooperate if $(A_2-A_1)<(D_2-D_1)$. In this case, we can see that even under putatively exploitative conditions, it may be in a state's self interest to cooperate, if the alternatives are worse.

This simple example highlights the complexity of

issues like trade and technology transfer. The authors of the essays that follow argue that we should be studying these issues and not engaging in polemics about whether Japan is exploiting Korea. Scholars should pay serious attention to the potential that trade may produce amity or friction under the conditions of a changed international order.

Another question involves the role and extent of interdependence among national economies. Generally, it is assumed that interdependence breaks down barriers among national economies. But, what is the nature of such interdependence; who is creating links with whom? Is it "states" and their national economies, or corporate actors occupying special niches in those economies? The end of the Cold War has brought to light linkages that were masked by the overpowering security concerns of nations. With the potential to be free of overarching national security concerns, attention has turned to the national economy as a source of international security. And, from a national perspective, it is unclear what maximizes economic welfare. Is neomercantilism, even though it perpetuates disequilibrium in the world trading system, the best way to promote national welfare? If so, why have so many corporations chosen to organize themselves on multinational principles? If IBM's main production and manufacturing units are located in Southeast Asia, how do investment, labor, and wages paid to IBM employees help the U.S. economy? Is Hyundai, which purchases parts from Malaysia and Singapore, and in turn exports cars to those states, a "Korean" company? Does Hyundai really care how the South Korean economy performs, or does Hyundai, as a self-interested, profit-maximizing entity, merely wish to make the most money possible, regardless of national source?

Robert Reich makes the argument that economies are not and could not remain national, and he discounts the idea of the economy as a "lifeboat."[4] However, in Asia and elsewhere the symbol of a national economy evokes strong passions, and, whatever the evidence, the concept remains important to scholars and practitioners. The evolution of business-state linkages during the next decade will have serious consequences for international politics. National security cannot be isolated from a deepening of interdependence among the Japanese, Chinese, Russian, and Korean economies.

A final issue of concern in many of the following essays is policy toward North Korea. Should Korean unification be pursued on a "two-plus-four" basis, with the involvement of North and South Korea, Japan, the U.S., China, and Russia? Or should negotiations be purely a bilateral affair? Should the Western powers attempt to bring North Korea into the community of nations by pursuing conciliation, in the hopes that North Korea will soften its stance, or should the Western powers exert additional pressure, pushing North Korea until it crumbles? These questions require more than tired analogies to Hitler and World War I—instead, the issue of policy toward North Korea requires a focus on the strategic interaction between North Korea and its leaders and the potential benefits and costs of alternative policies. In this context, Georgi Arbatov's argument that America's hawkish approach to the Soviet Union during the 1980s reinforced the resistance to change of Soviet hard-liners is very relevant.

---

4. Robert Reich, *The Work of Nations* (New York: Alfred A. Knopf, 1989).

The Papers

The essays deal with the issues described above in a variety of ways. All of the authors have a specific, substantive specialty, and they approach their concerns from unique national, ideological, and methodological perspectives. Of special interest in this book is the dialogue between Russian and Chinese and Japanese and Korean scholars. Although they never fully agree, the benefit from bringing together diverse perspectives and analytic frameworks is instructive.

Richard W. Mansbach (Chapter 2) confronts directly the argument that the U.S. is "bound to lead," as many have argued, after the Cold War victory.[5] Mansbach argues that the U.S. is almost surely in decline economically, militarily, and culturally. Soft power (culture and values and respect) may still be important components of U.S. foreign policy, but only because at one time soft power was backed up by hard power. Adjustment is inevitable for the U.S., especially when, in an unstable and uncertain world, the pretenders to the throne, Japan and Germany, demand a leadership role that is commensurate with their capabilities. Mansbach argues that even as we celebrate the burial of Marxism-Leninism, it is by no means certain that liberalism will win the day. Tribalism and ethnic violence and authoritarian experiments are equally probable prospects. The U.S., driven for half a century by the Cold War, will be both less likely to support its allies and more unpredictable. The U.S. will find itself increasingly in the role of player rather than acknowledged leader.

---

5. See, in particular, Joseph S. Nye, Jr., *Bound to Lead: The Changing Nature of American Power* (New York: Basic Books, 1990).

Regional powers like Korea may, in the short term, wish to seek security from and follow the U.S., but Mansbach predicts these smaller powers will come to recognize that they cannot rely on an endlessly willing and capable U.S. to lead the way. The specific problem for Korea is that it is in the midst of re-emerging traditional powers—Japan, China, and Russia—and perhaps Korea will emerge once again as an arena in which the larger Asian powers vie for supremacy.

Charles Doran (Chapter 3) argues that neomercantilism has worked best for countries over the last forty years, and these states are at an advantage when dealing with liberal regimes. The failure of the Uruguay Round of GATT and the emergence of the European Community has led to the NAFTA and APEC. Doran calls this "locomotive regionalism," where a large central state is the focus for much of the trade and finance in a region of states with increasingly harmonized macroeconomic and trade policies. Doran argues that this arrangement can also lead to frictions, as, for example, in trade diversion within regions, which may produce a reduction in the world volume of trade. Within this framework, Doran argues that Korea should not be worried about Japan; after all, the Japanese only want to profit as do others, and Korea is a good place for that. Although Japan may not be prepared to share all its technology with Korea, the Japanese-Korean economic relationship is, nevertheless, basically healthy. The most interesting aspect of this paper is Doran's suggestion that Korea should consider positioning itself to join the NAFTA as soon as possible. In this case, there exists a 'first-mover' advantage to joining a regime, in particular the ability to help set the rules and the agenda. Later joiners will have to take the rules as given; if Korea can join the NAFTA promptly, it might benefit greatly in the future.

Melvin Gurtov (Chapter 6) continues the discussion of the post-Cold War role of the U.S. in the same vein as Richard Mansbach. Gurtov argues that in many ways, the term "new world order" is a misnomer, for there exists a fair amount of disorder in the world. The U.S. continues to see "new world order" as meaning "we're number one," while other countries see the new order as meaning that many states, like Germany and Japan, are finally earning equality with the U.S. The problem, as Gurtov sees it, is that in matters of security, the U.S. continues to act as a world policeman, preparing to fight many wars at once, and justifying interventionism and large military defense expenditures on the basis of perceived threats. In the context of Northeast Asia, the ROK's nordpolitik and the collapse of the USSR have decisively undermined the conventional wisdom about the U.S. role in Asia. It has become clear that the U.S. is neither the only balancer in the region nor an imperialist of limitless ambition. The countries in Asia want the U.S. to remain, but more in order to keep them from falling into conflict with one another than to defend them from an external threat. The new world order has allowed two previously unthinkable possibilities to emerge—the withdrawal of U.S. troops from Korea and Korean unification.

Given all the problems in redefining security in Asia, Gurtov argues that a two-plus-four system of collective security, which explicitly includes discussion of Japan's and China's role, might be the most fruitful avenue to pursue in the future. Crisis consultations, limitations on conventional arms transfers, and other reassurance measures should be comprehensive. In particular, Gurtov wants to see Japan begin to assume some of its economic, political, and diplomatic burden in the area.

Yung-Hwan Jo (Chapter 4) analyzes the Korean and Japanese relationship and the problems in that relationship. Jo writes that cognitive dissonance characterizes the attitudes of many Japanese and Koreans. On the one hand, Koreans feel genuine bonds with the Japanese. On the other hand, many feel great hostility toward the Japanese. Studies have shown that Korean mistrust of the Japanese, however well grounded in history, has little basis in current relations. Cultural interaction will reduce the dissonance between the two countries. Although Jo takes a nuanced stance in his discussion of Japan, he dismisses the claim that Japan is intentionally perpetuating the division of Korea. Japan has little to fear from Korea, either divided or united. The problem, in Jo's eyes, is that Japan is still ambivalent about assuming leadership in Asia. Owing to the dissonance between respect and fear of Japan by her neighbors, efforts to overcome the information gap are important.

Hosup Kim (Chapter 11) also discusses Japanese-Korean relations. Kim argues that Japan and Korea will continue to enjoy good relations, even though there exist a number of impediments, such as the issue of Korean "comfort girls," and problems in trade liberalization. While North Korea and Japan continue to work toward normalization of relations, South Korea worries about North Korean military power and Japan's modernization of its Self-Defense Force. Kim would like to see Japan confront its militarist history directly, with more attention paid to the

Showa military period and to the potential that in the future, militarism could take root again. Additionally, Kim argues that without more technology transfer, trade between Japan and Korea will always be characterized by friction. The problem, according to Kim, is that Koreans blame Japan for the trade imbalance, while the Japanese blame Korea. Kim presents six Korean images of Japan—as a model worthy of emulation, a security partner, an economic partner, a competitor, an exploiter, and a threat. Kim argues that which of these images eventually becomes dominant will depend largely on how the Japanese and Koreans manage their relationship. Kim would like to see relations evolve gradually, over time, toward a more positive friendship.

Masao Okonogi (Chapter 10) analyzes the recent discussions by North Korea and Japan aimed at normalizing diplomatic relations. In thoroughly recounting these events, Okonogi contends that North Korea has been haphazardly pursuing negotiations over the last few years in response to the collapse of the socialist camp. While fearing the success of South Korea's nordpolitik and feeling increasingly isolated, North Korea, he contends, embarked upon an effort to gain some leverage for itself by initiating efforts to normalize relations with Japan. Japan, Okonogi writes, was initially surprised at the proposal to normalize relations quickly, and predictably reacted with customary caution. Although Okonogi does not speculate about the future, his discussion of the past emphasizes the role both domestic constraints and international pressures have had upon North Korean attempts to redirect foreign policy.

Young-Kwan Yoon (Chapter 5) turns his attention to recent developments in the international relations literature to buttress his discussion of international economic cooperation. As noted earlier, the promise of absolute economic gain for a country does not necessarily mean that a country will pursue it, because it may well be preoccupied with its relative gains vis-a-vis others. Yoon argues that for international economic cooperation—mainly a reduction in trade barriers—to occur, it is important to structure an arena in which the relative gains of each country will be equitable. Without such an equitable distribution, Yoon argues, the country receiving the lesser relative gain will not cooperate, and everyone will be worse off. When Yoon applies this argument to Northeast Asia, he sees an unequal distribution of gains between Japan and South Korea, with Japan gaining more of the benefit from free trade. Yoon, therefore, concludes that Korea must focus on expanding its market both at home and with North Korea in order to increase the bargaining leverage with Japan. Only in this way, Yoon argues, will free trade occur and benefit both Japan and Korea.

Georgi Arbatov (Chapter 7) argues that neither the U.S. nor the Soviet Union won the Cold War. The real winners were Germany and Japan. The two superpowers overextended themselves militarily and created serious problems for their economies. On the basis of personal observation, Arbatov argues that America's hard-line policies during the Reagan years only prolonged a repressive regime by strengthening the hand of the Soviet cold warriors. The Cold War allowed both the U.S. and USSR to pursue messianic ideological crusades and forced them to become involved in every small issue in the world, despite the marginality of many of these issues to their interests. Arbatov argues that Russia will continue to play an important role in Asia, because that vast country sits between Europe and Asia and is vitally involved in both. In addition, Russia remains a major player because it possesses nuclear weapons and still has an enormous military establishment. In line with one of the themes of the conference, Arbatov argues that the world is becoming multipolar, not unipolar. Russia will continue to look at the Pacific, but with an eye to deterrence, not expansion. For this reason, he favors confidence-building measures and regional approaches to maintaining order and peace.

Parris Chang (Chapter 8) did not participate in the conference but was asked to contribute a paper representing a Chinese point of view. He discusses both the considerations behind China's normalization of ties with South Korea and Beijing's relations with North Korea. Arguing that China's overriding foreign policy objective of the past twenty years has been the deterrence of a Soviet attack on China, Chang finds two major changes in China as central to explaining their diplomatic moves vis-a-vis South Korea. First, the attenuation of the Sino-Soviet rivalry allowed China to pursue a more adventurous foreign policy. Second, the domestic emphasis on economic development caused China to desire more foreign investment and trade. These two considerations overrode the long history of exclusive Chinese support for North Korea, leading to the normalization of ties between South Korea and China in August 1992.

Hideshi Takesada (Chapter 9) argues that the end of the Cold War has led to renewed regional conflicts and power vacuums. Takesada argues that, despite the reasons for concern that Japan seeks to rearm — among them the growing defense budget, the dispatch of troops to Cambodia, and increased conservatism in Japanese politics—these fears are baseless. He suggests that Japanese security policy is purely defensive in nature, with the sole purpose of repelling. The U.S.-Japan defense treaty remains the cornerstone of Tokyo's security policy, and there are no plans to significantly reduce the American troop presence in Japan anytime soon.

Turning our attention to the problem of North Korea, Byung-joon Ahn (Chapter 13) argues that rather than pursuing national goals of aggrandizement and communization of the South, North Korea is actually engaged in regime survival. Focusing on the difficult crises that North Korea faces in almost every aspect of national policy, Ahn observes that North Korea is on the defensive both for regime survival and national goals. Indeed, North Korea is making a significant change in its foreign policy by pursuing normalization with the U.S. and Japan. Evidence of these changes comes from North Korea's recent acceptance of IAEA inspections of nuclear facilities and changing attitudes toward the U.S.; additionally, high-level talks are being pursued with South Korea. North Korea's pursuit of nuclear weapons is the key obstacle to any real thaw in relations and, therefore, hinders regime survival at home and economic cooperation abroad. As a result, Ahn argues that South Korea ought to seek gradual change in North Korea, not "messy, quick change." By using a mix of positive and negative incentives, South Korea, Japan, and the U.S. should attempt to manage very carefully the transition of North Korea from the status of international pariah to that of contributing member of the international community. Only then can the goal of unification be effectively pursued.

Jae Jean Suh (Chapter 12) also concludes that North Korea is not about to collapse in the near future. Suh focuses on the social and political factors that militate against a rapid collapse, namely, the Communist Party remains securely in place, there are no critical ethnic cleavages, and the army remains relatively coherent and motivated. However, Suh argues that there does exist potential for change. Like Ahn, Suh writes that North Korea is pursuing dual policies—domestic political stability and economic growth through the creation of export industries and the opening of home markets to foreign investment. At the same time, North Korea is pursuing better relations with South Korea. Although at the present time North Korea has no plans to liberalize its economic system in the manner of China, some reform will be necessary. Suh argues that, if the program of gradual liberal reform fails, the possibility for rapid unification will increase. If liberalization succeeds and North Korea can strengthen its economy, there will be a greater prospect for extended South-North Korean coexistence.

Summary

These essays that follow are among the first to consider the changing international order in Northeast Asia. The issues they cover are both complex and important for both academic and practical reasons. Although the future order in Northeast Asia is still being shaped and there remain significant difficulties that the interested parties must solve, the overall prospects for Asia are brighter than they have been for many years. The U.S. should continue to focus on the region for both its own interests and for helping to mitigate regional tensions. The authors generally agree that greater Japanese involvement in international affairs will be a positive factor, that China and Russia have begun the slow process of institutionalizing reform, and that the possibilities for tension reduction on the Korean peninsula are brighter than at any time since the Korean War. In both economic and military affairs, the region has changed forever, and for the better.

CHAPTER 2

THE NEW ORDER IN NORTHEAST ASIA: A THEORETICAL OVERVIEW

Richard W. Mansbach

The end of the Cold War will provide a rigorous test as to whether a major global transition can take place in orderly fashion. Time will also resolve the question of whether the end of the East-West conflict marks the onset of a new and triumphant age of American hegemony and the spread of its ideological counterpart— political and economic liberalism—or the onset of merely a brief "unipolar moment" followed by the precipitous decline of the second superpower and the emergence of new global leaders and their preferred ideologies. The difficulty in determining the shape of the so-called "new order" is complicated by the fact that only in military affairs can we speak of unipolarity. In economic affairs, at least three global centers exist, and in political affairs, influence is even more diffuse. In no region will the test of adjusting to dramatically changed conditions prove more challenging than in Northeast Asia, an area that is home to a number of the likely contestants for future global hegemony.[1]

This region is the site of the world's most dynamic economic experiments and will be the source of much of the capital and technology necessary to keep the global economic system afloat in the coming decades. One optimistic scenario sees the wedding of this dynamism to a resurgent America and the cementing of a Pacific partnership based on open markets and political democracy. Whether this is a new incarnation of liberal progressive idealism or a realistic prospect remains unclear.[2] After all, Northeast Asia is also home to simmering nationalist ambitions and revanchist sentiments that will menace regional and global peace and stability. It would be perilous indeed to predict that we will "live happily ever after" in the face of omens like spiraling U.S. and Japanese "bashing" and stereotyping of one another, Chinese pursuit of superpower status, continuing Russian-Japanese suspicion, and all the accidents and foibles to which leaders and their plans are prey.

The Changing Global Equation

For countries like Korea, making the correct guess could be critical to future security and prosperity. And, as Korea inevitably moves toward reunification, it will be difficult to postpone designing policies that will either reinforce and stabilize the long-term and

1. See Byung-joon Ahn, "Strategic Trends in East Asia," *The Pacific Review*, 4:2 (1991), pp. 109-115.
2. See Takashi Inoguchi, "Shaping and Sharing Pacific Dynamism," *The Annals*, No. 303 (September 1989), pp. 46-55.

mutually rewarding link to Washington or move closer to the orbit of one of America's likely competitors, especially Japan and/or China. If, as Francis Fukuyama believes, we have reached "the end of history"[3] and are at the threshold of the globalization of Western liberalism, then one should seek to keep ties with Washington in good repair. If America's era of ascendancy is coming to an end, it would be foolish to wait too long before thinking of future alternatives. One paradox is that the decision that countries like Korea make and the bets they place will contribute importantly to the very process that they are seeking to predict.

In a general sense, Western power and Western ideas have been diffusing outward since the fifteenth century. Western technology, especially military capability, permitted imperial and colonial expansion that, if we regard the United States as the legitimate successor of its European cousins, has continued until recent years. American hegemony, which was neither desired nor sought, was the consequence of two world wars which produced the exhaustion of Britain and France and rebuffed the challenges of Germany and Japan. The economic bases of that hegemony were in place by the late nineteenth century and became apparent in the early decades of the twentieth century.

With the demise of the Hapsburgs and Ottomans, the creaky Russian empire was the last of its ilk and was rescued only temporarily from the same fate by Lenin and the Bolsheviks. The multinational and bureaucratic Soviet bloc, which was built on insub-

---

3. Francis Fukuyama, *The End of History and the Last Man* (New York: Free Press, 1992).

stantial economic and social foundations, was largely based on military power and ideological fervor. The two world wars sufficiently enfeebled Britain, France, and Holland and stimulated the nationalist movements that brought an end to the remaining European empires.

Inevitably, the outward movement of Western power was accompanied or followed by a diffusion of ideas and culture, the most prominent of which were probably the concepts of territorial nationalism and liberal ideology. By liberal ideology I am referring to a broad cluster of norms and institutions, including "individual rights," "private property," "free trade and markets," "democracy and limited government," that have their roots in the eighteenth century European Enlightenment and that are reflected in documents as different as the United Nations Charter and the Japanese Constitution. The triumph of liberalism, with its naive faith that harmony will inevitably flow from adherence to its simple principles, was by no means peaceful. Its victory required a ferocious series of wars in early eighteenth-century Europe, two world wars, and a Cold War (interspersed with a number of smaller hot wars).

As scholars such as Paul Kennedy, Robert Gilpin, and Charles Doran have persuasively argued,[4] economic performance and political influence are intimately related. In Gilpin's words:

---

4. Paul Kennedy, *The Rise and Fall of the Great Powers; Economic Change and Military Conflict From 1500 to 2000* (New York: Random House, 1987); Robert Gilpin, *War and Change in World Politics* (Cambridge: Cambridge University Press, 1981); and Charles F. Doran, *Systems in Crisis: New Imperatives of High Politics at Century's End* (Cambridge: Cambridge University Press, 1991).

The legitimacy of the "right to rule" on the part of a great power may be said to rest on three factors. First, it is based on its victory in the last hegemonic war and its demonstrated ability to enforce its frequently accepted order or international security. Third, the position of the dominant power may be supported by ideological, religious, or other values common to a set of states.[5]

And, notwithstanding the "free-trade" norm and the accompanying rhetoric of the postwar international trade regime, history, both distant and recent, clearly reveals that governments understand this and interpret the rules of the game accordingly. Mercantilism has never entirely ceded the field to the liberal ideal of free trade, and few politicians have ever accepted the liberal assumption that the spheres of politics and economics can be isolated from one another.[6] One noted economist frames the issue well:

> For economists trained in the conventional neoclassical tradition, the subject of international trade is inherently frustrating. On the one hand, we have our theory, descended from Adam Smith and David Ricardo, which stresses all the benefits of open markets and unrestricted exchange between nations based on underlying differences where forces of mercantilism and protection always seem rampant if not wholly dominant. Rarely in the economics profession do we encounter greater dissonance between what we are taught in principle and what we observe in practice. And try as we might to find logical reasons for all this in the tenets of our own dis-

5. Robert Gilpin, *War and Change in World Politics*, p. 34.

6. See James R. Kurth, "The Pacific Basin versus the Atlantic Alliance: Two Paradigms of International Relations," *The Annals*, vol. 505 (September 1989), pp. 31-45 for the argument that the mercantilist spirit is alive and well in the Pacific Basin, especially in Japan.

cipline, ultimately we are tempted simply to throw up our hands and proclaim: "It's all politics!"[7]

If we focus on economic trends and accept the idea that future global politics will be in the hands of what Richard Rosecrance calls the "trading state,"[8] we are forced to conclude that the brief era of American hegemony is coming to an end. The collapse of the "Evil Empire" disguised the long-term erosion of America's hegemonic status. This erosion is by no means obvious, punctuated as it has been by periods of listless political leadership and retreat (for example, the post-Vietnam years) and explosive spasms of foreign interventionism (for example, the Persian Gulf War).

The prominent Harvard political scientist Joseph Nye has vigorously denied the "American decline" thesis by arguing that what we see is really the "vanishing World War II effect," that is, the natural and inevitable ebbing of America's astonishing and abnormal dominance of global affairs in 1945.[9] Claims about America's imminent decline, he declares, really hide the key problem, which is a momentary loss of self-confidence and will to act. And, he continues, even if there is some relative economic decline, this is more than compensated by America's dominance of "soft power resources—cultural attraction, ideology, and international institutions."[10] However, as we shall

---

7. Benjamin J. Cohen, "The Political Economy of International Trade," *International Organization*, 44:2 (Spring 1990), pp. 261-262.

8. Richard N. Rosecrance, *The Rise of the Trading State* (New York: Basic Books, 1986).

9. Joseph S. Nye, Jr., *Bound To Lead: The Changing Nature of American Power* (New York: Basic Books, 1990), p. 72.

10. *Ibid.*, p. 188.

see later, "soft power" is likely to outlast "hard power"
but, as Great Britain discovered, only for a limited
period of time.

Nye's analysis is suggestive for what it omits. He
concludes that:

> These measurable dimensions of the current distribu-
> tion of power clearly show that only one country ranks
> above the others on all... dimensions... the United
> States. Japan and Europe are not in the top rank in
> basic and military resources; China is not the top rank
> in economic and technological power resources; and the
> Soviet Union is a dubious contender in technological
> resources.[11]

Yet it is increasingly clear that economic and technological resources are likely to prove increasingly
decisive in the future. Ultimately, they can be transformed into military and ideological clout, not vice
versa.

Even more important, Nye seems preoccupied by
absolute power at the expense of *relative* power
shifts. Even as America's absolute power continues
to rise, its relative share of global capabilities, especially though not solely economic, is declining. Nye's
own data, for example, reveals that the U.S. export
share of techonology-intensive products declined
from 27% in 1970 to under 21% in 1986, while
Japan's rose from under 11% to almost 20%.[12] The
major arms control agreements between the United
States and Soviet Union and domestic pressure on
Washington to cut defense budgets will almost surely
produce an even more precipitous decline in America's relative share of military resources. Yet, as

---

11. *Ibid.*, p. 110.
12. *Ibid.*, p. 77.

Charles Doran argues, it is relative power that counts, and the United States is well past its peak, and its share continues to decline:

> Analysis of the *full dynamic* of the state power cycle... is required for understanding the dynamic of international relations.... The rise of a state must be viewed as non-linear "logistic" growth which itself ultimately feels the constraint of an upper asymptote resulting from the limited number of systemic shares. The natural constraints on a state's relative growth limit or stimulate its absolute growth.... Relative and absolute change often contain conflicting messages, and ... these confusions hinder efforts to assess economic and strategic variables in historical interpretation and in the formulation of current policy.[13]

America's decline is not inevitable, but is is probable. Washington's difficulty in reversing economic trends is well documented and is the topic of increasingly acrimonious U.S.-Japanese negotiations—lagging savings and investment, mountains of debt and growing budgetary deficits, uncontrolled and uncontrollable entitlements, eroding infrastructure, racial strife, and a failing educational system.[14] Nye's hypothesis about insufficient will is poignant in this respect. Whatever the virtue of his argument, it is difficult to imagine an American politician willing or able to reverse American priorities sufficiently to reverse these trends.

---

13. Charles f. Doran, *Systems in Crisis*, p. 20. Emphasis in original. This volume is a major contribution to our understanding of the power cycle and the phenomenon of power transition.

14. See, for example, David P. Calleo, *The Bankrupting of America: How the Federal Budget is Improverishing the Nation* (New York: Morrow, 1992).

Pretenders for the Mantle of Hegemony

What will life be like "after hegemony?" An optimistic view is that global regimes, including an open trading system, will persist owing to the benefits they provide actors.[15] Perhaps the fear of coming instability will compel major actors to cooperate and to resuscitate institutions like the United Nations. A less benign prospect, however, is the emergence of rival trading blocs in Asia, Europe, and North America, perhaps with military counterparts, each led by a regional power that is incapable of claiming the mantle of global hegemony.

Key economic players in the New World Order are likely to be Japan and its trading partners in East and Southeast Asia and Germany and its partners in the European Community (EC). "The next stage of history," declares James Kurth, "will involve a return to an era when Germany and Japan were leading powers and Mitteleuropa and East Asia leading regions of the World... ."[16] Germany's effort to gain a "place in the sun" and challenge Britain and France for world leadership in two world wars seems, finally, to have produced a society with deeply democratic roots. National reunification has made Berlin once more the key weight on the European scales. Economic integration has gone just about as far as it can, and Europe may be on the verge of a great adventure in social, political, and military coordina-

---

15. Robert O, Keohane, *Beyond Hegemony: Cooperation and Discord in the World Political Economy* (Princeton: Princeton University Press, 1984).

16. See James R. Kurth, "Things to Come: The Shape of the New World Order," *The National Interest*, No. 24 (Summer 1991), pp. 3-12.

tion. If this, in fact, takes place, Germany will be the engine of a great economic machine on which Eastern Europe and possibly Russia as well will depend. Other potential contenders, based on military or ideological influence, include a possible Islamic grouping with countries like Iran and Pakistan at its core, or an economic and military union revolving around Russia and its neighbors.

From the perspective of this region, as well as global politics more generally, Japan and China will surely be contenders for hegemonial patrimony. The United States and Russia will continue to be key players regionally and globally. History, geography, and, most importantly, trends in economic, militiary, and political influence, all conspire to give confidence in these predictions. And, it is important to recognize that America's postwar dominance in Northeast Asia, though justified as a deterrent to Soviet ambition, had the equally important function of keeping apart the traditional regional rivals—Russia, Japan, and China. Tokyo and Beijing are already aware that America's retreat will remove the buffer that stands between them and that there is no apparent successor to play this role. Korea is fated again, whether it wishes to or not, to be wooed and coveted by its neighbors.

Japan has begun to sense its destiny. Its militant effort to use the power developed during the Meiji Restoration to force its way to the top of the global hierarchy ended in disaster, but the trauma of that defeat is quickly fading. Its overseas investment and economic assistance programs have grown dramatically in recent years. Its willingness to provide financial support for America's crusade against Saddam Hussein underscored both Tokyo's search for a greater role and America's economic feebleness. Japanese citizens are increasingly active in international organizations, and Japan's recent interpretation of its constitution to allow the dispatch of troops to serve the United Nations in Cambodia may usher in a new era.[17]

Whatever the shape of things to come, China will be a key factor. Although it will take a long time for Beijing to become an economic superpower, its immense population, historical self-consciousness and sense of destiny, military power, and rapid economic growth will make it a formidable competitor. In the words of Paul Kennedy, "it is only a matter of time."[18] What makes prognostication more difficult is that contemporary China is genuinely schizophrenic. On the one hand, ambitious market reforms have created a boom economy, at least for certain regions and economic sectors. On the other hand, Beijing's powerful octogenarians remain unable to reconcile economic growth through a free market with stultifying political authoritarianism and outmoded Stalinist dogma. This contradiction will, without a shadow of a doubt, intensify in coming years.

We can be confident that the world is in the midst of a major power transition and, inevitably, a major revision of habits and rules. And even as we celebrate the burial of Marxism-Leninism, we have no cause to assume that the triumph of liberalism is more than a passing phenomenon. A return to tribalism characterized parts of Africa, and Islamic fundamentalism is anathema to liberal and democratic traditions. One

17. See, for example, Sadako Ogata, "The Changing Role of Japan in the United Nations," *Journal of International Affairs*, 37:1 (Summer 1983).

18. Paul Kennedy, *The Rise and Fall of the Great Powers*, p. 458.

should not be deceived by the rush to adopt democratic institutions and rhetoric in Eastern Europe and elsewhere by societies in which liberalism has only very shallow roots. The bloody power of nationalism on human imagination is amply reflected in the former Yugoslavia and Soviet Union.[19] Those who will probably claim the mantle of hegemony have no wish to share the Yugoslav or Soviet experience, and have very different historical and philosophical touchstones than the European heirs of the Enlightenment. Few have reason to feel warmly toward the Western societies that most vigorously espouse liberal domestic and international institutions and policies or to see utility for them in such institutions and policies. In addition, whether looked at from the perspective of economic growth or political stability, the liberal democracies may not, at a distance, appear to be attractive models.

China is, of course, very much in mind in this context. There is no reason to believe that those who will assume the reins of power in Beijing as the current generation of leaders passes will be "liberal" or "democratic" as we understand those concepts. They will recognize that Marxism-Leninism is bankrupt, but many will probably look for guidance to non-liberal alternatives, such as imperial tradition, an inherited sense of national superiority, a love-hate relationship with the West, and clear regional aspirations. Other than material prosperity and high technology, there may be little in what the West offers of interest to up-coming Chinese or other Third World

---

19. John J. Mearsheimer, arguing from a European context, makes much the same claim. Mearsheimer, "Back to the Future: Instability in Europe After the Cold War," *International Security*, 15:1 (Summer 1990), pp. 5-56.

leaders. Recent noises of approbation from Beijing about the governing style and philosophy of Singapore's Lee Kuan Yew suggest interest in a contemporary mandarinate with a hybrid combination of benevolent despotism, corporate politics, and free enterprise.[20]

America and The End of the Cold War

For almost a half century, American foreign and domestic policy was a captive of Cold War imperatives. Although policy was conditioned by a host of factors both within and without the United States, it had to be filtered through the Cold War prism and legitimized in terms of its impact on the "Great Game." Of course, bureaucratic, economic, and domestic political factors were important in shaping American defense budgets and the weapons systems they provided; but, ultimately, those budgets had to find justification and political support in a Soviet "threat" and in fear of the "Evil Empire."[21] Similarly, amounts and targets of foreign aid might reflect the clout of

---

20. Arguing along similar lines, Donald J. Puchaia describes what is emerging in China as "a form of developmentalistic fascism." "Cultural Diversity, Conflict and Cooperation in the Post-Cold War World," paper delivered at the 88th Annual Meeting of the American Political Science Association (Chicago), September 3-6, 1992, p. 32.

21. Military budgets in the United States are determined in a complex and highly political process. Nevertheless, one could reasonably predict the absolute size and direction of such budgets (with an appropriate lag) by observing the Soviet military budget (or at least CIA estimates of that budget). For this reason, some have argued that U.S. military budgets "were made in Moscow." It was almost certainly the case that Soviet military planners used their American counterparts in the same manner.

ethnic lobbies and thereby mirror electoral realities, but the foreign aid program could scarcely have been sustained in the absence of the justification provided by putative Soviet threats.[22]

The sudden collapse of the demonized USSR has removed the rudder of the Cold War, not only by altering the external realities that the United States must confront, but also by dramatically changing the relative influence of different domestic factors and the overall relationship between the international and domestic realms. From 1948, for instance, American presidential elections were inevitably bound up with Cold War issues—"the loss of China," "failure to win in Korea," "Castro's communism off the coast of Florida," "the endless war in Vietnam."[23]

All this has changed, and, for the next few years, American foreign policy is likely to be less predictable (and possibly more dangerous) than at any time since World War II. As it is, the Bush Administration has largely "reacted" to events during the last few years, and, as witnessed by policies such as that intended to maintain Iraqi territorial integrity and maintain Baghdad as a "balancer" against Iran, has failed to understand how far beyond the Westphalian world global politics has moved. A Clinton presidency promises a more rapid scaling down of American

---

22. Whatever the mix of factors behind American foreign assistance programs, humanitarianism did not rank high. Leading recipients were virtually never among the poorest countries, however one measures poverty.

23. This meant that it was extremely difficult for Moscow to deal with Washington during an election year. With few exceptions (e.g., George McGovern), candidates sought to depict themselves as "hard-liners" and "hawks"; fortunately, winners routinely assume more moderate positions after the election.

commitments overseas, including Asia, and, at least, a partial return to the less realpolitik rhetoric and style of the Carter years.

In the near future, American leaders (whether Republican or Democratic) will be seeking new moorings in an effort to discern new norms and cues in the external realm. Republicans will no longer enjoy the advantage of looking "strong on defense," and Democrats will no longer have to prove their anti-communist credentials. The disappearance of the Cold War has already enhanced the relative impact of domestic factors on American foreign policy. Previously, domestic policy was often shaped to enhance America's ability to wage "cold war." In the coming years, that equation will be reversed; foreign policy decisions will be taken more frequently in order to enhance domestic interest.

As long as a Soviet "threat" lurked just over the horizon, an elite foreign policy consensus (though muzzled since Vietnam) assured continuity from administration to administration by demanding that "politics stop at the water's edge." The Cold War provided a number of general, largely nonpartisan, axioms:[24] (a) The United States should negotiate from "positions of strength;" (b) American involvement must be global and sustained;[25] (c) domestic impera-

---

24. These axioms were, of course, the product of an earlier debate over foreign policy that had effectively ceased with bipartisan measures such as the National Security Act (1947), the Marshall Plan (1947), and NATO (1949) to cope with postwar crisis.

25. There were, of course, significant differences over the particular meaning of this axiom which came to a head during the Vietnam War. However, there was never a question of retreating from responsibilities, as had occurred in 1919, or of abandoning core allies.

tives must yield pride of place to the overriding need for security from the Soviet threat,[26] and (d) the Cold War was not only a politico-military contest, but one between competing ways of life as well. Indeed, the last of these effectively precluded consideration of a left-wing or "socialist" agenda for confronting America's domestic problems.

Together, these axioms constituted a general but consensual notion of "national interest" that, though unable to provide specific policy guidelines, placed limits on what policies were permissible. They made it difficult for American politicians to force a reluctant "ally" to "shape up" by democratizing, reining in corruption, rationalizing economic policies, or curbing human rights abuses lest the "friendly" regime collapse or the country fall prey to communism.[27] They also effectively precluded responding to domestic pressures in ways that were perceived as alienating important American allies.[28]

The diffuse threats to American interests that have

---

26. It is for this reason that domestic experiments such as Harry Truman's commitment to full employment and Lyndon Johnson's "Great Society" were abandoned in the face of rising international tension.

27. The list of authoritarian regimes that American administrations supported for fear that they would be "lost" to communism is lengthy indeed—the Chiang Kai-shek regime in China and then Taiwan, the Rhee government in South Korea, Suharto in Indonesia, Franco in Spain, Salazar in Portugal, Mobuto in Zaire, the Shah in Iran, Haile Selassie in Ethiopia, the "generals" in Greece, Batista in Cuba, and innumerable short-lived governments in South Vietnam, to name a few.

28. Washington's failure, for example, to pressure Turkish withdrawal from Cyprus in the face of agitation from the large American Greek community, or to act early and vigorously against South African apartheid illustrate the primacy accorded the foreign realm.

replaced the USSR cannot be trotted out to temper domestic pressures for adopting particular foreign policy measures. In the absence of a new "threat" that can capture the imagination of large numbers of Americans, the American public will increasingly ignore foreign policy issues. As the "audience" shrinks, bureaucracies will be increasingly responsive to interest group politics, and those that can make a case that they are most "affected" will enjoy the greatest de facto influence on particular issues. In consequence, foreign policy will be designed to satisfy particular sub-groups.

Under these conditions, it will become increasingly difficult to curb protectionism aimed at Western Europe, Japan, or the newly industrializing countries (NICs) by reference to their critical roles as American allies; instead, it will be necessary to mobilize other domestic constituencies that might be harmed by such protectionism. Thus, the states of Washington and California, which are home to key, high-technology export industries, are enrolled in efforts to combat the rising protectionist sentiment in "Rust Belt" states (like Michigan and Pennsylvania) and in industries (e.g., automobiles). For countries like Korea, the absence of a natural lobby in the United States poses special problems of access.

As new issues come to dominate Washington's foreign policy agenda, there will be a marked shift in the Washington balance-of-power among players. The "traditional" foreign policy brokers—the State and Defense Departments, the CIA, and the like—will be hard pressed to defend their prerogatives (and their budgets). Defense will be pressured in two ways. In the first place, inflated public expectations of a "peace dividend" will sorely test the military's ability to defend itself against domestic assault. A more difficult challenge, however, will be posed by the Pentagon's need for a coherent and persuasive global strategy to justify large budgets.[29] It is not that there is a shortage of threats to American interests so much as these threats are diverse and not amenable to a single, attractive, strategic idea like "containment."

The Changing Imperatives of Global Politics

What the collapse of the Soviet Union and bloc may disguise, at least in the short term, is the relative decline of the United States as well. This decline augurs a diminishing ability on the part of the United States to determine global outcomes and a greater reluctance to shoulder global burdens. Even more important, however, is that the end of the Cold War removes the key physical and psychological constraint upon important American allies to coordinate policies and interests with Washington. For over forty years, fear of American withdrawal and/or Soviet political[30] and military pressure provided a strong discipline to the behavior of Germany, Japan, and others. The end of this discipline, combined with the continued accretion of economic and military assets by America's allies, is almost certain to produce greater political assertiveness on their part.

---

29. Recent "leaks" of a Pentagon strategic plan to perpetuate *pax Americana* were greeted with derision, and the idea was subsequently withdrawn. Clearly the colonels will have to go back to their drawing boards.

30. The metaphor of "Finlandization" expresses the nature of his fear.

Members of the former "free world" coalition will increasingly assert traditional interests that may or may not be compatible with American preferences. A united Germany—relieved of the threat from the East and having achieved its most prominent postwar priority—has already taken steps toward restoring its historic economic and political influence in central Europe and Russia.[31] This action has already renewed the historical anxieties of former German adversaries and has slowed the drive toward a united Europe. Equally significant is the intensification of Japanese nationalism, repressed for decades by reliance on American military might. Japanese economic ambitions and a growing willingness to assert political independence are likely to be wedded in its policies toward China, Russia, and Southeast Asia.

The assertiveness of powerful American friends, combined with reduced overall threat perception, will likely reduce American inhibitions about pursuing policies that conflict with those of allies and intensify pressures to reduce the highly visible (and expensive) American presence in Europe and Asia. Indeed, a race is already on to withdraw American forces from Europe, South Korea, and Japan—a development that most mainstream American politicans would have regarded as unthinkable only a few years ago.[32] Such withdrawal will intensify allied assertiveness,

---

31. The choice of Berlin as capital is highly symbolic in this regard, as is the increasingly independent German policy toward the fragments of what had been Yugoslavia.

32. It was routine for the administrations simultaneously to paint the allies' contribution to the common defense to Congress as generous in order to contain pressures to reduce the U.S. overseas commitments, while arguing with allies that they were not contributing enough.

which will, in turn, hasten the withdrawal. Some
measure of Japanese rearmament (until the end of
the Cold War, an American objective) and the growing
willingness of Germany and Japan to utilize their
power assets (including military), at least regionally,
will intensify the cycle. In the short term, this will
lead to a peculiar situation in which Washington will
bring pressure on allies to do more for themselves
(as it did during the Persian Gulf War); and if they
do, that very behavior will increase American sentiment to reduce overseas commitments further.

As ties between the United States and its allies
erode, another consequence of the end of the Cold
War is likely to become visible. In the short run,
regional powers like Korea and Syria are likely to perceive themselves as more dependent on the single,
remaining superpower, but this perception will then
decline as they recognize the long-term erosion of the
American position and the growth of alternative centers of influence that they can play off against one
another. As a result, the recent willingness of gover-
ments like those of Syria, India, Pakistan, and Vietnam to dance to Washington's tune is likely to be
short-lived, even while creating potentially dangerous
illusions of omnipotence in Washington.[33]

During the Cold War, the United States and Soviet
Union competed with each other in most regions and
adopted local clients, like North and South Korea, to
act as regional surrogates. Such clients, whatever
their public professions regarding "communism" or

---

33. The willingness of the Philippines to sever ties with the United States is something of an anomaly in this regard and can only
be explained by reference to features of their long and sometimes
tumultuous historical relationship.

"capitalism," used their superpower relationship to pursue their own interests. For the most part, however, Washington and Moscow kept clients on a short leash. The superpowers are no longer available to restrain former clients, and those, in turn, are increasingly anxious about a world without a patron's protection. A number of alternatives are available to them, the most dangerous of which is the acquisition of nuclear weapons. The frantic scramble of Iraq, Iran, North Korea, and Pakistan "to go nuclear" makes it possible to conjure up some frightening scenarios. The long term consequence of the end of the Cold War, then, may be to reduce the ability of *anyone* to channel and control regional conflicts.

Alternatives and Choices

The end of the Cold War has made international politics more complex than in previous decades. Complexity is dangerous because it taxes the ability of leaders to understand what is going on and produces anxiety by reducing predictability. In the coming years, foreign policy behavior—whether in Japan, China, or the United States—will surely reflect all the uncertainties and anxieties that accompany an era of rapid change. In the United States, for example, the seductive isolationist message of Patrick Buchanan and his ilk will collide with the ambitious globalism of internationalists who wish to maintain the illusion of unipolarity. It is highly improbable that any major country will retreat into the sort of isolationism that characterized U.S. policy after 1919. The "lessons" of that era have been learned (though not necessarily correctly). More importantly, Americans, Japanese,

Koreans, and even Chinese are now so deeply enmeshed in world trade and finance that there exists in each a strong constituency for "internationalism" that was not present after World War I.

For the single remaining superpower, the real question is the *extent* and *nature* of involvement in world politics in the absence of a "Red Menace" to provide cues. The answer is still unclear, not so much because of the vagaries of electoral politics in the United States, but because external and internal factors pull in different directions. On the one hand, the collapse of the Soviet Union has removed the only military counterweight to American unilateralism. Although the Cold War competition induced each superpower to involve itself in issues merely because of the involvement of the other, that joint presence produced caution on the part of both. Mutual caution was especially evident in the years after the Cuban Missile Crisis (1962), as both sides sought to avoid triggering dangerous escalatory spirals. It was for this reason, too, that both sides constrained the behavior of regional clients.

There is already evidence, however, that the elimination of the USSR may have reduced Washington's self-restraint. The significant upsurge in American activity througout the Middle East may be a harbinger of things to come. Washington is now apparently willing to twist arms in ways it would not have in earlier years—pressuring allies to contribute to the Gulf War, using strong-arm tactics against Israel, continuing to intervene in Iraq, and stationing troops in the Gulf region. No longer preoccupied by fear of Soviet intervention or requests for Soviet support, the United States has resorted to blunter tactics than in the past in relations with countries such as Pakistan, the Philippines, and Zaire. There is also less reluctance to be assertive in relations with Western Europe and Japan, and, as recognition of decline sets in, there will be a temptation to try to reverse it. There is, then, a risk of serious over-extension and, with it, a heightened prospect of failure and disillusionment because America's relative capabilities are diminishing, the most important problems in global politics can not be resolved by using blunt instruments, and a clear foe upon which to focus efforts is absent.

Happily, the inversion of the relationship between domestic and foreign policy in the United States may tug in the other direction, helping to limit adventurism. The American public will be reluctant to embark on foreign adventures in the absence of a coherent ideological theme of the sort which "anti-communism" provided. This reluctance will be reinforced by serious economic constraints, enormous budget deficits, and a growing need for investment in America's domestic infrastructure. It will take time for the balance between domestic and international realms in the United States to be restored; and, until it is, American foreign policy will lack continuity and will be disturbingly unpredictable.

Northeast Asia and The Korean Dilemma

For Korea and other regional powers, unanswered questions, such as whether or not the United States is in decline, are neither trivial nor academic. Indeed, the prosperity and perhaps even the survival of countries like Korea depend heavily on guessing well and accurately. A wrong guess will have the sort of outcome for the country that Germany's wager on Austria-Hungary had for Berlin in World War I. Like China, Korea is also approaching a crucial moment in its internal evolution, a moment that will arrive with reunification. Which model will it choose for domestic development? Will the stirrings of democratic liberalism yield pride of place to traditional nationalism and authoritarianism? Clearly, the answer to this question is connected to Korea's choice of external allies and models.

Korea, always a geopolitical stake in the China-Japan-Russia triangle, will be significantly more important in the future owing to its rising status in the international economic order. The paradox is that Korea's rapidly growing economic and political (and potentially military) capabilities simultaneously provide the means to maintain independence while making it a greater prize in any contest that might involve its larger neighbors. As in the past, America's distance from the Korean peninsula and, therefore, its inability to exercise dominion make it a desirable partner and protector, but, as Chung-in Moon so felicitousy puts the question: "Can South Korea continue to enjoy free-riding in an age of waning U.S. hegemony?"[34] If weakness and an absence of will remove the American shield, which exists, after all, and is workable only because of the American presence in Japan, Korea will have the unenviable task of maintaining its autonomy among a number of suspicious and potentially predatory regional powers.

---

34. Chung-in Moon, "Between Supporting and Spoiling: Military Alliance and Economic Competition Between the United States and South Korea," Miles Kahler ed., *Beyond the Cold War in the Pacific,* IGCC Studies in Conflict and Cooperation Vol. 2 (Berkeley: University of California Press, 1991), p. 23.

Recognition of this coming danger gives a special urgency to the Korean reunification process. In reviewing its options and making policy adjustments, Korea will have to emphasize subtlety. Militarily, all three regional powers may be formidable. Japan will find itself under growing domestic and foreign pressure to rearm. Nationalism at home and the absence of American protection of its overseas interests will encourage Japanese exploration of alternative ways of providing security, possibly including acquisition of nuclear weapons. From an economic perspective, Russia and China are likely to provide enormous markets for Korean products, but endemic Korean trade surpluses may become a thorn in relations with either or both. Russia and China will also compete for Korean and Japanese investment and technology. For its part, Japan will remain a key source of high technology for Korea and an important trading partner. However, Korea's ability to usurp Japanese markets may produce serious friction between the two.

Conclusion

It is clear that we are in the midst of one of those rare transitional disturbances in global politics in which the world is turned upside down and only barely resembles its former self. Similar periods witnessed the erosion of the Roman Empire in the years following the birth of Christ, the collapse of the medieval Islamic empire in the eleventh century, the decline of Hapsburg/Spanish imperium following the Armada, and the collapse of four empires in World War I followed by the decay of several others in the ensuing years.

Such epochs are peculiarly dangerous. Existing norms and expectations suddenly become irrelevant. Existing repertoires of policies and habits that may have served for years will suddenly become dysfunctional. Stability and predictability precipitously decliné to be replaced by disagreeable shocks to the system, fears for the future, and increasing resort to unilateral behavior to protect interests. And, there is also a risk that unpleasant surprises may be misperceived as acts of malevolence. It is precisely such conditions that are most conducive to large-scale warfare of the sort we escaped during the Cold War.

For major powers, the risks include over-commitment and over-extension of actors in decline, or the unwillingness and inability of those in the ascendancy to accept new responsibilities. But those most at risk are regional and smaller powers for which such periods pose peculiarly knotty puzzles. Such actors can no longer depend on past allies or friends whose interests and capabilities are rapidly changing. In closing, two telling epigrams come to mind. The first, from the British historian Thomas Babington Macaulay, reminds us that policy should be based on an uncertain future rather a certain past: "A single breaker may recede; but the tide is evidently coming in." The second, by the French essayist Anatole France, is something of a warning: "The future is a convenient place for dreams."

CHAPTER 3

THE UNITED STATES, JAPAN, AND KOREA: THE NEW INTERNATIONAL POLITICAL ECONOMY

Charles F. Doran

Entitled "No More NICs," a pessimistic article appeared a few years ago in a U.S. policy journal expressing fear that the world economy was closing, that artificial substitutes were replacing many natural commodities, that cartels were exercising market power against new entrants, that barriers to entry in many industries were increasing, and that, in general, the world economy was more difficult to penetrate.[1] The message was that new industrial countries ought to look to their internal markets for growth. The gap between the poor and the rich was widening. International trade was no longer the "engine of growth."

Periodically, the same message is heard in many places around the globe. Yet the pace of economic

---

1. Robin Broad and John Cavanagh, "No More NICs," *Foreign Policy*, Vol. 72 (Fall 1988).

growth in many Asian countries continues to be phenomenal, South Korea among them, the current
recession notwithstanding. Export-led growth appears successful. Surely the liberal trade order has
facilitated an enormous growth in external trade
world-wide over the last four decades and great prosperity for the countries that have participated in that
trading system.

The thesis question for this paper is what role the
United States and Japan will play in the future
evolving trade order. What impact will the United
States and Japan have on Korea and countries like
Korea in that emerging trade regime?

Politics of the New International Economy

Neo-mercantilism. Without question, neo-mercantilism has been the most successful strategy for economic development in the post-1945 period. For it to
be successful, all of the internal economic, institutional, and cultural factors must be supportive. Not
all societies qualify. Japan has pioneered this form of
development. Many other governments are trying to
emulate it with slightly greater or less success.
Strangely, very little has been written about it with
definitiveness. Nobody, to my knowledge, has received
a Nobel Prize in economics for it. Yet neo-mercantilism has been extremely kind to its adherents.

The principal characteristics of neo-mercantilism
need only be enumerated here, they are so familiar.

(1) Neo-mercantilism is economics in the service of
the state. Politics is not at odds with economics; the
government is not at odds with the market—in contrast to the liberal, market states. The purpose of

government is to further economic advantage.

(2) The objective of neo-mercantilism is to import so that one can export. Liberal economies, in contrast, export so they can import and increase consumer choice. The neo-mercantilist imports raw materials so as to be able to export higher value-added manufactured goods and services.

(3) Constraints on imports in selected industries via non-tariff barriers and traditional societal limitations are coincident with an attempt to target foreign markets using dumping and other aggressive strategies to grasp and hold market share. Market share rather than profits is the objective of the firm.

(4) Persistent, non-clearing bilateral deficits with individual market countries are the unintended result of neo-mercantilism. Trade deficits are normally regarded as clearing only in multilateral terms. Yet the persistence of bilateral trade deficits of an aggravated sort result from asymmetric trade policies backed up by very efficient production techniques and high quality output in the neo-mercantilist country. Bad macro policies in some of the consumer countries, sluggish adjustment by management and labor, institutional resistance to structural change, and a gap between personal income and productivity have worsened the situation for the consumer countries.

Together, all of these effects have created a problem of self-perpetuating disequilibrium in the world trading economy.

When a firm in a traditional liberal market state competes with a firm in a neo-mercantilist state, the latter firm, other things being equal, has an advantage. When the neo-mercantilist economy confronts a traditional liberal market economy across a range of manufactures and services, the former economy, other things being equal, has an edge. These advantages obtained by the neo-mercantilist economy will enable it to aggregate wealth that must be recycled either at home, leading to accelerated imports for building the local economy, or in the world economy, through capital movements and foreign investment. The net effect in trade terms is to put great pressure on the liberal, market economies, which begin to lag in investment and begin to suffer significant loss of economic competitiveness.

Emergence of the European Community. In part a response to the sad history of intra-European warfare, in part an effort to bolster economic strength in the face of a perceived security threat from the former Soviet Union, in part an attempt to obtain economies of scale to offset the great size and market power of American industries, the EC was born. While "deepening" has always been the objective, "widening" has always proved easier, as the EC grew from 8 to 12 and now perhaps to 15 members. Instant benefits from a common external tariff, slowly lowered or in some cases replaced with non-tariff barriers, leads to some trade creation and some trade diversion. As the EC grows larger, the potential for trade diversion grows as well.

Very soon, the EC becomes a vehicle for meeting the greatest trade challenge, namely, that stemming from the neo-mercantilist country. In the process, the response of the firm in the neo-mercantilist country as well as other foreign firms is to hop the external trade barrier and to invest inside the market so as to exploit import-substitution opportunities.

Given the preoccupation with filling the regional market, harmonizing trade, financial, and investment norms internal to the EC, and trying to deepen the arrangement by moving toward a single currency and a single central bank, the EC Commission has little time or clout to support external, liberal, free trade initiatives world-wide. Coping with the regional market demands most of the energy and attention of the European political leadership.

Failure of the Uruguay Round. Although the brunt of the responsibility for the failure of the Uruguay Round has been placed on Paris, responsibility is much broader and ought to be shared throughout the EC and beyond. But neo-mercantilism and the rise of the EC have contributed to the new protectionism in the liberal market economies and the corresponding demise of universal free trade as an organizing principle of the trade order.

The sticking point is agricultural subsidy. At base the problem is that farming is one of the few industries experiencing perfect competition. No individual farmer has enough output to affect price. Each farmer maximizes output to try to make as much income as possible, and vast overproduction results. Governments then erect various subsidy schemes both to limit agricultural output and to subsidize the farmer's income. Usually further output increases occur.

In each of the democracies, agricultural interests are over-represented in the parliaments where they tie the hands of government regarding mutual subsidy reduction in trade negotiations. As one of the low-cost agricultural producers, the United States is adamant that this form of flagrant market distortion be curbed. France speaks for many farmers in Europe and other European governments (but not for all, as indicated by the Danes, the Dutch, and the

British) when significant subsidy cuts and moves to transparency are rejected.

But increasingly clear also is the rejection of progress toward liberalization of rules in intellectual property rights and in services. Unless other low-cost producers in areas such as manufactures come forth to push for broad-based trade liberalization, which is strongly in their economic interest, this round of universal trade liberalization is lost. The momentum is likely to shift elsewhere, in this case toward regional alternatives and, lamentably, toward managed trade.

FTA, NAFTA, and North American Regionalism. The FTA started out as bluff, or perhaps as a second-best alternative, either to nudge the Uruguay Round forward, or to provide some back-up in a period of long drawn-out negotiations in Geneva. It was not really regarded as a stand-on-its-own prototype for regional free trade. But in a sense the international trading system "called" the bluff, and the United States and Canada found themselves with the FTA as the strong card for future trade liberalization.

An objective of the FTA was to eliminate all tariff barriers between Canada and the United States by the year 2000 in phased-out steps depending upon type of industry. Phasing out of tariffs is ahead of schedule. New rules concerning national treatment of foreign investment accompany the agreement. On the other hand, exemptions also were made concerning investment treatment in two areas, the so-called "cultural industries" and energy. In the latter case, some restrictions still prevail in the foreign ownership of Canadian companies. Investment Canada, the foreign investment screening agency, a de-fanged variety of the old Foreign Investment Review Agency, still exists, but it no longer has much clout. In the former case, an entire sector is exempted from investment liberalization on grounds that the cultural industries are essential to the promotion of national identity in Canada, and that foreign ownership of newspapers, magazines and TV stations, among others, was threatening to the capacity of the country to forge a sense of unity.

But clearly the most progressive aspect of the FTA is the dispute resolution panel arrangement. This provision was included at the explicit request of Canada. Canada was unhappy about being "sideswiped" by American trade legislation that was meant for broader policy coverage but that ended up including Canada because of the size of its volume of trade with the United States. Secondly, Canada wanted to provide more security in its access to the U.S. market, since 70 percent of its trade is with the United States. Thus the United States ended up signing an agreement with Canada that yielded considerable sovereignty in trade matters.

The trade dispute panel approach uses panelists from both countries. After domestic routes to resolution have been exhausted, the dispute panel approach can be triggered. The governments act as the gatekeepers for the industrial disputants. The trade law of the challenged country is the standard against which each case is measured. Two grounds are sufficient for panel recommendation of adjustment: (1) improper interpretation of the law, and (2) new data that have a bearing on the case. So far the disputes have split pretty evenly between the two countries in terms of outcome. The respective governments have followed the recommendations of the binational panels, for the most part. The dispute resolution machinery has not decreased the number of claims, however, although we have no way of knowing how many claims would have been placed in the absence of the machinery. On the Canadian side, the trade disputes are quite visible. On the U.S. side, they have been overshadowed by other preoccupations. In general, the two governments seem satisfied with their trade dispute resolution procedures and apparatus.

While a more detailed discussion of NAFTA occupies a subsequent section, what can be said here is that the agreement with Mexico is highly likely to be ratified in all three countries. It is modeled after the FTA but goes beyond it in a number of areas, such as services and intellectual property rights. Like the FTA, the NAFTA is a second-best approach for the respective governments. An indicator is that Mexico went first to the European Community for an affiliation and was rebuffed. Mexico then came to the United States with a proposal, not the other way around. Canada joined largely to protect its gains in the FTA.

But second-best or not, the NAFTA is innovative. It is the first major regional trade agreement in which a large, poor, Third World country is partner with rich neighbors. Per capita income in Mexico is about one-seventh of that in the United States. It is very clear that without the far-reaching economic reforms in Mexico, most of which were unilateral, involving the reduction of tariffs, elimination of non-tariff barriers, reduction of subsidies, moderation of foreign investment laws, and privatization, neither of the other partners would have acceded to this agreement.

ASEAN and APEC. Regionalism in the Pacific area is as much the result of the weakening of the universal trade impulse as it is a contributor to viable alternate strategies to further trade liberalization. Neither organization is a bargaining instrument for the respective governments. Nor is the degree of institutionalization and the machinery regarding trade policy implementation notable. ASEAN reached a turning-point in June 1992 when security affairs were for the first time placed on its agenda. Since China is not a member, further prospects for security discussions may or may not advance, depending upon the perceived concerns of the members. Some will worry about giving ASEAN an anti-Chinese orientation. Others will be concerned that the economic and trade focus may get lost.

APEC is the favorite of the United States to help integrate what is otherwise a very far-flung and diverse region. But APEC is a forum for discussion, not a realistic, policy-making vehicle in the trade sphere at present. It complements GATT because it does not get in the way, as some other regional organizations are on the verge of doing. But is APEC genuinely an instrument for extending trade liberalization in the Pacific region?

Among regional trade and economic organizations, the EC is most tightly integrated, the FTA and NAFTA are in the middle, and ASEAN and APEC are probably at the lower end. Whether these latter regional entities will ever receive enough member support to move as actively into the field of trade and commerce as their counterparts in Europe and North America, remains to be seen.

In short, the politics of the new international economy is led by an array of new bargaining and institutional entities, most of which have a strong regional flavor. The advent of neo-mercantilism, a more trade-diverting European Community, managed trade and problems of bad macro-economic management in a number of the liberal market states, and regional trade associations have all contributed to the weakening of the universal free trade impulse.

Emergence of Locomotive Regionalism

What is emerging in the new international economy can best be described as *locomotive regionalism*. Locomotive regionalism is composed of two attributes: (1) a group of states located within a single region with increasingly harmonized policies, and (2) a large, central state which is the focus for much of the trade, commerce, and finance within the region. The regions are not just composed of a number of equal states. Nor is the locomotive state limited in its principal contacts only to the region. A feature is that each locomotive state reaches far beyond its own region in a way not matched by many of the other members of the region (in this some ASEAN members diverge from the model). Another feature of locomotive regionalism is that the other members seek contact with the locomotive state to assure market access and the benefits of the dynamism of the locomotive state. One by one, additional actors are drawn into the regional grouping as the scope of the regional arrangement expands. As the train moves down the track of development, more and more cars are added, some from widely varying regions, but all with a commitment to the discipline associated with the direction and momentum of the track.

In Europe, Germany is the locomotive pulling the regional train. If a single central bank ever is established, it may be physically located in London. But

European monetary policy will be German. The price of a Europeanized Germany is a Germanized Europe. The alternative is no Europe at all, but what the Germans call "renationalization." For most Europeans, this is a high political price to pay. Hence the European Community will continue to struggle toward its goals.

Germany not only has principal ties with each country inside the Community. It also has reached out to Eastern Europe in a way that no other government has. Thus Germany extends its commercial and trade links outside the Community just as the other European countries are concentrating upon their position inside the Community. Germany is bound to grow rapidly, with its internal-external strategy, while retaining leadership of the European drive toward regional centralization.

In Asia, can there be any doubt but that Japan is the locomotive state regionally? It scarcely matters whether a formal regional organization is constructed. Japan has a clear conception of what it wants from the region. It wants to establish a hierarchic set of economic relationships based on specialization and technological capability. In such a framework, Japan retains all of the most sophisticated technology, and it manufactures the most sophisticated products with the highest value-added. Below Japan are ranked the other regional actors, each with a place in the scheme of regional specialization and development. All are linked to the Japanese firms and trading companies through inputs and outputs. Japanese capital supplies many local enterprises, which in turn may produce for other Japanese firms. The purpose of the production is to export outside the region. Gradually a form of trickle-down production occurs as less-rich states in the region take on production, such as at the lower end of the automobile manufacturing ladder, that Japan no longer wishes to produce because of shrinking margins.

In North America, the locomotive is the United States. By expanding its market, it hopes to increase economies of scale and learning curve efficiencies for firms operating there. Firms in Mexico and Canada that previously were branch plants of U.S. firms producing for the local market are now rationalized to produce intra-firm products or to specialize directly in some product area for external markets. The United States, Canada, and Mexico hope also that domestic firms now operating outside North America, and foreign firms, will increasingly relocate inside North America. Part of the purpose of regionalization is commercial rather than trade-related.

Over time, NAFTA will add other countries, starting perhaps with Chile. Countries within the region may get first option for affiliation. But NAFTA will reach outside the region to like-minded states as well. Gradually the sphere of trade and commerce will widen, just as liberalization and harmonization internally proceed.

In sum, each region contains a locomotive state that leads the others down the track of trade and commercial liberalization. That locomotive state is larger and much more prone to international ties beyond the region than many of the other regional actors. Politics mixes with economics. But if the regional approach does not provide some perceived economic benefits to all the participating members, it will not have much chance of success.

Problems with the New International Economy

Problems with the new approach to international political economy are multifold.

First, there is a great danger that over time, especially as the regional associations become larger, trade diversion will exceed trade creation.

Second, managed trade becomes attractive as larger regional entities can bargain effectively with counterparts. The problem is that political capacity to actually reduce non-tariff barriers is not great because decision-making inside these units is of the "lowest common denominator" variety, either de jure, when all are reflected directly in the bargain as with the European Commission, or de facto, when the locomotive state bargains for everyone.

Third, distortions arise for the late-comers to the association. They must essentially accept the terms that the others have agreed upon. What the others have agreed upon fits the existing industrial structures of the locomotive state and the early members of the association.

Fourth, insofar as the regional unit is not a full common market, rules of origin agreements become so cumbersome that large bureaucracies will be necessary to monitor and enforce the agreement.

Fifth, the regions promote an inward-looking preoccupation within the core state (witnessed recently even for Japan, the titular export-oriented model) and among the other regional members. Regionalism then becomes a self-fulfilling conclusion.

Sixth, multinational firms, by locating within these regions, may earn oligopoly profits because of the large internal market, the relaxed attitude toward cartelization, and the existence of non-tariff barriers or rules of origin that exclude foreign competition. Surely the automobile industries in North America and Europe are examples, and the semi-conductor market in Asia suggests this pattern.

In short, locomotive regionalism, responding to the changes in the new international economy, has begun to crowd out other conceptions for world trade and commerce. Despite its shortcomings as a means of promoting global welfare, the locomotive regional approach is gaining ground. Trade liberalization occurs, but it is preferential. It occurs within regions but not between regions. At some future time, inter-regional negotiations might once again pick up the baton of global trade liberalization. But currently that promise appears faint.

Interests in the Korean Peninsula

Japan. The interests of Japan in the Korean peninsula are far-reaching and combine economic, political, and security objectives. Contrary to those who hold the "dagger thrust at Japan's heart" thesis regarding Korea, I believe Japan is genuine concerning its desire for a united Korea under a democratic, market banner. The notion that the Cold War was kind to Japan because it kept the two Koreas apart ignores much political reality, and the Japanese are realists. For one thing, the Cold War is over and the Koreas are still divided. It was not the Cold War that kept them divided, but a Stalinist regime in the North that, although its government form is anachronistic by today's standards, continues to demand unity on its terms. But more than this, a divided Korea is a dangerous place, not the most dangerous in the world context, but dangerous still. A divided Korea is the last of the flashpoints left over from Yalta. Until the division is mended, under present circumstances of opposed ideologies and regime styles, the potential for trouble exists. Japan does not like trouble.

In addition, Japan is currently capable of defending itself against any conventional assault upon its territory by Korean forces mounted from anywhere in the peninsula. Its navy, after all, has responsibility for a naval defense out to a perimeter of 1000 miles of its shores, including a defense against much better armed and sophisticated forces than those available militarily in the Koreas. A conventional assault is not Japan's concern.

What does preoccupy Japan greatly, however, is the prospect that North Korea will develop nuclear weapons. In a setting where American troops are withdrawing from South Korea in a phased reduction (now held in abeyance), this means that no nuclear capability, tactical or otherwise, would be left on South Korean territory. This would give the North an asymmetrical advantage. Worse from the Japanese point of view, an unstable regime in Pyongyang could attempt to blackmail Tokyo when backed up by nuclear capability. Worse still, South Korea too might decide to build or buy nuclear weapons. Then Tokyo would face four nuclear powers in the region: Russia, China, North Korea and South Korea.

The potential for misinformation, uncertainty, and paranoia under these circumstances is hard to exaggerate. Japan might abruptly opt for a very sophisticated form of nuclearity and delivery at such a time. Everybody's security, regionally and globally, would be diminished by such a chain of nuclear proliferation.

*The way to manage future crises is to avoid the cir-
cumstance and preconditions of such crises.* Nowhere is
this lesson more evident than regarding the nuclear
situation in North Korea today. Sadly, the Kim Il-sung
government does not seem to understand the sincerity
of international concern about its intentions.

Commercially and financially, South Korea is very
important to Japan as well. Joint ventures and
financial loans make South Korea, because of its
very rapid economic growth, an attractive place to do
business. As mentioned before, through its model of
neo-mercantilism, Japan has a distinct idea of what
relationship the Korean economy ought to play in the
overall strategy of Japanese growth and development.
Korea has a privileged place in this strategy. But it is
not to be treated on a par with Japan's own economy
and firms. Korea is to take up the slack in output that
is more labor-intensive than that produced by
Japan. Korea in turn is expected to provide a very
attractive market for Japanese high-tech goods and
for equipment used to manufacture other goods for
export that possess a lot of technological content.
This does not mean that Japan intends to ship the
most advanced technology itself to South Korea.

From the economic viewpoint, this trading and
investment relationship may not seem very attractive.
Indeed, it may appear frustrating. Yet there is a great
deal of money to be made in the arrangement. Where
money is to be made, principles do not always weigh
too heavily. Hence the future for Japanese and Korean cooperation in the trade and commercial field
seems full of prospects for expansion. Over time,
Korea may close the gap between itself and Japan in
terms of per capita income and technological development. But to some extent, this will have to come

from additional contacts with other trading partners.

United States. An overriding objective for the United States is that South Korea enjoy security and that the peninsula remain in peace. The United States did not lead the defense of South Korea in the early 1950s only to have that result overturned in the 1990s.

On the other hand, a lot has changed. South Korea is now rich and growing rapidly. The Soviet Union is gone. The United States has many internal preoccupations as well as global responsibilities. All of this means that South Korea is in a position where it will have to assume more of the direct responsibility for its own defense, the knotty problem of North Korean nuclear intentions notwithstanding.

In the longer run, Washington is aware that South Korea, or perhaps eventually an amicable united Korea under the South Korean flag, will become something of a balancer in the Asian region. This means a counterweight to the giant powers, Japan, China, and Russia. Today such a role seems presumptuous, even perhaps foolhardy. But over time, especially if all of Korea is united, this role will become more palatable, conceivably obvious. For, the greatest problem that Asia can face is a situation where these three powers fall into grave dispute. Korea will always have to be the "fixer."

To some extent, on a limited scale, that is what Korea has been doing already. The strategy ought to be made explicit so that it is not bungled for lack of comprehension. By making commercial and political advances in Manchuria with the Russians, Korea is outflanking North Korea. But there is a risk of offending the Japanese, who are caught up in their own complexities with the Russians over the Kuriles. By calling upon the Chinese, at the cost of alienating Taiwan, to assist in carrying a message to Pyongyang, Seoul is isolating the North Koreans. But how will Kim Il-sung react to isolation? That is a question that South Korea should perhaps also address.

For this strategy of isolation to have maximum value, North Korea must also be offered a way out that is attractive and benign. From the U.S. perspective, an inward-looking, paranoid, and isolated regime in the north may not be a regime willing to forgo a "trump card" such as nuclear weapons development. What the strategy of diplomatic isolation, plus alertness and military strength, ought to be combined with is openness to increased commercial and trade ties. It is important to be tough and not to let defenses down. It is important to specify exactly what is needed to make mutual inspections work. It is also important to give Pyongyang a face-saving way out of the corner in which it is trapped. Hence, looked at from the perspective of another country, far from the tensions of the local setting, beware of being too successful in the art of diplomacy. Always leave a door open, the door you choose, to a perhaps defeated but still lethal opponent.

Regarding an economic interest in the peninsula, the United States has no elaborate or ready answers. South Korea is regarded as an important trading partner. Persistent trade imbalances will of course get an increasingly hard look even though the United States is well aware that it must give productivity a boost on its own side so that its manufactures become more competitive. Insofar as South Korea is an important importer of American agricultural products, including cigarettes, this will be extremely helpful to the relationship. Many American multinationals with operations inside South Korea are good emissaries on behalf of Korean interests. In general, the United States expects of South Korea, increasingly what it expects of its senior GATT partners. South Korea, because of the size and robustness of its economy, is beginning to move into this rank.

Korea and NAFTA

In the longer run, given the emergence of locomotive regionalism, South Korea might well consider the development of a countervailing strategy. This strategy could carry the policy forward well into the next century. The strategy, not now acceptable to North Americans, but potentially important within the decade, is for South Korea to position itself for entry into the NAFTA.

This is not a strategy which would today bring a positive response in Washington, Toronto, or Mexico City. Yet this is scarcely a reason to give it up. Changes occur. The trajectory of trade and commerce is quite self-evident within NAFTA. NAFTA is going to be transformed into an umbrella organization. Inclusion of Mexico is going to make inclusion of other Third World and, indeed, Newly Developing Countries far easier. The queue may be long, but those first on the list will have many advantages.

What this strategy does is to confound all pundits. First, it challenges the notion that NAFTA is going to be closed and inclusive. Second, it erases the idea that NAFTA must be regional in the geographic sense. Third, it stands on its head the claim that South Korea is neo-mercantilist and therefore unwilling to observe the same rules as the more liberal, market-oriented economies. Fourth, it rejects the view that South Korea is captive in another region that has a different geographic focus. Fifth, it makes excellent use of the commercial and investment potential that exists in Korea and in the United States. Finally, it is strategically and economically audacious and therefore probably of great benefit to the positive restructuring of world economic relationships.

In the meantime South Korea ought to "tend its garden" in the best tradition of international interdependence and trade and commercial interaction. By positioning itself for a thrust upward and outward during the next upturn of the business cycle, South Korea will be able to enjoy to the fullest the benefits of its own hard work and the opportunities created by powerful trading partners.

Neo-mercantilism as a generalized trading concept cannot work. Everyone cannot be a neo-mercantilist. Who will buy all of the exported goods and services? Rather, in the new international economy, groups of countries will try to practice internal trade liberalization. To paraphrase the Chinese parable by P'u Sung-ling, "The Stream of Cash," money must flow, it cannot be hoarded. Trade imbalances cannot become permanent. They will generate opposing policies and strategies that will imperil the world trading regime and may themselves become even more constraining than the neo-mercantilist policies for which supposedly they are an answer. South Korea will find itself swimming in the main current of the new international economy with many future choices and many opportunities.

CHAPTER 4

JAPAN AS AN ECONOMIC SUPERPOWER: IMPLICATIONS FOR THE KOREAN PENINSULA AND BEYOND

Yung-hwan Jo

Japan has become an economic superpower in the world. What role will Japan play in Northeast Asia and Korea in addition to spawning economic development? Will there be a time when, strapped for resources, the Japanese will once again seek hegemony over neighboring nations, including the two Koreas? Can Japan continue to shape the space and nature of the economic development of the two Koreas through trade, investment, and science/technology without affecting the political environment of these countries? If Japan's attempt to keep its economic boom alive creates conditions that further the economies of its neighbors, will there be a regional economic bloc? For Koreans, these are the important implications of Japanese economic supremacy.

The Japanese Economic Power

It will be less relevant to this paper, if not premature, to ask if and when Japan will become the new Great World Power replacing the United States. What is more relevant is the sustainability of Japan as an economic superpower.

Statistically, Japan edges out or equals the United States in per capita income, although its GNP is second in the world, being 58% of the U.S. GNP (*Table 1*). But in terms of per capita "affluence," Japan is ranked tenth. A reasonable extrapolation of past and current trends will have Japan in second or third place by the early years of the 21st century.[1]

However, Japan's "less-economic" factors will sustain its economic success for the following reasons. (1) Unlike the United States, Japan's best and brightest often opt for the civil service and, in turn, provide Japanese industry with useful economic advice and financial assistance. (2) With more production and better educated citizens plus an export-oriented economy, Japan is better prepared for the interdependent world economic order than any other power. (3) Companies in Japan benefitted from better work ethics and better relations with workers who are more secure in their jobs. (4) The government spent very little of its tax monies on social-welfare programs or military defense. (5) A stable family structure produced psychologically stable and reliable employees. (6) The reservoir of Japanese pacifism and remorse over past military adventurism will not be depleted under the impact of chauvinistic bicker-

---

1. Paul A. Samuelson, *Hard Truths for Korea* (Seoul: Shisa Yongu, 1992), p. 64.

Table 1. Comparative Indices of Economic Powers

	Japan	ROK (SK)	DPRK (NK)	Taiwan (ROC)	USA	PRC (China)
Population	123,800,000	43,300,000	21,800,000	20,454,000	255 million	1,130,865,000
GNP ($)	2,920 billion	200 billion	28 billion	119.1 billion	4.2 billion	258 billion
Per Capita	$20,000	$4,600	$1,240	$6,200	$19,560	$350+
Area	145,874 sq. mile	38,031	44,358	36,000	9,372,614	9,572,900
Life Expectancy	76 (M) 82 (F)	66 73	69 75	70 76	71.5 78.5	68 70
Military Expenditure	1% of GNP	5% Central Gov't Expenditure	22% C G E	39.4% C G E	29.1% C G E	14.6% C G E
Export	$270 billion	$62.3 billion	$2.4 billion	$66.1 billion	$250.4 billion	$51.6 billion
Import	$210 billion	$61.3 billion	$3.1 billion	$52.5 billion	$424 billion	$58.2 billion

Sources: The 1992 Almanac (New York: Houghton-Mifflin)
D. Collinwood, *Japan and the Pacific Rim* (Dushkin, 1991).

ing. Fortunately, Japan shows no evidence of aspirations to build a Japanese Empire. (7) Enormous amounts of money and energy were invested to educationally alert the people that in a resource-poor country like Japan, sacrifice could be called for even in peacetime, and that they must always be prepared for long-range planning with research and development in science and technology.[2]

An important underlying assumption behind the sustainability of Japanese economic supremacy is that Japan remains in the American security system, thereby obviating the need for Japan to undertake a substantial rearmament program.

Since 1985, Japan has been the leading creditor nation, possessing the world's ten largest banks in terms of deposits (valued in dollars). Japan is the second largest donor to the Inter-American Development Bank and the African Development Bank, holding the same position in the World Bank and probably also in the International Monetary Fund. During 1989, Japan became the largest provider of foreign economic assistance, the total amounting to about half of its military budget in terms of percentage of GNP. In 1991, it amounted to $6 billion. In 1984, Japan passed the United States in terms of GNP spent on research and development.[3]

---

2. David Halberstam, *The Next Century* (New York: Avon, 1991), pp. 84-87; Dean Collinwood, *Japan and The Pacific Rim* (Guilford, Conn.: Dushkin, 1991), pp. 20-21.

3. Mike M. Mochizuki, "Heisei Japan," a paper prepared for the conference on the "Strategic Quadrangle," organized by the Research Institute on International Change of Columbia University, March 9-10, 1989.

Cognitive Dissonance Between Japan and Korea

The above-mentioned indices of Japanese economic power are necessary but not sufficient for Japan's drive for economic dominance, which is feared in Korea should there be a political will to use it on the part of the Japanese. Japan has never had a De Gaulle or a Yeltsin. The Japanese political culture and system prevents the exercise of strong, executive, leadership and a more activist foreign policy, especially vis-a-vis the two Koreas. The Japanese side could say that their government has been in a "reactive state." The Korean side would argue that, with the rising influence of the right-wing nationalists, Japan could have a leader stronger than Yasuhiro Nakasone.

What values, either of the Japanese public or the state, will guide Japan's drive for domination of its neighbors and/or the world? The Japanese leaders have no experience in handling a global, superpower position. But an emerging consensus in Japan appears to be that Japan must develop a foreign policy more commensurate with its economic capabilities.

Prime Minister Nakasone urged Japanese scholars to redefine or develop a Japanese value system that would be universally appealing for a twenty-first century "mission" of sorts. His cultural aim was to evolve and transform Japanese culture from a particularistic, idiosyncratic culture into a universal and international one befitting the Japanese rise to an economic and political powerhouse. To Toru Haga of Tokyo University, Japan is a spiritually rich society where each person can find fulfillment in life. More specifically, he thinks that the Japanese sense of aesthetic harmony, domestic harmony, and harmony with and veneration toward nature, with ecological implications, are exportable Japanese values.[4]

Some of Nakasone's followers wanted to reinterpret such ancient history books as *Nihon Shogi* and *Kojiki* of the Jamon culture, which can be identified as the origin of Japanese culture. But even to fellow Confucianists in Korea, these books might appear to be too situationalistic and particularistic to attract those living in neo-Confucian societies such as the two Koreas, Taiwan, Hong Kong and Singapore.[5]

But in fact, a large number of Koreans are receptive to Japanese popular culture, as evidenced in the number of satellite TV sets linked up with Japan. There is some evidence of homogeneity in the two countries' popular songs, so that a Japanese song could become a hit song in Korea, and vice versa. Koreans should be more amenable to the notion of "free" culture and balance of culture than is the case in the area of trade. Seoul National University's recent exclusion of the Japanese language from its list of secondary foreign languages is about the worst manifestation of cultural chauvinism. This is not defensible for Korea's economy, since its research and growth depends so much on Japanese publications in science and technology.

Cultural interactions and exchange of visits on all levels could reduce cognitive dissonance and cultural barriers, the removal of which is as important as removing the tariff barrier in order to promote vari-

4. See his "A Vision of Japan and the World in the 21st Century," a paper presented at an International Conference on "Korea and the World in the 21st Century," October 21-23, 1991, sponsored by the Presidential Commission on the 21st Century, Seoul.

5. "Japanese Cultural Imperialism." *Newsreview*, September 12, 1992.

ous types of cooperation between Japan and Korea. Fortunately, in 1990 almost equal numbers of tourists were exchanged between Japan and Korea: 978,000 Japanese visited Korea while 978,984 Koreans visited Japan.[6] A recent statistic shows that almost 70 percent of Koreans in Japan marry Japanese. This is twice the rate of mixed marriages in 1965, which was 34.6 percent.[7]

In spite of such a favorable trend, an area of cognitive dissonance still remains on the question of Korean reunification. According to a recent survey, as many as 79 percent of the Koreans interviewed think that the Japanese government would oppose Korean reunification, whereas an almost equal number of the Japanese surveyed in fact favored the idea of Korean reunification.[8]

Kuroda Katsuhiro argues that what Japan really wants is a peacefully united and secure Korea. Otherwise, North Korea's absorption by South Korea is preferable to Tokyo, rather than the other way around, in that a united Korea dominated by the South could come more readily under the Japanese economic sphere. Unlike the Koreans, who have almost always felt threatened by Japan, historically the Japanese never viewed Korea as a direct threat to Japan's security.[9] To most Koreans, a united Korea could be a very

6. Myonghwon Chi, "Japan misunderstands Korea," *The Real Power of Japan* (Korean) (Seoul: Chosun Ilbo, 1992).

7. Yung-hwan Jo, "Japan," in Jay Lifton, ed., *International Handbook on Race and Race Relations* (New York: Greenwood Press, 1987).

8. Ikeda Tokujiro's paper presented at the 1991 Conference on "Big Powers' Roles in Korea," Pusan National University. Cf. *Asahi Shinmun*, March 1, 1992.

9. Kuroda Katsuhiro, "Japan and the Japanese as Misconceived by the Koreans," *The Real Power of Japan, op. cit.*

formidable neighbor to Japan, while to most Japanese, the two Koreas, even after reunification, cannot be threateningly larger to the "super" Japan.

Economic Implications

Of all the former members of Japan's Greater East Asia Co-prosperity Sphere, probably no nation other than Korea resented Japan's leadership. Nevertheless, today's geopolictical and economic realities dictate (1) that it is to their mutual advantage to develop closer ties and the habit of cooperation, and (2) that Japan returns to Asia since it cannot enjoy global responsibilities in place of the United States. If Japan's economic role is accepted by Korea, it will be more readily acceptable to Japan's other neighbors.

Since the establishment of diplomatic relations between Seoul and Tokyo in 1965, however, the trade volume has increased so that Japan has become Korea's second largest trade partner as of 1988. But the trade deficit increased from $575 million in 1970 to $ 55,494 million in 1990.[10]

As defended by Japan, such a phenomenal increase was largely due to Korea's emphasis on heavy chemical industries and its need for raw materials and parts in order to expand Korean exports. Also, in the area of technological transfer, Japan confines transfers to already standardized technologies rather than the core or high technologies. Japan is being pressured by Korea and its neighbors to

---

10. KEIST, "Imports from Japan and Technological Transfer; the Current Situation and Policy Solution," (in Korean) Seoul: KEIST, 1991), p. 26.

open more markets and to be more lenient in its technological transfers, while at the same time Korea is striving to improve the quality of its products and the reliability of its own technology.

In the meantime, multilateral economic cooperation is being sought in this region. But Japan will likely opt for functional rather than structural cooperation until the grass roots demands for organizing an economic bloc occur. But some Koreans argue that even a new Greater East Asia Co-prosperity Sphere, however open or soft a form of regionalism it may be, would invariably make the Korean economy far more dependent on Japan, the core nation of the economic regionalism, by turning a Korea with a relatively high purchasing power into a market for Japanese goods. Japan transferred a large amount of its capital and technology used for manufacturing industries in Korea to Southeast Asia. Japanese and other economists might ask if these are better alternatives for Korea, in view of the increasing trade friction with Japan and its neighbors, and, in addition, with the United States.

The income and technological gap and the complimentarity of economies in the East Asian region also add to the theoretical advantages of joining a regional economic bloc, although they are necessary but not sufficient conditions for a successful economic community, unless accompanied by the political will of the members. Hardly anyone would question the need and desirability of countering the trend toward protectionism and of helping solve trade issues, especially those that could lead to the "coming economic war between the United States and Japan."[11]

---

11. See G. Freedman & M. Lebord, *The Coming War with Japan* (New York: St. Martin's Press, 1991).

Whatever type of regional organization, be it Asian "new order" or Asian *grossraumwirtschaft*, the proponents should aim at building a loose and open institutional umbrella under which the members have improved forms of cooperation, negotiation, and consultation. In addition to its economic capabilities, Japan is qualified to become the core nation. Japan's heavy reliance on its neighbors' resources and good will, plus its awareness of the damages it inflicted on them in the past, would prevent Japan from becoming a Frankenstein monster. South Korea can best play a mediating role between the core nation and less developed members of the economic "bloc" (open and soft regionalism).[12]

Toward the end of his tenure, the U.S. Ambassador to Japan, Mike Mansfield, articulated a view that the best way to prevent the coming war with Japan is to create a free trade zone between the U.S. and Japan. This was his preference over the recently proposed NAFTA. Mansfield's view, which was once brushed aside, is receiving more attention in the ruling circles of Japan.

Challenges in the Future

Future trade and investment prospects between Japan and Korea will be strongly influenced by the evolving pattern of trade specialization. In the meantime, Korea's trade imbalance with Japan will decrease, as will Japan's non-tariff barriers. Korea

---

12. See Yung-hwan Jo, "Building a Cooperative System in the Pacific Basin," Proceedings of the Fifth Joint Conference, Korean Political Science Association, Seoul, 1983.

will likely follow the path of Japanese trade structure.

As to the future prospects of economic regionalism, Japan is still ambivalent about assuming the leadership role in setting up an organization, and that reluctance is due not only to the still-prevailing neo-mercantilistic nature of its economic system, but also to its traditional reliance on its U.S. ties. In view of continuing trade disputes, Japan would rather see somebody else promote East Asian economic zones or some sort of bloc. The intra-Asian volume of trade is increasing, and China is getting a larger share of it.

Japan will continue to absorb more exports from NICs and supply more capital goods to them, which it began doing in 1990. The most frequently mentioned institutional framework for an economic region is the APEC (Asia Pacific Economic Cooperation). But APEC is more likely to develop into a consultative forum on trade issues and economic policies, especially for those areas not covered under the GATT.[13] In 1990, when the Malaysian government proposed forming an economic bloc called "the East Asian Economic Caucus" that excluded the U.S., Canada, Australia, and New Zealand, Washington openly opposed the proposition. Tokyo could be receptive to the idea in the future.

Lastly, North Korea must be factored into this paper, however briefly. Pyongyang began to emulate the Chinese policy of economic reforms, as evidenced in the Tumen River Project and laws allowing private ownership. Though small in scale, such things were

---

13. Marcus Noland, "Economic Cooperation and Conflict between the U.S., Korea, and Japan," a conference paper on the topic sponsored by Pusan National University, October 22-23, 1992.

unthinkable a few years ago. With the settlement of
the nuclear issue, North Korea will succeed in exact-
ing economic concessions from South Korea, Japan,
and the United States.

North Korean leaders have been frustrated by the
slow progress of their efforts to normalize economic,
if not diplomatic, relations with Japan. During my
recent visit to Pyongyang, I received a distinct impression that there must be some solution to the
nuclear issue for North Korea's diplomatic and economic survival, and that the priority was being shifted from negotiations with Tokyo to those with Washington, since the latter has been "directing" the
former.

The economies of South Korea and North Korea
will be interconnected through the linkage provided
by Japan. In the meantime, Japan will become a permanent member of the U.N. Security Council, which
will symbolically provide Japan with the status of a
political *big* power in addition to that of an economic
super power. Tokyo-Pyongyang relations are a cause
and an effect of Seoul-Pyongyang interaction. Japan
should, and will, be willing to finance some of the
unification costs if unification occurs as a result of a
precipitous collapse of the North Korean regime.

Policy Issues and Options

Japan's role in Korea and other neighboring countries is linked up with the United States. The new
U.S. President has an opportunity to reshape the
power configuration in Northeast Asia. Now that economics will be in command of Clinton's foreign and
security policies, will this shift cause America and

Japan "bashing" to spiral?

The Japanese economy is too large, too varied, and too fast-growing to be contained in a region. The Japanese leaders think that Japan needs a military power to match its enormous economic clout and that Japan must increase its military might to fill the power vacuum left behind by the U.S. and the former Soviet Union. Yet Japan has not developed its international strategy. There has been no consensus on Japan's world role or on Japan's foreign economic policy.[14] The only consensus has been on its economic domination of the East Asia-Pacific region, which served to make Japan less vulnerable to the NAFTA and EC protectionism.

Under these circumstances can Japan become a real superpower? Alvin Toffler lists two drawbacks for Japan's becoming a world power. One is that only 125 million people speak Japanese, and the other is the Japanese antagonism to social, economic, and cultural diversity, to say nothing of racial diversity.[15] Sustaining a more structurally integrated U.S.-Japanese alliance will reduce such antagonism on the part of the Japanese and make them more bilingual, thereby increasing Japan's qualifications as a future world power. And Japanese security ties to the U.S. provide additional insurance against the long-standing Chinese and Korean fear of Japanese militarization.

A slowdown in the Japanese economy, with next year's projected growth as low as 1.0 to 1.5 percent, will hamper Clinton's efforts to boost the sluggish

---

14. Alvin Toffler, *Power Shift* (New York: Bantam Books, 1990), pp. 433-437.

15. *Loc. cit.*.

U.S. economy; Japan will then curb demand for U.S. exports, which is an important element in economic recovery. The U.S. economy must be based more on domestic demand.

Even if Japan were to become entirely self-reliant in its defense, how much would it save the U.S. and thereby contribute to the U.S. economy? By 1995, Tokyo will be paying nearly $4 billion a year to cover the expenses of American forces in the country, and it is doubtful whether it will make it much cheaper to bring the forces home than station them in Japan?[16] It appears, therefore, that it would be much better for each to improve its domestic policies and for both to agree to continue the American security role in Japan for the forseeable future.

However, there is a school of thought in Japan arguing that the justification for the U.S.-Japan alliance is outdated, that Japan must look after its own national interest in the post-Cold War world, and that the United States can no longer provide Japan with a sufficient guarantee of security. sixty-eight percent of the Japanese people expect a reduction or a complete withdrawal of U.S. forces from Japan.[17]

Parallel to this view of a self-reliant Japan is Francis Fukuyama's view that Japan has the best qualifications to lead the world in this "Post-history" era. To him, the ideological struggle has been replaced by the consumer culture that prevails throughout the world. That consumer culture is characterized by economic calculation and concern for issues of technology and ecology. Japan is the epitomy of the con-

---

16. *Time*, November 16, 1992, p. 46.

17. F. McNeil, "Beyond Containment," *Foreign Affairs Journal*, (December 1990), p. 16.

sumer culture, economic value being its central cultural value.[18]

Turning to China, Clinton will link China's most-favored-nation treaty status to its human rights record, good trade performance, and restraint in weapon's exports. Clinton has called for the establishment of a "Radio Free Asia" and a "Democracy Corps," patterned after the Peace Corps, to promote democracy in Asia and elsewhere.[19]

What if such programs result in the Balkanization of China? A chaotic China, like Russia, would destabilize the entire region, especially Korea and Japan, both of which have established close economic and political relations with China in recent years. The Chinese "boat" people could flood South Korea and the western part of Japan. China is too critical for Northeast Asian economic and security relations for the U.S. to undergo such a breakdown with China. Besides, for North Korea and its relations with South Korea, China has the key outside influence. How can we induce North Korea to join the Missile Technology Control Regime without first obtaining China's cooperation in it?

After the 14th Party Congress, China showed renewed determination to push forward with its own economic reform. Americans must understand that a large number of Japanese and Korean elite do not agree with the emphasis Clinton places on enhancing human rights in China, because they prefer a stable, authoritarian China to an unstable, democratic China, the negative consequences of which would be frightening.

---

18. F. Fukuyama, *The End of History and the Last Man* (New York: The Free Press, 1992), p. 242 and ff.

19. *The Far East Economic Review*, November 12, 1992, p. 11.

As for North Korea, its nuclear weapons program was probably discovered before the North Koreans were able to develop it as a viable counterweight to the South's conventional capabilities. Pyongyang may therefore be able to use the nuclear program as a diplomatic card to exact maximum concessions from Seoul, Tokyo, and Washington. President Roh Tae Woo has offered to cooperate with North Korea on economics and almost all other levels, but only after North Korea settles the problem of mutual inspections of nuclear facilities. Would not Japan and the U.S. follow suit? The new Presidents of Korea and the U.S., namely Kim Young-sam and Bill Clinton, along with Miyazawa of Japan, should be able to coordinate their actions, even on matters other than non-nuclear issues, vis-a-vis North Korea.

Since North Korea's economic collapse and the onset of political turmoil would create security issues for South Korea and neighboring countries, what kind of preparation or joint action can we take, especially if and when these occur in a surprising manner?

Conclusion

Even though there is, as yet, no agreement on a multilateral security arrangement such as CSCA (Conference on Security and Cooperation in Asia), Japan, South Korea and the U.S. should first create among themselves a variety of vehicles for dialogues — as well as for other multiple efforts — that include China and Russia when appropriate.[20]

---

20. Scalapino, op. cit., p. 4; cf. Melvin Gurtov's paper on "Prospects for Korea-U.S.-Japan Trilateral Security Relations," in this volume, p. 126 and ff.

In this period of transition and uncertainty in Northeast Asia, where the economic and security relations of Japan are so inter-related, dialogue between Japan and its neighbors, especially the two Koreas, must be activated and accelerated.

If the NAFTA or EC "protectionism" do not facilitate the growth of a Japanese-American consortia or cooperative hegemony in the world, Japan as an economic superpower is likely to develop "equal distance" economic relations toward both China and the United States. In the distant future, the "United States" of Korea likewise could pursue an economic policy of equal distance vis-a-vis China and the United States.

CHAPTER 5

THE EMERGING ECONOMIC ORDER
IN EAST ASIA IN THE 1990S:
A POLITICAL ECONOMY PERSPECTIVE

Young-Kwan Yoon

Introduction

Two important events in the late 1980s have changed the basic structure of the world political economy. One is the transformation of the socialist command economies in the Soviet Union and Eastern Europe and the other is the EC's drive toward economic and political integration. The efforts to reform the Soviet economy led to the dissolution of the Soviet Union itself and a shift of power dynamics in international relations. Since the old rules of the game have become irrelevant but have not yet been replaced with new ones, there is an increased level of uncertainty in the international system.

In Europe, the EC member countries adopted the Single European Act in 1986 to remove barriers between them inhibiting free movements of goods, services, labor, and capital. Furthermore, they are pursuing the even higher goals of realizing a single European currency and political integration, as mandated in the Maastricht Treaty. These efforts toward economic and political integration in the EC have inspired North America, in one way or another, to enlarge its free trade area into Mexico.

Such trends of regionalization in other parts of the world economy have aroused discussion about the prospects for economic cooperation in East Asia. This paper will analyze both the current state of economic cooperation and the nature of the emerging economic order in East Asia from a political economy perspective. It also attempts to clarify the implications of this analysis for Korea's economic strategy.

Recent discussions in Korea concerning economic cooperation and regionalization are mostly based on the economic approach that emphasizes the principle of comparative advantage and the division of labor. Naturally, such an approach tends to disregard the political dimension of international economic cooperation.

The political economy approach adopted in this paper is based on the assumption that politics and economics interact closely. State and market, the two most important organizing principles of human activities, affect each other in various ways. The tradition of political economy in this sense has been a part of intellectual history in Europe since the 18th century. It was only about a century ago that scholars in the United States divided the academic field of political economy into politics and economics, establishing a new tradition. However, this new tradition in American social science has turned out to be less and less effective in explaining the complex and comprehensive nature of the social activities of human beings in the late 20th century. Even in the field of international relations, scholars, by the 1970s, began to realize the importance of analyzing the political aspects of international economic relations or the economic underpinnings of international political relations. Thus, a new field called international political economy was born. This meant, in a sense, a return to the old European tradition of political economy.

Viewed from the political economy perspective, international economic cooperation has both an economic and a political dimension.[1] When nations cooperate with each other to establish a common market or a free trade area or even to make capital investments, each nation expects net gain as the result of cooperation. Without net gain, a rational actor will find no motive to cooperate. This concept of net gain is an economic explanation about cooperation. The political economy approach, however, raises another important issue unexplained by the economic approach. That is, how the total sum of the net gain resulting from cooperation should be divided among participants. Each actor is concerned about not only absolute gain, but also relative gain.[2] For

---

1. The concept of international economic cooperation has a broad meaning in this paper. It includes not only an advanced level of institutional cooperation such as economic integration and free trade areas, but also an introductory level of cooperation, as in bilateral trade and investment relations.

2. In the area of international political economy the issue of relative gain has been the focal point in recent debates about the possibility of cooperation among major actors in an international system. See Robert O. Keohane, *After Hegemony: Cooperation and Discord in the World Political Economy* (Princeton: Princeton University Press, 1984) and Joseph M. Grieco, "Anarchy and the Limits of Cooperation: A Realist Critique of the Newest Liberal Institutionalism," *International Organization*, Vol. 42 (1988), pp. 485-508.

example, let's suppose a net gain of 10 units of value was produced as the result of economic cooperation by two actors. Whether 10 units of value will be allocated on a 9:1 basis or a 5:5 basis is of great concern for rational actors in the real world. In essence, if games of unequal distribution of net gain are continued, they will affect the balance of power between the two actors in the long run. In this sense, economic cooperation is not simply an economic issue; it is also an important political issue.

Most recent discussions about the possibilities for regional economic cooperation are based on the simple economic logic that emphasizes the existence of comparative advantage and economic complementarity among nations in East Asia. They also argue that East Asia should strengthen its bargaining position against the EC and the NAFTA by promoting economic cooperation. However, these approaches barely mention the political and strategic dimensions involved in the bargaining processes through which regional economic cooperation can be achieved. This paper attempts to fill that gap in research by focusing on the analysis of the political dimensions of the issue and providing recommendations for Korea's foreign economic policy.

The Current Situation and Structure of Economic Cooperation in East Asia

Each of the three regions in the world economy has achieved a different level of economic cooperation: EC the highest level, NAFTA an intermediate level, and East Asia the lowest. While the EC is at the stage of economic integration, East Asian countries are just starting to expand economic interactions, mostly on a bilateral basis through trade and capital investment.[3]

Even with East Asia, there is a regional breakdown of economies. In this, Japan stands apart as the most advanced industrial country, and, within the region, there are three other clusters of countries at different stages of economic development. One cluster includes the NICs (Newly Industrializing Countries) — Korea, Taiwan, Hong Kong, and Singapore. The second cluster numbers among its members Southeast Asian countries such as Indonesia, Malaysia, Thailand, the Philippines, and Brunei, whose economies have been growing rapidly in recent years. The last cluster consists of the (former) socialist countries, including China, North Korea, Russia, Mongolia, and Vietnam. Among these (former) socialist countries, China has been pursuing economic reforms and has been rapidly opening in the last decade.

There has been much economic interaction between these clusters' constituent countries in recent years. When we analyze the trends of these economic transactions closely, we can identify two prominent economic spheres of cooperation emerging in recent years. The first one is based on the close economic ties between Japan and ASEAN countries. In the

---

3. At the 4th ASEAN summit meeting held in January 1992, the six ASEAN countries agreed to cut tariffs on 15 groups of manufactured products to no more than 5% within 15 years. However, this agreement on the ASEAN Free Trade Area will not be effective in its current form. According to the agreement, each country can delay the tariff cuts as long as it wants and important sectors, such as the automobile industry, are excluded. *The Economist*, February 1, 1992, p. 25.

1980s, especially in the period when the yen was
strong after the Plaza Meeting, Japanese firms
invested heavily in these countries having rich natural resources and abundant labor. Recently they
have also begun to expand their investments in both
manufacturing sectors, such as electronics and
automobiles, and service sectors, such as finance,
construction, and transportation.[4] Through these
investments, the structural ties based on the vertical
division of labor between the Japanese economy and
ASEAN countries have been strengthened.[5]

Table 1. Japanese Foreign Direct Investments in East Asia[6]

(1951-89, total, billion dollars)

Countries	World	E.Asia	Korea	Taiwan	H.K.	Singapore
Amount	253.9	39.9	3.9	2.3	8.1	5.7
Share (%)		100	9.7	5.7	20.2	14.3

Countries	Indonesia	Malaysia	Thailand	Philippines	China
Amount	10.4	2.5	3.3	1.3	2.5
Share (%)	26.1	6.3	8.2	3.3	6.2

---

4. *The Korea Economic Daily*, July 9, 1992.

5. In the period 1989-90, Japanese foreign direct investments
occupied 32%, 26%, 23% and 26% of the overall foreign investments in Thailand, Malaysia, Indonesia, and the Philippines. See F.
Wu, "The ASEAN Economies in the 1990s and Singapore's Regional
Role," *California Management Review* 34:1 (Fall 1991), p. 105.

6. Calculated from Table 2 in Toshio Watanabe, ed., *Kyokuchi
Keizaiken no Jidai: Nurikawaru Ajia Keizaichizu* [Emerging Local-
ized Economic Zones: The Changing Map of Asia] (Tokyo: The
Simul Press, 1992), p. 7.

The second economic sphere in East Asia is the so-called "Chinese Economic Community," where the two Chinese NICs have been investing heavily in China's coastal areas in recent years. Hong Kong has invested huge amounts of capital in Guangdong province and Taiwan has rapidly increased its investments in Fujian province. China has actively induced Taiwanese capital by granting tax favors and other preferential treatment. It is interesting to note that this economic sphere has emerged on the basis of the nationality principle.

Table 2. Foreign Direct Investments in China (1979-89 total) [7]

(On the basis of contract, million dollars, %)

Total Sum	Hong Kong*	Japan	U.S.	Korea
34,101 (100)	20,879 (61.2)	2,855 (8.4)	4,058 (11.9)	25 (0.07)

* Includes investments from Macao.

Other notable economic transactions in East Asia include Korean investments in Shandong and Liaoning provinces, Thai investments in the Southern area of Vietnam, and Japanese investments in China. Moreover, South and North Korea, China, Mongolia, and Russia are also collaborating in efforts to develop the Tumen River area on a multilateral basis

7. Calculated from Table I-3-2 in Icksoo Kim, "Dongbugga jiyok eui tooja mit jabon hyeobryok," Korea Institute For International Economic Policy, *Dongbugga Gyongje Hyobryok eui Yeokeon gwa Jeonmang,* 1991. 12, p. 95. The amount of Taiwanese investment in China in 1992 alone is expected to be as much as 2.5 billion dollars. *The Korea Economic Daily,* October 5, 1992.

under the institutional framework of the UNDP (United Nations Development Program). These economic transactions, however, are still less conspicuous than those of the above two economic spheres.

When we look into the current state of economic cooperation in East Asia, we find the following important patterns. First of all, economic cooperation in this area, apart from the cases of the Tumen River Development Project and the ASEAN Free Trade Area, takes the form of bilateral investment cooperation. This indicates that economic cooperation in East Asia is at an earlier stage than that in the EC and North America. This is mainly because countries at different states of economic development, including socialist countries, coexist in this area. Institutional economic cooperation such as exists in the EC and the ASEAN will be possible only after this type of bilateral cooperation progresses further, deepening interdependence. At the current level of interdependence, it still seems premature for countries to form an economic institution such as a free trade area in East or Northeast Asia.

The second important aspect of East Asian economic cooperation is the application of the principle of nationality, as seen in the case of the Chinese Economic Community. The trend toward unification or division along the lines of nationality has become a worldwide phenomenon in the post-Cold War period. This has been the result of the decreasing importance of the old "rule of the game," ideological confrontation, in international relations. The dissolution of the Soviet Union, the national struggle in Yugoslavia, and the unification of Germany are well-known examples.

Close economic cooperation between China and the

market economies of the Chinese NICs shows that this principle has become important even in East Asia.[8] Though China has sought to attract as much foreign capital as possible, it has given higher priority to Chinese capital from abroad than to Japanese and Western capital, as we can observe from its special treatment of Taiwanese investments.[9] A political economy interpretation of this behavior is that not only has the Chinese government considered it important to improve mutual relations between Taiwan and China on the basis of nationality, but also it has sought investment from economies more similar to itself in economic size or developmental stage. In other words, the Chinese government may be afraid of the possibility of economic dependency on advanced capitalist countries like Japan.

From a political economy perspective, deepening economic dependency can be interpreted as the continuation of unequal distribution of gains produced by mutual cooperation between the advanced and the industrializing countries. To soothe fears on the

---

8. The rivalry between two major nations, Japan and China, will become more visible and important as the rivalry between two ideological superpowers, the United States and the former Soviet Union, loses its relevance in East Asian politics.

9. In July 1988, the Chinese government announced "The Regulation on Encouraging Investments by the Taiwanese Compatriots" and granted special treatment to Taiwanese investments. Since the revision of the law in April 1990, local governments have been providing special treatment through administrative guidance. See Imai Satoshi, "Chudaio musubu ryogan keizaiken," in Toshio Watanabe, *ibid.*, pp. 105-6 and *International Herald Tribune*, July 3, 1992. On July 16th, 1992, the Taiwanese national assembly also passed a new law "Ordinance on Relations between Peoples in Taiwanese Area and the Mainland Area", which expands travel and political-economic relations between the two areas. See *Dong-A Ilbo*, July 17, 1992.

weaker side over such a possibility, the stronger side has often had to make side payments to or otherwise compensate the weaker. However, in many cases, conflicts have arisen in the bargaining process on the amounts and the methods of such side payments or compensation. This is why cooperation between countries with a big gap in economic power is more difficult than cooperation between countries sharing similar economic power and developmental stage. This is an important point that should be considered, but is quite often disregarded, in economic policy-making in Korea.

The third important aspect of East Asian economic cooperation is that economic relations between Japan and the ASEAN countries are quite different from those among other countries. Economic cooperation in other regions of East Asia is mostly based on capital investment by the market economies of the NICs in the (former) socialist economies. Thus, the intensity of this type of cooperation and its importance to each participant's economy are still relatively insignificant. Conversely, the cooperation between Japan and ASEAN countries is not only intensive, but also is built on a close structural linkage based on a vertical division of labor. This has led to the integration of ASEAN economies into the Japanese economy. Especially during the period in which the yen was strong, Japanese firms invested huge amounts of capital to produce parts, intermediate goods, machinery, and equipment in these labor-abundant ASEAN countries, and reimported these products back to Japan.[10] This

10. On the explanation of how the rise in the value of the yen has affected economic integration in East Asia, see Rediger Dornbusch, "The Dollar in the 1990s: Competitiveness and the Challenge of New Economic Blocs," in Federal Reserve Bank of Kansas City,

type of foreign direct investment is called out-sourcing. Owing to this massive capital investment from Japan, ASEAN countries have achieved very high rates of economic growth in recent years and now appear to be the new core of growth in the world economy. This intense cooperation and the structural dependence it entailed was the background for Malaysian Prime Minister Mahathir's proposal to form an East Asian Economic Caucus centered around Japan. Economic interaction in this area has advanced enough to suggest establishment of an institution formalizing economic cooperation.

Even though economic relations between Japan and the NICs also exhibit certain features of a division of labor, the industrial structures of Japan and the NICs are somewhat similar. Thus, products from both sides are quite competitive with each other in many industries. This is especially the case with respect to Korea and Japan. Naturally, products from the NICs have not been able to penetrate the Japanese market, and the United States has been the major importer of products from the NICs. For instance, while Korean manufacturing depends much on Japanese parts and materials, mainly because of lagging technology, Korean exports are absorbed more by the United States than by the Japanese market.[11] The contrast with ASEAN coun-

---

Monetary Policy Issues in the 1990s (Kansas City: Federal Reserve Bank of Kansas City, 1989), pp. 266, 270.

11. For example, total Korean exports were about $62.4 billion in 1989. Of these exports, those to the U.S. market amounted to about $21.0 billion while those to the Japanese market amounted to about $13.5 billion. See Korea Institute for International Economic Policy, *Northeast Asian Economic Cooperation: Perspectives and Challenges* (Seoul: KIEP, 1991), Table 1, p. 228.

tries, where parts and intermediate goods are manufactured by Japanese foreign investments and
exported back to Japan, is dramatic. Thus, Japan is
the dominant market for exports from ASEAN countries; their dependence on the United States is much
less important.[12] The exclusion of the United States
in Prime Minister Mahathir's proposal may have
reflected this situation.

Moreover, two countries among the four Asian
NICs, Taiwan and Hong Kong, have been rapidly
strengthening their economic ties with China. Singapore, another newly industrializing country, has
deepened its relations with the Japanese economy as
a member of the ASEAN. In this sense, Asian NICs
have become polarized and more deeply involved in
two different economic spheres. This is why it has
become difficult to identify Asian NICs as a group in
the same way as the ASEAN. Thus, it is inaccurate to
argue, as do some Japanese scholars, that there
exists a structural tie of vertical division of labor
between Japan and the NICs that is similar to the
one between Japan and the ASEAN countries.[13]

---

12. In 1988, 24.6% of total exports from four ASEAN countries
(Indonesia, Malaysia, the Philippines, Thailand) was exported to
Japan, and 19.7% went to the United States. In the same period,
19.6% of total exports from Korea went to Japan, while 35.1% went
to the United States. See Table 2c in William E. James, "Basic
Directions and Areas for Cooperation: Structural Issues of the Asia-
Pacific Economies," in Korea Institute for International Economic
Policy, *Asia-Pacific Economic Cooperation: The Way Ahead* (Seoul:
KIEP, 1990), p. 59.

13. For example, Toshio Watanabe, *Tenkan suru Ajia* [Transform-
ing Asia] (Tokyo, 1991).

The Role of Japan in East Asian Economic Cooperation

Some Japanese scholars argue that the structure of East Asian economies is hierarchical and that those economies are tied to each other based on a structural and vertical division of labor. The argument is based on the so-called flying wild geese model, which is embedded with ideological assumptions. According to this model, Asian economies have been developing in a pattern similar to flying wild geese. That is, the leader, the Japanese economy, is followed by the NICs, which, in turn, are followed by the ASEAN economies. Nowadays, proponents of this model assume that China and other socialist economies constitute the last group following after the ASEAN economies.[14] In this way, the industrial structures of these groups, which are at different stages of development, are structurally linked and change following the pattern of a product cycle.[15]

For example, Toshio Watanabe assumes the existence of "structural combination" between these groups of countries in East Asia based on a vertical

---

14. For an explanation of the flying wild geese model, see Kaname Akamatsu, "Shinkou Kogyokoku no Sangyou Hatten [Industrial Development in Newly Industrializing Countries]," in *Ueda Teijiro Hakushi Kinen Ronbunshu* [Essays in Honor of Dr. Teijiro Ueda], Vol. 4 (Tokyo: Kagagushugi Kogyosha, 1943), and Kiyoshi Kojima, "Reorganization of North-South Trade: Japan's Foreign Economic Policy for the 1970s," *Hitotsubashi Journal of Economics*, 13:2 (1973), pp. 1-28.

15. For a representative work and a review of the model, see Ippei Yamazawa, *Economic Development and International Trade: The Japanese Model* (Honolulu: East-West Center, 1990) and Young-Kwan Yoon's review in *Journal of Asian Studies* (February 1992), pp. 181-3.

division of labor.[16] According to him, U.S. efforts to reduce its budget deficit will have a deflationary effect which will reduce the capacity of the traditional U.S. market to absorb exports from the NICs and the ASEAN countries. At that time, the Japanese market will become more important and replace the U.S. market as the sole major absorber of exports. Japan has already taken this new role, according to Watanabe, since the strengthening of the value of the yen in the mid-1980s. Since then, Japan has appeared to be the axis of economic growth in East Asia, in the sense that it has taken the role not only of the supplier of capital goods to the NICs and the ASEAN countries, but also of the absorber of their exports.[17]

However, there are some problems with this argument. Firstly, as I have already discussed, it is too early to argue that a similar structural combination exists between the Japanese and NICs' economies as exists between the Japanese and ASEAN's economies. Watanabe overestimates the complementary aspect in the Japan-NICs' relations. If we just look at Korea's continuing trade deficit with Japan, we can easily refute Watanabe's argument about Japan's role as the absorber of exports from the NICs. Secondly, it is important to keep in mind that Japan, unlike the United States and other Western economies, has been pursuing a neo-mercantilist economic policy for a few decades. As a result, neo-mercantilistic values, institutions, and customs are deeply embedded in every aspect of the Japanese economy and society. If Japan really wants to replace the United States as

---

16. Watanabe, *ibid.* p. 19.
17. *Ibid.*, pp. 7-10.

the demand absorber in East Asia and deepen structural ties with the NICs, important changes must
take place in Japanese economic, social, and political systems. In other words, Japan's political economic system, with its emphasis on producer interests,
exports, and savings, would need to change to one
that emphasizes consumer interests, imports, and
consumption.[18]

Moreover, the Japanese government does not seem
to be active in pursuing the goal of an exclusive and
autonomous economic bloc in East Asia at present.[19]
For example, when Prime Minister Mahathir first
announced his proposal, the Japanese policy-makers
tended to think that the proposal was not beneficial
to the interests of Japan because Japan had benefitted most from the postwar multilateral free trade
regime. The U.S. government also expressed opposition to the proposal.

Within Japanese academia, there are divergent
views about whether Japan should emphasize its ties
with East Asian countries or continue to focus on
maintaining favorable relations with its traditional
ally, the United States. At present, the latter view
seems to be the mainstream, and the Japanese government is not actively trying to form an exclusive
East Asian or Northeast Asian bloc. Rather, the

---

18. If I borrow the terminologies of the hegemonic stability theory
in Western international political economy, Japan has no ability yet
to provide East Asian countries with the public goods that are necessary to build and maintain an economic bloc. This is due to the
neo-mercantilistic nature of its domestic political economic system.

19. Discussions in Japan about the potential for regional cooperation in Northeast Asia seem to be mostly initiated by the institutions related to local governments and private interests rather than
by the central government.

Japanese private sector is taking the initiative by cautiously increasing its investment in this region on the basis of profitability. However, it is also possible that the conflictual aspect of U.S.-Japan relations in the economic area will override the cooperational aspect. This can be especially true in the post-Cold War situation where they each try to readjust the other's military and political roles because the collapse of their common enemy, the Soviet Union, reduced their incentives to cooperate. In conclusion, how actively the Japanese government will try to form a regional bloc in East Asia will depend on its external relationships with the United States and the EC.

Even if the Japanese government actively pursues the goal of an East Asian bloc, the issue of whether participation in it will be beneficial for Korean national interests remains to be analyzed. Participation in a Japan-centered bloc with its vertical division of labor will limit Korea's role to that of a semi-peripheral country and transform its economy into one that acts as a subcontractor to the core. The division of gain produced by economic transactions between Japan and Korea will continue to be unequal and unfavorable to Korea, and will widen the gap in power between the two countries. Trapped by the functional network of a vertical division of labor, it will be very difficult for Korea to rise into the ranks of advanced industrial countries through technological development. Japan wants Korea to be a follower, not a challenger, and this explains Japanese reluctance to transfer technologies to Korea. Also, the autonomous pursuit of economic policy will become much more difficult if the Korean economy becomes trapped by the functional network of a self-reliant economic bloc. In this sense, choosing the option of a Japanese centered bloc means giving up other policy options for Korea. Of course from a short-term perspective, utilizing our comparative advantage, there would be an absolute gain in becoming a subcontractor for the Japanese economy. But Japan's absolute gain from this type of interaction would be much larger than Korea's. Moreover, Korea's short-term absolute gain would be achieved only at the cost of giving up long-term improvement of welfare and efficiency through the dynamic creation of comparative advantage.

Let us suppose that Japan's relations with the United States and the EC worsen and Japan tries to build an institutional cooperative body, such as a free trade area in East Asia. Even in this case, Korea should ask for compensation or side payments for the possible unequal distribution of net gains that would result from the construction of the institution. For example, in the process of negotiation, Korea should ask for Japan's guarantee of the transfer of high technology and its cooperation in the process of structural adjustment toward higher-level industry. Korea would also have to ask for the expansion of Japan's role as the demand absorber for Korean exports to remove continuing trade deficits. In other words, Korean negotiators should try their best not to limit Korea's economy to the role of a semi-peripheral subcontractor, but to leave the options open for Korea to become a core country.

Viewed from this perspective, international economic cooperation, by its very nature, is not a simple economic issue but a political issue. For example, the Latin American Free Trade Association, which was established in 1960, began to weaken in less than 10 years. This was mainly because relatively less developed members, such as Bolivia, Ecuador,

Paraguay, and Uruguay (after August 1967), or member countries with smaller domestic markets, such as Chile, Colombia, Peru, and Uruguay (before August 1967), tended to think that most of the benefits from the establishment of a free trade area were captured by the relatively more developed countries, including Argentina, Brazil, and Mexico. In other words, the weaker countries perceived exploitation by the stronger countries through the creation of a free trade area.[20] In the case of the European Monetary System (EMS), a weaker country, Italy, was permitted to have a wide margin of exchange rate fluctuation (6%) that was more than twice that permitted other member countries (2.25%). About one billion dollars worth of subsidies were provided to Italy and Ireland so that these weaker countries might not have to contract their domestic economies to keep their currencies in line with the EMS. At the same time, more severe duty was applied to the stronger surplus country, Germany, so that the distribution of the cost of stabilizing exchange rates would not be unfavorable to the weaker members.[21] The current crisis in the EMS prompted by the U.K. and Italy's departure from the ERM (Exchange Rate Mechanism) was basically caused by their perception that the burden for maintaining a fixed exchange rate was distributed unequally. In their eyes, they were

---

20. Joseph Grunwald, Miguel S. Wionszek, and Martin Carnoy, *Latin American Economic Integration and U.S. Policy* (Washington, D.C.: The Brookings Institute, 1972), pp. 52-3.

21. Hugo M. Kaufman, "The European Monetary System and National Policy Constraints," *Comparative Social Research*, Vol. 5, pp. 107-28 and George Zis, "The European Monetary System, 1979-84: An Assessment," *Journal of Common Market Studies*, Vol. 23 (1984), pp. 45-72.

pushed to accept too much of the burden while Germany was accepting too little. Even in the case of the Tumen River Project, both China and North Korea argue that their own territory in the triangle should be developed first. The methods employed to solve this difference of opinion will affect the prospects for the Project. All these examples show that economic cooperation among countries is, in reality, not reached simply through the normative application of the principles of the division of labor, but through political bargaining based on a cold calculation by each member of its national interest.

The Choice for Korea

What, then, should be Korea's first priority in foreign economic policy from a long-term perspective? As we have already discussed, in becoming a member of an East Asian (or even Northeast Asian) bloc centered around Japan, Korea faces the problems of sacrificing long-term economic welfare and efficiency, losing autonomy in economic policy-making, and experiencing a widening power gap between Japan and Korea. At the moment, the Japanese government itself is not visibly trying to build any bloc. Besides, the possibility of forming a bloc depends on how the nature of Japan's domestic political economic system changes and how Japan's relations with the United States and the EC unfold. However, Japan would welcome a spontaneous development of this kind of hierarchical economic order in Asia, whether its government pursues it deliberately or not.

Considering all these factors, Korea should put the highest priority on economic cooperation with North

Korea in accordance with the nationality principle, as currently being practiced by the Chinese. It is very important to expand the market size of both Koreas through economic cooperation, utilizing comparative advantages on each side. Only through the expansion and integration of the market in the Korean peninsula can Korea reinforce its bargaining power in the future negotiation process to establish a new economic institutional mechanism in East Asia. It is very likely that the Japan-ASEAN sphere and the Chinese Economic Community will become the two fundamental axes whose dynamic interrelations will decide the shape and the nature of the new economic order in the region. Only through achieving economic cooperation and integration on the nationality basis will Korea be able to strengthen its bargaining power and have a greater influence in the negotiation process. In this way, the new institutional cooperative mechanism will more properly reflect Korea's national interests.

From North Korea's point of view, reduction of the danger of being the victim in an unfavorable distribution of net gain from economic cooperation is possible by putting a higher priority on South Korea; there is a smaller gap in economic power between South and North Korea than between Japan or the United States and North Korea. Furthermore, even in cases when an unequal distribution of net gain occurs, South Korea would be an easier partner to ask for side payments or compensation because of the common cause of national unification. This is why, from a long-term strategic perspective, economic cooperation between the Koreas would be a more rational and less risky strategy for both. To pursue this strategy, North Korea would have to provide a favorable environment to investors from the South so that they may invest freely in line with the dictates of the market principle and profitability. It would also be desirable to grant preferential treatment to capital investments from the South, as the Chinese government did to those from Taiwan. Strengthening economic cooperation between the South and the North would help to restore a common sense of national identity between the two and reduce the cost of the upcoming unification. After all, the issue of regional economic cooperation is not much different from the issue of national unification for Korea.

If there is little advancement in economic cooperation between the South and the North, and if a new economic order, either in the form of a free trade area or in some other institutional form, is created in East Asia, then the latter will reflect the interests of the Japan-ASEAN sphere and the Chinese Economic Community, but not Korean interests. Our ancestors fell prey to the expanding Western international system of nation-states in the latter half of the 19th century when they were captivated by the Confucian notion of tributary international order. If we are captivated by the Cold War mentality and cannot prepare for the formation of the coming order in this region, Korea will remain, once again, a backward nation. For Korea, the process of becoming a unified nation-state overlaps with the process of preparing for a new international order that may partially transcend the nation-state system.[22]

---

22. It may be inappropriate to pose an either-or question about whether the realist perspective emphasizing the nation-state as a basic unit in international relations or the liberal perspective emphasizing the role of institutions is more relevant in explaining the current trend toward regional integration. Probably it is more correct to

If the two Koreas can achieve the goal of intensive economic cooperation, then they will also be more effective in pursuing a foreign economic policy with other economic powers. For example, if Korea promotes economic cooperation with China, Russia, and the United States on the basis of Korean economic integration, it will strengthen Korea's bargaining power. But if the two Koreas pursue their own strategies of cooperation with other economic powers on an individual basis, without North-South economic integration, their economies will each become structurally incorporated into the bigger economies. In this case, neither Korea will have the bargaining power to reflect its own interest in the formation of a new order.

Nowadays, a country's position in the world economy depends not only on its efforts to utilize its comparative advantage from a static viewpoint, but also on its efforts to generate comparative advantage for the future from a dynamic perspective. As the utilization of current comparative advantage is the foundation for current foreign economic strategy, future foreign economic strategy for Korea will be sustained only through continuing domestic efforts to create future comparative advantage. Future comparative advantage will be successfully pursued only when Korea continues in its efforts to accumulate high technology, prevent the hollowing-out of industries, find new products establishing niches in the world market, and reform the domestic political economic system to promote efficiency.

---

explain that the realistic pursuit of national interests to the fullest extent led to the self-denial of nation-states or a partial relegation of sovereignty which realizes the liberal forecast for regional integration. In other words, this is a self-contradictory aspect of the historical development of dynamics in international relations.

CHAPTER 6

PROSPECTS FOR KOREA-U.S.-JAPAN TRILATERAL SECURITY RELATIONS

Melvin Gurtov

The "New World Order" and International Security

The end of superpower rivalry and Cold War alignments is the most promising development in world politics of the last half century. It has led to dramatically reduced international tensions and opportunities for shifting attention and resources to a host of other global security issues. But the end of the Cold War has not, in and of itself, created a "new world order" (NWO) in a number of regions, including Northeast Asia.

This paper addresses security prospects and potentialities in Northeast Asia. To do so, we first need to consider what the NWO means and does not mean.

Reflecting on the Persian Gulf War, President Bush said it was about "more than one small country; it is a big idea; a new world order ... [with] new ways of working with other nations ... peaceful settlement of disputes, solidarity against aggression, reduced and controlled arsenals and just treatment of all peoples." In fact, the Gulf War itself, not to mention events since then, only partially fulfilled the President's ambitious definition. Operation "Desert Storm" was a successful exercise in collective security, but not in the use of nonviolent means of settling disputes. While carried out under various United Nations resolutions, "Desert Storm" was first and foremost designed by the Bush Administration to accomplish national objectives: to win a "test case" of post-Cold War aggression; to preserve access to a vital resource, oil; to maintain nation-state sovereignty (Iraq's as well as Kuwait's) and a Middle East "balance" against Iran; to demonstrate the virtues of using rapidly deployed, high-technology weapons; and, especially, to establish U.S. leadership of the new order by keeping control of forces under the flag of the United States. In these respects, "Desert Storm" was closer to an old-fashioned containment action against the "communist threat" than to a "new order."[1]

Events since the Gulf War are testimony to the problems of universalizing its significance. For every instance of a "new order" there is an instance of disorder. Perhaps this explains the Bush Administration's virtual silence on the NWO in the last year. Consider the record of international security in the terms used by the President to define the NWO:

• **"peaceful settlement of disputes, solidarity against aggression":** On the positive side, the United Nations is involved in twelve peacekeeping efforts,

---

1. See Strobe Talbott, "Post-Victory Blues," *Foreign Affairs*, 71:1 (1991/92), pp. 53-69.

a significant number of armed conflicts and hostile relationships have moved to the negotiating table (including Cambodia, Afghanistan, Israel-Palestine, Mozambique, Western Sahara, El Salvador, and, of course, the two Koreas), and sanctions have been applied by the UN in three cases and the Organization of American States in one case (Libya, Iraq, Serbia, and Haiti, respectively). International peacekeeping is marred, however, by continuing violence where negotiations are ongoing (such as Cambodia and Afghanistan); and by civil war and repression in numerous countries (including Peru, Somalia, Burma, Iraq, Indonesia's East Timor, and South Africa). Competing ethnic nationalisms have replaced Cold War tensions throughout central Europe and the former USSR. The case of Yugoslavia stands out as a particular failure of collective sanctions thus far to stop Serbia's "ethnic cleansing" in Bosnia-Herzegovina.

• **"reduced and controlled arsenals":** The record on arms control is as murky as ever. Global military spending has apparently levelled off; but U.S. spending remains at Cold War levels. Nuclear-weapons stockpiles have been reduced about 10 percent under U.S.-Russia agreements, and the nuclear danger is being further relieved by the withdrawal of nuclear weapons from Europe and South Korea. But, overall, the means of international violence continue to spread, while planning for the conversion of military industries has proceeded fitfully, at best, in several countries. Proliferation of nuclear technology and materials remains a serious problem; Iraq's covert acquisition of a nuclear capability and its subsequent forced denuclearization demonstrate the depth of both ends of the proliferation problem. Conventional arms transfers are again on the rise. As the cases of Russia, China, and the U.S. show, arms sales are being increasingly driven by profit-making, employment, and domestic political considerations now that military forces are being trimmed. Despite Bush's initiative, in May 1991, to reduce conventional and other arms transfers to Third World countries, in fact the U.S. has sold or transferred about $6 billion worth of arms to the Middle East since the initiative, and about $19 billion all told to that region since Iraq invaded Kuwait. Globally, U.S. arms sales amounted to about $63 billion in 1991.[2]

• **"just treatment of all people":** The prospects of a new world order look dimmest on this score. True, the human condition has improved in some respects over the last several years. Notably, elements of democratic governance have newly emerged in parts of Eastern Europe, Africa, Asia, and Latin America. But systematic violations of human rights by repressive military and civilian authorities are no less prominent today than in previous periods.[3] Economic development in the Third World outside the four Asian NICs and China has generally not kept pace with population growth, and has suffered from worldwide trade protectionism, spiraling external indebtedness, and a redirection of international aid to Eastern Europe. Thus, at the level of individuals

---

2. On Middle East sales, see the report of the Arms Control Association in *The Oregonian*, February 15, 1992, p. A10. For global figures on U.S. arms transfers (including government and commercial sales), see *The Defense Monitor*, 21:5 (1992), pp. 1-8.

3. For documentation, see Ruth Leger Sivard, ed., *World Military and Social Expenditures 1991* (Washington, D.C.: World Priorities, 1991).

and families, the global product continues to be enjoyed by fewer people. According to the Worldwatch Institute, the concentration of wealth and the rate of absolute poverty are both still rising globally. About 1.2 billion people, or over 23 percent of the world's population, are estimated to be living in absolute poverty, that is, at the very margin of survival.[4]

A comprehensive understanding of international security, and therefore of the NWO, would take additional factors into account. For instance, "just treatment of all peoples" needs to include environmental factors, such as lack of access to clean water for 1 billion people in developing countries, lack of access to sanitation for 1.7 billion people, and the consequent deaths of over 3 million children a year from diarrhea.[5] Remedying the unequal treatment of women in most countries in the world is central to effectively confronting both underdevelopment and environmental decline. Global environmental issues such as deforestation, global warming, and the thinning ozone layer are matters of international security too. At best, the UNCED summit in Rio de Janeiro in June 1992 is only a start toward regulating greenhouse gas emissions and destruction of tropical forests in ways that balance human, national, and global interests, North and South.

Finally, it must be observed that although the term "NWO" is widely used, it is open to diverse interpretations based on competing national interests. The view of President Bush and other senior U.S. officials,

---

4. Alan B. Durning, *Poverty and the Environment: Reversing the Downward Spiral* (New York: Worldwatch Institute Paper No. 92, November 1989), pp. 18-20.

5. World Bank, *World Development Report 1992: Development and the Environment* (New York: Oxford University Press, 1992), p. 5.

deriving from the Persian Gulf War, that NWO means the U.S. now "calls the shots"—which led Canadian Prime Minister Brian Mulroney to say recently that the G-7 might better be called G-1—may not be all that widely shared. Some governments are undoubtedly wary of a solitary superpower that believes itself to be in charge of enforcing the rules of the new order. Other governments will accept U.S. leadership on some issues, but will be much more cautious when it comes to matters of national sensitivity. In Asia, for example, Malaysian Prime Minister Mahathier has been an outspoken critic of U.S. (and Western) notions of human rights and environmental protection. The Chinese government likewise rejects the notion that a "new order" permits outside interference in its domestic decisionmaking, especially on human rights. Beijing may also have in mind its future freedom of action in Tibet and Hong Kong. While Japan struggles for a consensus on its international role (see below), it is obvious from the steady criticisms of U.S. economic management that many leading Japanese concede to U.S. *military* leadership but believe Japan deserves co-dominion when it comes to GATT and other fixtures of the global economy.

For all its ambiguities and contradictions, however, the NWO is still a meaningful term. After all, international security in the 1990s *is* qualitatively different from previous decades. At least five changes in world order come to mind that affect security in Northeast Asia:

• The end of the Cold War in most parts of the world has opened up unprecedented opportunities for national economic renewal through increased interdependence in science, technology, trade, and investment.

• Regional and sub-regional integration has helped to leapfrog borders, subordinate some political frictions, and create new patterns of interaction. But nationalism is likely to remain a powerful force often in competition with regionalism.

• Military power is growing less salient to national and international security as other, global factors come into play, such as environmental protection, energy resources and needs, economic management and productivity, scientific and technological innovation, and access to information.

• World politics is multipolar, not unipolar. Although the U.S. is the only superpower, Russia remains a first-rank military power, the EC and Japan are economic superpowers, and some Third World countries, such as Korea and Taiwan, have moved to the front ranks of international trade.

• Superpower rivalry in Europe and the Third World has been replaced by cooperative approaches to security, greatly enhancing prospects for a collectively enforced rule of law through the UN and other bodies.

Superpower(s) in Asia

William Pfaff, writing in *Foreign Affairs*,[6] asserted that the end of superpower rivalry also marked the end of superpowers. That interpretation of the NWO is not official Washington's. There, the prevailing view since the Persian Gulf War has been that the world remains a dangerous place and only the United

---

6. "Redefining World Power," *Foreign Affairs*, 70:1 (1990/91), p. 35.

States has the muscle and political will to enforce the peace. As one journalistic spokesman for this concept of unipolarity puts it, "American preeminence [is] based on the fact that it is the only country with the military, diplomatic, political and economic assets to be a decisive player in any conflict in whatever part of the world it chooses to involve itself."[7]

The U.S. definition of superpower status was clarified when a draft Pentagon strategic plan on U.S. military needs was leaked to the *New York Times* in early 1992.[8] The plan is a vintage Cold War document in several respects. Its key assumption is that the United States needs to retain the capacity to act decisively in a crisis, unilaterally if necessary. A new world order, in the sense of a more or less permanent coalition of powers acting through the UN to counter threats to the peace, is judged not reliable. "The United States should be postured to act independently when collective action cannot be orchestrated," the document reads, since future coalitions of the Gulf War type may not be achievable, may not share similar objectives, or may not be capable of acting. The document also echoes longstanding U.S. concerns about rival hegemons. It asserts that the United States "must maintain the mechanisms for deterring potential competitors from even aspiring to a larger regional or global role." In other words, Japan, Germany, and possibly Russia should not be regarded as potential co-equals; they may even emerge as threats

---

7. Charles Krauthammer, "The Unipolar Moment," *Foreign Affairs*, 70:1 (1990/91), p. 23.

8. *New York Times*, February 17, 1992, p. 1 and February 18, 1992, p. 1; *Oregonian*, March 8, 1992, p. A4 (from the *New York Times*).

to U.S. supremacy. Finally, the Pentagon document makes the case for continued high military spending to support a 1.6 million-man military and a five-year budget of perhaps $1.5 trillion. It speaks of retaining a capacity to fight two major wars simultaneously and two lesser conflicts—a scenario last unveiled in the Kennedy years.

The Pentagon document can be dismissed as simply a justification of high military budgets, or as merely a contingency plan. Following a storm of Congressional protest over the "naivete" of the document, it was publicly criticized by White House and State Department officials, forcing a Pentagon spokesman to backtrack somewhat.[9] The fact remains, however, that the document circulated among the senior civilian and military leaders of the Defense Department. No one revised the view in the draft document that the United States should deter pretenders to superpower status and challengers in regions of primary U.S. interest. In fact, at a press conference on March 1, 1992, President Bush, while saying he had not read the document, backed its essential conclusions. He said:

> We are the leaders and we must continue to lead. We must continue to stay engaged. Now that does not preclude working closely with multilateral organizations. For people that challenge our leadership around the world, they simply do not understand how the world looks to us for leadership.

The problem with this self-conception is that when other governments (Japan and Germany among them) *do* look to the United States, they see not only

---

9. *New York Times*, March 11, 1992, p. 1.

unparalleled military power, but also serious economic and social problems that limit U.S. leadership
in world affairs and impose unfair burdens on them.
The U.S. budget deficit in 1991 was just under $300
billion, and in the coming year will be over $320 bil-
lion; the external (national) debt surpassed $4 tril-
lion in mid-1992; and federal government borrowing,
which now absorbs over 40 percent of all capital, has
created annual interest payments of $286 billion, or
14% of the budget. (The sharp reduction of Japan's
investments in the U.S. in 1991 spells further trouble for the U.S. budget.) Large-scale military spending reductions, which could be applied to the national debt, are not on the agenda of either political party
(The next U.S. military budget will be nearly $290
billion). Nor has any major political leader, or candidate for the Presidency, endorsed a strategy for military conversion. Thus, there is no peace dividend in
spite of the Soviet collapse and a full plate of urgent
domestic needs.[10]

A kind of political paralysis has taken hold in
Washington as Congress and the President endlessly
debate spending priorities but have proven incapable
of dealing effectively with the twin threats of human
insecurity and fiscal irresponsibility. In turn, according to one of America's foremost pollsters, a "crisis of
legitimacy" has gripped voters who are literally

---

10. These include $750 billion in savings and loan banking fail-
ures; numerous "superfund" hazardous environmental sites that
have not been cleaned up; rising real unemployment, which now
stands at about 11 percent; rising violence and crime; the high
number (one in five) of children living in poverty; a poverty rate
overall of 14.2 percent (35.7 million people) in 1992, the largest
number of people since 1964; and the approximately 36 million
people without health insurance.

frightened about the future.[11] Such fear and anxiety bodes ill for continued good relations with major economic partners.

Implications for Northeast Asia and Trilateral Security

But perhaps the most important factor weighing against American unipolarity is the tide of events in particular regions and countries. Here we turn to East and Northeast Asia.

Two developments above all others have altered the political landscape of East Asia: the collapse of the USSR, and the ROK's Nordpolitik. These are not the only important signs that the Cold War is over in Asia: the U.S. withdrawal from bases in the Philippines, the Cambodia settlement, the emergence of "Greater China" (PRC, Taiwan, Hong Kong), and PRC-ROK normalization are others. What makes the Soviet collapse and Nordpolitik so pivotal is that they were the first concrete indications of real hope of constructing a stable peace in East Asia around new structures of regional cooperation. They are signs that the strategy of containment is no longer necessary; that once-formidable ideological barriers in state-to-state relations are coming down; that new centers of power (including Japan) are emerging, if not yet in politically definable ways; and that economic and technological forces are exerting an irresistible appeal across borders, replacing military power and narrow nationalism with strong regional mechanisms.

---

11. Daniel Yankelovich, "Foreign Policy After the Election," *Foreign Affairs*, 71:4 (Fall, 1992), p. 4.

These developments have decisively undermined longstanding, contending views of U.S. power in Asia—both the traditional view that "no power other than the United States is now able or welcome to play the role of regional balancer," as Assistant Secretary of State Richard Solomon said in October 1990 and since, and the critical view that emphasizes U.S. interventionism and hegemonic ambitions. The traditional view is geared to contingencies whose relevance is rapidly disappearing. Communism is no longer either ideologically or militarily menacing. Defense of Japan hardly seems urgent, since Japan no longer has obvious enemies to defend against. In fact (see section 5 of this paper), Japan in the future seems certain to have a more independent national security policy, even while remaining within the bilateral treaty. And the strategic function of the United States as enforcer of the balance of power can no longer be assumed; it now requires a persuasive rationale that has not yet been forthcoming. If some kind of "balancing" or "deterrent" presence *is* needed in the region, it may be performed with more political efficacy and at lower cost by a *grouping* of states rather than by the United States alone.

As for the critical view of U.S. policy, it has largely been bypassed by events. The U.S. removal of its nuclear weapons from Korea, the various ROK initiatives since proclamation of the Northern Policy, and the momentum to an all-Korean solution of some outstanding issues have undermined the notion of U.S. domination. These events also contradict the view that no change is possible in the "strategic stalemate" that had long prevailed on the peninsula. The deadlock has in fact been broken, and by the Koreans rather than by outside powers.

Oddly enough, the traditional and the critical views hold in common two important truths about U.S. policy: its slowness to change, and its seeming imperviousness to thinking beyond the Cold War. Traditional Realpolitik continues to dominate official U.S. thinking *in spite of* recognition of a new era in Asia, suggesting either that Washington fears being excluded, or wants to forestall Japan's emergence as a regional political leader. Secretary of State James Baker's *Foreign Affairs* article on future U.S. policy toward the Pacific community, while expressing more sensitivity to multilateral ventures than the Pentagon, shows the continuing reliance on geopolitical premises and Ameri-centrism in U.S. strategic thinking.[12]

Granted, there is considerable support within the Asia-Pacific community for a continued strong U.S. military presence. Contrariwise, there is as yet no region-wide agreement on a multilateral security arrangement—such as a "Conference on Security and Cooperation in Asia" or an informal forum for

---

12. James Baker, "America in Asia," *Foreign Affairs*, 70:5 (Winter, 1991-92), p. 3. Baker's fundamental point is that the United States anchors all three pillars of the Pacific community. He asks us to "visualize…a fan spread wide, with its base in North America and radiating west across the Pacific." The essential ingredient of regional security remains the "loose network of bilateral alliances with the United States at its core." The "primary rationale for [U.S.] defense engagement in the region [is] to provide geopolitical balance, to be an honest broker, to reassure against uncertainty." Hence, as the Pentagon document also makes clear, the U.S. envisions the maintenance of significant, although reduced, military strength in the region to deal with conflict scenarios such as North Korean aggression and a coup in the Philippines. The U.S. role does not exclude multilateral arrangements, such as in Cambodia or even Korea; but it is the self-perception of being the balancer (and ultimate arbiter) of power in the region, notably without major Japanese participation, that sets the United States apart.

mediating disputes—that would replace or supplement the five existing bilateral defense treaties between the United States and Asian countries. But these considerations need to be balanced against some others.

First, the original purposes of the bilateral treaties, as of the SEATO pact—to deter and defend against attack by communist forces—no longer are relevant except in Korea. As Robert Scalapino writes, "the risk of a major power conflict in Asia is at its lowest point in this century."[13] Flashpoints of possible conflict remain, of course —such as civil war in Cambodia and Burma, differences between Japan and China over the Senkakus, and multiple territorial claims in the South China Sea. And political instability is characteristic of every society in East Asia, including Japan. But the sources of international conflicts in the region are for the most part being successfully addressed through diplomacy and negotiation. Political instability today is purely domestic in origin, not the product of external machinations. Most importantly, East Asia's security concerns are less salient to the region's future than are other issues that call for cooperation and multilateralism: regional economic partnerships, Japan's economic penetration east and south, trade imbalances, environmental protection, surplus labor migrations, weapons transfers, nuclear nonproliferation, and the de-ideologization of bilateral relations. Addressing these issues requires diplomacy, not "balancing" power.

Second, the reasons why Asian countries want a continuing U.S. military presence vary in kind and

13. Robert Scalapino, "The United States and Asia: Future Prospects," *Foreign Affairs*, 70:5 (Winter 1991/92), p. 26.

persuasiveness. Some governments perceive a modernizing China as a security threat, with designs on oil in the South China Sea (the Spratley and the Paracel island groups). Yet the spectre (again) of an aggressive China is rather premature, and certainly does not justify the kind of U.S. naval buildup being advocated (and to some extent being implemented) in Southeast Asia.[14] It should be balanced against China's development needs and its diplomatic offensive since 1989 that has normalized relations with a number of Asian neighbors.

Other governments, such as the ROK, are more concerned about a revival of Japanese expansionism, especially since the Japanese parliament's passage of the Peacekeeping Operations (PKO) bill. But the PKO bill is an extremely modest and carefully conditioned response to international pressures on Japan to sacrifice more on behalf of global stability. Still other governments may, as in years past, have interest mainly in the economic and political value of having U.S. bases on their territory. From the standpoint of actual and potential threats to regional security, however, as opposed to the narrow interests of particular governments and bureaucracies (such as the U.S. Department of Defense), none of these reasons seems to justify a *unilateral* U.S. role as the stabilizer or balancer of power in the Asia Pacific region.

Asian governments are only in the beginning

---

14. U.S. military cooperation with Malaysia, Thailand, Indonesia, Singapore and other countries is expanding—and a potential "China threat" is the stated reason. See Nayan Chanda, "U.S. Maintains Broad Asian Military Pacts," *Asian Wall Street Journal*, April 8, 1992, p. 1, and an interview of Vice-Admiral Stanley Arthur, commander of the U.S. Seventh Fleet until July 1992, in *Far Eastern Economic Review*, August 13, 1992, pp. 18-19.

stages of working out a new pattern of post-Cold War relationships. A number of possible multilateral groupings to deal with emerging security issues may evolve, as we already see in ASEAN's intercession in the six-nation dispute over ownership of the Spratleys. Any such efforts may or may not directly involve the United States, but they are bound to take into account both U.S. interests and the fact the United States will have a military presence in the region for years to come. It is presumptuous to believe, however, that Asia's future security depends on a balance of (U.S.) power. New regional linkages are developing, dialogue is working, and nationalist sensitivities (including Japan's) are as keen as ever to external intervention.

Prospects for Korean Security

Changing circumstances in global security, the Asia region, and the U.S. economy coincide with dramatic successes in Korea's diplomacy and progress in its democratization. Together, these propitious developments point to a recasting of U.S.-Korea-Japan relations.

Nordpolitik under President Roh Tae-Woo has made "thinkable" two developments that until recently seemed like only distant possibilities: U.S. withdrawal from Korea and Korean unification. On the first point, the Korean security situation has taken a dramatic turn for the better. The "threat from the North" has not entirely ended; but direct ROK-DPRK diplomacy has replaced the trading of threats with bargaining, concessions on both sides, and mutually beneficial agreements. Soviet decline and China's "opening" to Korea and the rest of the world economy have greatly eroded North Korea's international support and standing in the world community. These developments, and others in the global economy, have isolated the DPRK, put it on the defensive, and exposed its economic and political weaknesses. The DPRK's military forces remain formidable; but by most accounts, ROK forces are more than a match for them and, as importantly, have the technical and financial resources to continue growing if necessary.

In recognition that Korean security is greatly improved, the United States has already withdrawn nuclear weapons from Korea, cancelled "Team Spirit" for 1992, and placed the joint command under Korean leadership. These are all helpful, tension-reducing measures. Yet there remains an American preoccupation with containment and nuclear deterrence. Early in 1992, General Colin Powell stated, and the draft Pentagon planning document repeated, that Korea is still regarded as one of the two arenas (along with the Persian Gulf) in which a major regional war might be fought. North Korea, in a time of growing economic crisis, may resort to some "irrational" act. (Cuba and China are also placed in the category of potentially irrational actors.) The war scenario depicts an all-out North Korean attack directed at capturing Seoul and launched at a time when the U.S. is preoccupied with an Iraqi attack on Kuwait and Saudi Arabia. Pyongyang, the document says, might use "5-10 [nuclear] weapons deliverable by aircraft or missiles" if its situation became desperate. To counter that possibility, the U.S. defense planners not only suggest a large-scale dispatch of ground and air forces. They also urge adopting contingencies for a general preemptive attack (or threat of preemption) on North Korea generally or on its nuclear weapons plants.[15]

Contingency planning of this kind was sensible during certain periods of high Cold-War tension; but it seems out of place today. Actual circumstances in and around Korea, not worst-case scenarios, ought to be driving security planning. The Korean peninsula is not the Persian Gulf. North Korea's nuclear capability is cause for concern, but not alarm. As CIA chief Robert Gates was careful to say in testimony, "Even after North Korea accumulates enough plutonium, making a device would require several additional steps that could require months or even years."[16] Although Pyongyang has thus far barred the door to mutual "challenge" inspections of nuclear facilities in the two Koreas, it has accepted international inspections. Given Russian and Chinese interests in regional stability, their growing enmeshment in the East Asian and global trading systems, and the DPRK's interest in joint ventures with South Korean industries, North Korea's exercise of the nuclear option—even in a token force for symbolic purposes —much less a suicidal use of force against the South, is difficult to imagine. In the improbable case of a nuclear crisis or a resumption of fighting on the peninsula, the use of counterforce can be planned for within multilateral frameworks, both regional and international (see below). Security planning, however, now ought to comprehend economic and political incentives for cooperation and not dwell on military

15. See the various articles by Patrick E. Tyler in *New York Times*, February 17-18, 1992, p. Al, and (as reprinted) in *The Oregonian*, March 8, 1992, p. A4.

16. *New York Times*, March 2, 1992, p. A14.

deployments.

The second long-range prospect that Nordpolitik has telescoped is the opportunity for Korean unification. It is not likely to happen soon; but unification is now a possible dream, and from the standpoint of Korean interests, North and South, it makes sense to pursue that dream vigorously.

From this angle, the continued presence of U.S. forces in South Korea may soon become a political liability. As national unification becomes more realizable, or at least *imaginable* to Koreans, U.S. forces in their country will be seen by increasing numbers of them, and not only young people, as an obstacle to unification. Partly this will be the natural concomitant of Korean self-confidence and nationalism, both of which make foreign forces (and arrangements such as the status-of-forces agreement) an easy target. Partly this discontent will be embedded within the continuing volatility of Korean society, politics, and economy.[17] And partly it will be due to memories of the meddling of U.S. forces in Korean political affairs. Further fueling the fire is the (almost inevitable) reappraisal of the U.S.'s historical role in Korea, an increasingly negative perception of the United States among Koreans, and rising popular demands for national unification.[18]

---

17. For an excellent review of developments and prospects, see Sung-Joo Han, "Korea's Democratic Experiment: 1987-1991," *Democratic Institutions*, vol. I (1991), pp. 63-78.

18. T.C. Rhee, "The Future of U.S.-Korea Relations," paper prepared for the Conference on Korea in the Asia-Pacific Community, Portland State University, Portland, Oregon, U.S.A., April 1991, pp. 15-18. A milder view of these phenomena is James Cotton, "Conflict and Accommodation in the Two Koreas," in Stuart Harris and James Cotton, eds., *The End of the Cold War in Northeast Asia* (Longman: Cheshire, Melbourne, 1991) pp. 169-70.

U.S. troop withdrawals should not await reunification, the full realization of Korean democracy, or an incident that touches off popular discontent. In fact, precisely *because* national unity is the principal responsibility of the two Koreas to negotiate, and because the democratization of Korean politics is not yet fully institutionalized, U.S. forces should eventually be completely withdrawn to avoid even the appearance of interfering in either process. The best time for friends to restructure their relationship when change is apparent is while they are on good terms and not after a multitude of latent resentments have been magnified out of proportion.

I am not talking here about a sudden abandonment of the ROK by U.S. forces. Rather, the central issue, in the wake of vastly different circumstances inside and outside Korea, is how best to promote Korean security in a probable context of growing nationalism. The answer, I suggest, lies in working toward a multilateral structure that will substitute for the bilateral defense treaty as tensions on the peninsula continue to ease. Under a Two-Plus-Four nation formula, the two Koreas would negotiate further tension-reducing steps and terms for unification (including possible confederation), while the United States, Russia, China, and Japan would jointly safeguard the results.[19]

Both the two Koreas and the four powers that determined Korea's postwar politics ought to sign

---

19. A four-power structure has been mentioned by others: see, for example, Baker, *op. cit.*, p. 13, and Stephen W. Bosworth, "The United States and Asia," *Foreign Affairs*, 71:1 (1991/92), p. 188. Roh Tae-Woo also referred to a Northeast Asia peace conference of the major powers in his October 19, 1988 speech before the UN General Assembly.

peace treaties, perhaps under UN auspices, to end the Korean War. The 1991 ROK-DPRK accord on "non-aggression and reconciliation" falls short of being a peace treaty. A peace treaty would also formally complete cross-recognition by all the parties. The ROK-DRPK treaty would also include provision for further confidence-building steps at the non-governmental as well as the governmental level. These might include larger-scale and more diverse exchanges of visits than previously have occurred, the conversion of military industries and facilities to civilian use, and military force and budget reductions; a time-table for the final withdrawal of "all foreign forces and bases" from Korea; reassurances of mutual noninterference and nonaggression; and an outlining of next steps in reunification.

The purpose of the four-power arrangement would be to guarantee the peace. It could accomplish this in a number of ways, including requirements for consultation in a crisis, limitations on conventional arms transfers to Korea, mechanisms of military verification, and cooperation on projects (such as the conversion of military industries) that promote Korean development. Although the four-power arrangement would nullify bilateral defense agreements involving Korea, nothing in it would prevent action by the United Nations (the precedent is Security Council Resolution 687 against Iraq's invasion of Kuwait) in the event North Korea were to initiate hostilities. (With normalization of PRC-ROK relations, the prospect of a Chinese veto becomes small.) Nor would the arrangement prohibit the continued basing of U.S. air and other nonnuclear forces in Japan, precisely to maintain the ability to react in a crisis.

The four-power structure, in which the two Koreas

would be represented, might specifically address the establishment of a Northeast Asia nuclear-free zone. The basis for a NFZ clearly exists: the principle of Korean denuclearization was agreed to in the December 1991 joint declaration; Japan maintains its three nonnuclear principles; and China reiterated its support of NFZs when it acceded to the Nuclear Non-Proliferation Treaty in March 1992. Russia (at least under Gorbachev, in his 1986 Vladivostok speech) is also on record as favoring a northeast Asia nuclear-free zone; and President Boris Yeltsin called for a nuclear-free Korea as recently as August 15, 1992.[20] A nuclear-free zone in Northeast Asia would foreclose the nuclear option for Japan and the two Koreas. By prohibiting U.S., Russian, and other nuclear-armed submarines from entering regional waters, the NFZ treaty would add to Japan's and Korea's security.

Another area in which Korean security would seem to call for international involvement is arms sales and transfers from and to the region. This issue cannot be solved with the participation of a few countries, even if (as in the proposed four-power regime discussed above) these countries are the principal weapons suppliers. Both Koreas, after all, are important weapons producers and exporters; and North Korea, not being a member of the Missile Technology Control Regime, has been actively selling missiles and missile manufacturing equipment to Middle East countries. The arms transfer issue, therefore, also needs to be brought into the larger UN effort. Modest progress has been made in the Security Council with agreement on the idea of an arms register to monitor official data, and on arms export guidelines. The two

---

20. *North Korea News*, No. 645, August 24, 1992, p. 1.

Koreas, along with the major powers, ought to sub-
scribe to these and other controls on transfers. But
all sides will have to accept that achieving major
reductions in this area—for example, with respect to
the import of dual-use technologies—is a matter of
political, not technical, progress.[21]

The final ingredient in multilateralization of Korea's
security and strengthening prospects for peace
through diplomacy is improved U.S. and Japanese
relations with North Korea. Pyongyang must be
assured that it will not be swallowed up by the South
with great-power support, especially now that Russia
and China have "abandoned" it. Several steps can be
proposed. One is the immediate establishment of
diplomatic ties with the DPRK by the United States
and Japan. Another is confidence-building mutual
force reductions and redeployments away from the
DMZ. (These military moves would be part of the
agenda in Two-Plus-Four talks and a peace treaty.)
Economic and technical assistance to the DPRK by
the United States and Japan constitutes a third step.
They might create a fund parallel to the ROK's Common Fund for Reunification, which seems pitifully
small. The U.S. and Japan can also offer support for
the DPRK's participation in Asian Pacific Economic
Cooperation (APEC) and possibly other regional economic groups. The DPRK should have the option of
becoming part of the "Yellow Sea" region and thereby
of the world economy. The alternative, North Korea's

---

21. See Herbert Wulf, "Challenges to and Prospects for Control of
Conventional Weapons Proliferation," in Hua Di, et al., *Arms Sales
Versus Nonproliferation: Economic and Political Considerations of
Supply, Demand, and Control*, Proceedings of the Program on Sci-
ence and International Security, American Association for the
Advancement of Science, Washington, D.C., 1992, pp. 7-13.

economic collapse and the onset of political chaos, would not seem to be in the interest of any outside party.

The Question of Japan

As is evident from the above discussion, I regard Japan's active involvement as important to Northeast Asia's future stability. The ongoing second-guessing in Japan about its belated support of the UN coalition in the Gulf War, and the difficult passage of the PKO bill into law, are indicative of the great sensitivity of Japan's venture into international security matters. That sensitivity is, of course, shared outside Japan, especially in Korea. Yet, between the extremes of a militant Japanese nationalism and a thoroughly self-absorbed and passive Japan lie a number of options — the 2,000-man Japanese noncombat peacekeeping force authorized in Cambodia is one of them—by which Japan can assume more "new-order" responsibilities.[22] It is idle to expect Japan, with its enormous economic and technological reach, to remain simply a writer of checks.[23] Likewise, one cannot expect Japan to be unmoved by talk around the Pacific about deterring "Japanese militarism."

The Four-Plus-Two arrangement proposed here provides a second option for Japan. It seeks to accommo-

22. For an intriguing discussion of Japanese foreign policy options, see Takashi Inoguchi, "Four Japanese Scenarios for the Future," *International Affairs*, 65:1 (Winter, 1988-89), pp. 15-28.

23. See Masahide Shibusawa et al., *Pacific Asia in the 1990s* (London: Routledge, Royal Institute of International Affairs, 1992), esp. Ch. 7, and Yoichi Funabashi, "Japan and the New World Order," *Foreign Affairs*, 70:5 (Winter, 1991/92), pp. 58-74.

date the two inevitabilities of greater Japanese visibility and international involvement, and concerns in Asia—and Japan itself—about a revival of Japanese militarism. Four-Plus-Two also accords Japan an appropriate big-power status. But unlike the other three guarantors of peace in Korea, Japan would have a strictly economic role. Indeed, a restriction on a Japanese military role could be explicitly incorporated in the Four-Plus-Two regime.

Japan's interest in and importance to Korean stability and prosperity are obvious. Its full participation as a big power may facilitate not only North Korean economic development, but also the adjustment of its unbalanced trade with the ROK and coordination with the ROK and others of aid and investment to Pyongyang.

Between now and 2000, it seems likely that Japan will take on additional responsibilities for its own defense. The debate in Japan will focus on the extent of the responsibilities—and therefore on the degree of autonomy from U.S. forces. Not only national pride, but also nationalistic pressures for a self-sufficient defense and U.S. concerns over basing costs are likely to fuel the debate. So long as the Security Treaty is maintained, however, and close working relations continue among the U.S., Korea, and Japan, there need be no alarm sounded over what will amount to a natural evolution of Japan's reemergence as a great power.[24] In fact, it might be appropriate, in light of the politically and economically interlocked interests of the three countries since World War II, to establish an ongoing consultative body for the post-

---

24. Shigeki Nishimura, "U.S. and Japan As Partners," *Far Eastern Economic Review*, July 30, 1992, p. 13.

Cold War period of changing relationships.

Japan can also gain recognition of its great-power status and, just as crucially, build up trust among its neighbors, through active involvement in regional diplomacy and environmental protection. Japan's support of ASEAN initiatives on security during 1992; its discussions with Russian leaders to break the deadlock on the Northern Islands; its involvement in the United Nations Development Programme multilateral project to develop the Tumen River Basin; and its emphasis on ODA assistance to China and the rest of Asia—these are contributions to regional stability. Japanese energy and environmental technology can also contribute. For example, Asia has become the world's principal source of carbon dioxide emissions, mainly due to rapid industrialization by China and other developing economies using coal-fired power stations. These emissions account for a large proportion of global warming gases and pose a serious threat of transboundary acid rain.[25] Japanese technology can come into play in a number of ways, including energy conservation (MITI has already proposed funding a research and training center for ASEAN members) and pollution controls on power plants.[26]

---

25. *International Herald Tribune*, June 3, 1992, p. 2.

26. To date, however, Japan's record in environmental assistance is far from exemplary. A number of its aid projects have been environmentally destructive, have insufficient oversight and environmental expertise, and are insensitive to local peoples and cultures. See Richard A. Forrest, "Japanese Aid and the Environment," *The Ecologist*, 21:1 (January-February, 1991), pp. 24-32.

CHAPTER 7

THE END OF THE COLD WAR: RUSSIAN-AMERICAN RELATIONS AND THEIR IMPLICATIONS FOR NORTHEAST ASIA

Georgi A. Arbatov

The major event in international relations in the last decade was the end of the Cold War. This meant also a drastic change in relations between the Soviet Union (and, after 1991, Russia and those states that became independent after its dissolution) and the United States of America, the major adversaries, the major warring parties in that strange, but very costly, dangerous, and not always cold (who knows it better than the people of Korea?) war.

I cannot take seriously the statement that the Cold War was won by the U.S. I think both superpowers lost. For decades, both superpowers squandered their resources and bled each other white in futile attempts to win military superiority in an era when the institution of war, at least war between big countries, became obsolete, meaning the same collective suicide, irrespective of who had superiority in overkill. If somebody won the Cold War, it must have been Germany and, above all, Japan, countries that spent much less on the military establishment and assured for themselves, instead, very strong competitive positions in the world market.

I also do not agree with claims made by some esteemed political figures in America that it was President Reagan's policy that, having tremendously intensified the arms race and military and political confrontation, undermined the position of communism and led to the collapse of that system. As a witness "from inside", I can assure you that the hostile, militant policy of the United States in the early 1980s only strengthened the positions of our hard-liners and militarists, helped them to prolong the days of a despotic regime, made its rule more cruel and oppressive.

Apart from an outright military defeat, totalitarian regimes cannot be destroyed by outside influences. They are doomed because of their inherent internal weakness, because of the seeds of self-destruction each of them carries at its very roots.

However, the Cold War, whatever the causes of its termination, is over. And the major participants — the former USSR and the United States — now stand alone, each without its archenemy, without a threatening enemy.

That means an enormous change. Both superpowers, and many of their allies, had become so conditioned to the Cold War that a life without an enemy meant a radical change in practically all spheres of existence — in their economy, in foreign and even domestic policy, and in their psychology and spiritual life.

The period of readjustment turned out to be rather complicated for both countries. One reason was the shift in priorities. Suddenly, long-neglected domestic problems — economic, social, moral etc. — shifted to the center of national attention, demanding drastic changes in policy and in the behavior of the political leadership. We, in Russia, feel it very acutely. I, as one of the chief Russian "America watchers", can assure you that this is true also about America. If there was need to prove it, the 1992 presidential election campaign has given ample evidence.

What are the consequences of that change for the foreign policy of the two superpowers?

The policies of the superpowers were affected in different ways by the Cold War. First of all, the Cold War distorted their understanding of national interest. It offered unparalleled opportunity to pursue messianic, ideology-driven, foreign policy concepts that had very little to do with the domestic needs of the USSR and the U.S. For the Soviet Union, the Cold War was a climax of confrontation between the two systems, a struggle between the "forces of progress" and the "forces of reaction". For the United States, the Cold War was a no less uncompromising struggle against the "evil empire". At all times, the messianic aspirations of both countries' political leaders were quite coherently linked with their imperial ambitions. An expansion of one's own "sphere of influence" was justified by lofty ideological goals, while any success in global expansion became a proof of the virtue of the chosen ideology. That created a vicious circle that proved very difficult to break out of. (One may recall the attempts of Khrushchev and Eisenhower in the late 1950s; or the Brezhnev-Nixon detente of the early 1970s that failed because of the powerful inertia of the Cold War.)

Second, the Cold War secured the USSR and the

U.S. a special status in the international system, made their relationship a distinctive axis for the entire body of world politics. The two superpowers invariably turned out to be major players in conflicts, negotiations, and international organizations, even in cases when their immediate interests were affected only marginally. I would not say that the USSR and the U.S. used this special status successfully in their interests. But, it was highly valued by the leaders of both countries, and it was used for domestic political purposes as well. At least the Soviet leadership constantly referred to foreign policy achievements in order to distract the population from mounting domestic problems.

At the same time, the Cold War led to unprecedented, peacetime militarization of both superpowers, which affected our economies (in the former Soviet Union, at least 40% of industries worked for defense), political life, and even our ways of thinking. But worse never came to worst; a military coup in the U.S. only took place in novels and movies, while in my country an attempted coup failed in August 1991. But the militarization profoundly affected both societies. Perhaps we were able to see it more clearly after the end of the Cold War, when both we and the Americans found ourselves confronted with the task of dismantling the huge war machine built up in recent decades.

Also, the Cold War had an impact on the superpowers' allies. They, too, had to pay their share of the price—and it was not a small one—for the deformation of the international system. From them, their senior partners demanded strict discipline and submission and, "in case of need," interfered in their internal affairs in the name of the "higher interests of democracy", or the "interests of social progress". Only very few countries (Yugoslavia, France, China) managed to break the orbit of the superpowers' political influence during the years of the Cold War.

At the same time, some of the countries allied or having friendly relations with one of the superpowers made use of them, dragging them into policies and sometimes even conflicts (including military ones) that served the "smaller guys'" selfish interests. It was not too difficult to do, because the Cold War imposed on the behavior of the superpowers a certain logic, according to which you had to support every enemy of your enemy.

The situation bred regional conflicts. On the one hand, such conflicts were used by the superpowers to create bridgeheads all around the world. On the other hand, regional and local powers, to win in their local political games, did not hesitate in attempts to globalize their own policies and conflicts, connecting them in one way or another with the "central confrontation", that is, the confrontation between the United States and Soviet Union, West and East, in the geopolitical sense of these words.

The Cold War also gravely affected the fate of developing nations. There is also no doubt that the U.S.-Soviet confrontation accelerated the dissolution of the old European colonial empires. Hoping to take the leadership of the Third World, both superpowers attempted to place themselves at the forefront of the decolonizaton process. Therefore, they had to exercise greater generosity in economic aid to the developing countries, occasionally permitting or even helping the latter to strengthen their positions in the international system.

On balance, however, the impact of the Cold War

on the developing countries was very destructive. To begin with, they turned into bridgeheads of most bitter confrontation. While in Europe a Soviet-U.S. conflict was too dangerous and, therefore, was to be avoided, in the developing world, military conflicts with direct or indirect involvement of the superpowers practically never stopped. In a few cases (Korea, the Middle East, Central America, Southeast Asia, Afghanistan), the conflicts grew into bloody wars that took away millions of human lives.

In addition, the Cold War significantly distorted the Third World countries' domestic development. This negative impact was particularly fatal in the countries just beginning to establish their statehood, having neither stable political institutions, nor traditions that could help to withstand external pressures. The distortion of domestic development manifested itself in extreme militarization, disproportionate growth of military spending by the poorest countries of the world, and the excessive role of the military in the politics of these countries. Numerous military coups and dictatorships in Asia, Africa, and Latin America in the years of the Cold War were at least partially its direct outcome.

Moreover, in general, the Cold War bred tolerance to, if not encouragement of, dictatorial authoritarian regimes. Under Cold War conditions, your enemy's enemy almost automatically became your ally and friend. In the Third World, the superpowers too often followed Roosevelt's old principle for Somosa: "Yes, he is a son of a bitch, but he is our son of a bitch." Too often, democracy and human rights became secondary issues as compared to the interests of geopolitical rivalry.

And finally, economically, the developing countries'

losses from the Cold War were greater than their gains. Yes, for sure, they got economic perquisites as a price for their political loyalty, but the drain of Soviet and U.S. resources into the military sphere sharply reduced their potential for providing economic assistance to the Third World. Also, whatever assistance reached the Third World was very often determined by political interests, limited to military aid that fanned up militarism or prestigious projects driven by "gigantomania", and proved ineffective and even counterproductive in many cases.

Because of all this, the whole world, I think, must feel safer and happier now that the Cold War has ended.

At the same time, I have to say that the end of the Cold War was not only a blessing, but also a challenge. It is a challenge to build a new world order, which must be not only much safer, but, by necessity, will also have to be much more complicated than the old one. The Cold War imposed on all nations a certain discipline. But now, not only are there many centers of power, but also there is unprecedented freedom for almost all nations to pursue their own national interests.

That can lead to a new international disorder, not order, if this pursuit of multiple interests cannot be managed. Managed not by superpowers, of course, but by international law, international organizations, treaties, and agreements; by the joint will of the international community as a whole, as well as by communities of nations in different regions.

This is the challenge we face now.

To return to U.S.-Russian relations, I have to say that neither country can, or will, dominate the new world order. But both have to play a significant role, and therefore both must shoulder serious responsibilities.

The role of the United States is obvious. Although that country has become more conscious than ever, since World War II, about the importance of internal (including economic) problems, I am sure it will not become isolationist. Too strong is its economic and political interdependence with the outside world, too great is its interest in the stability of a world oversaturated with weapons (including nuclear weapons), and too deep is its interest in other international problems.

The important role Russia has to play, I would even dare to say is doomed to play, is at this moment not so obvious, due to the extreme difficulties my country faces at this moment.

Why do I think that despite these difficulties Russia will play a very important role in the world?

First of all, my country cannot escape its responsibility. Russia promised to guarantee political continuity in regard to former Soviet Union commitments to signed treaties and agreements—its international political and economic obligations. Russia has also inherited the Soviet Union's place in the Security Council of the United Nations. After the Ukraine, Kazakhstan, and Belorus, in accordance with signed treaties, destroy or give up their nuclear weapons, Russia is supposed to take over the responsibility for the strategic forces of the former Soviet Union.

At the same time, Russia comprises less than half the former Soviet power in terms of population, more than half—but much less than the Union—of its economic and scientific potential and, especially after the Warsaw Pact was dissolved, hardly can regard itself as a superpower.

These facts lend weight to the point of view that Russia is no more and will be no more a global power, that it can claim a role no bigger than a regional power, albeit an important one. I do not deny this point of view, but I offer some serious reservations.

First, Russia is doomed to be a very influential regional power in two of the most politically, strategically, and economically important regions of the world: Europe and the North Pacific. This, alone, makes its role practically tantamount to that of a global power. And it makes it all the more so because the U.S.A. has critically important interests in both regions.

Second, Russia, for the observable future, until nuclear weapons are completely banned and scrapped (I hope that it will happen sometime), will remain practically an equal to the U.S.A. as a nuclear superpower. Russian military potential—and this I say being a very vocal and convinced critic of militarism, big armies, big military expenditures—will remain very impressive, making it one of the strongest nations militarily in the world. Although I hope it will be used for deterrence and peacekeeping (under U.N. guidance) only, this strength, nevertheless, makes the country rather important.

Third, despite the tremendous difficulties our economy faces, Russia has to become, and will become, one of the economic superpowers. That will be the result not only of our abundant natural resources, but also because of Russia's very impressive intellectual potential. Russian science is in many fields second to none and, in other fields, second only to American science. Russia has an army of engineers, a trained labor force (especially in defense industries, which are in the process of conversion), and a world famous culture. In addition, its internal market is vast.

Fourth, Russia has a very good chance of becoming a center of attraction to many neighboring countries, which in time can lead not only to close cooperation, but also to the establishment of a new confederation (or, later, federation). To a large degree, it depends on Russian policy toward its neighbors; I think our leadership understands this responsibility. Only after having persuaded the countries that were once part of the Soviet Union that Russia respects their independence and does not plan a resurrecton of the empire, can we open the way for the natural trends for integration, which worked so effectively in Western Europe.

Fifth, and last, but not least, I think that in the post-Cold War world the old notions about superpowers and power relationships become obsolete. The bipolar world has passed away, and I do not believe that we are moving into an era of a "one superpower world", as some people started to think in the wake of the Gulf crisis of 1990-1991, predicting that international relations will be dominated by a single superpower, the United States of America.

The very concept of a superpower is very closely linked to the Cold War system, to the bipolar international structure, the "enemy image". Without an enemy, without a rival, one country will hardly be able to mobilize the resources and national will necessary to sustain a superpower status (even the Gulf War had to be financed and supported politically and militarily by many countries of the world).

The second reason why a "one superpower world" is most unlikely to happen is that if only one superpower is left in the world, this will be almost tantamount to its domination of the world, which will inevitably cause other "power centers" to rally against it, as well as to fear and distrust it. The history of international relations offers a lot of such examples.

There is a third reason, and it is that the end of the Cold War did not so much lessen the global appetites of Americans as make them aware of domestic problems in their own country, which, as it turned out, were plentiful.

Summing up, I would say that the post-Cold War world should not, and will not, become a one superpower establishment. Much more probable is a "multipolar" world, though not in the classical sense, not a replica of the past, which brought us innumerable conflicts and wars. More likely, the world will be more complicated than the traditional models: there will be a place for multipolarity and international organizations, regional and subregional unions and institutions, and non-governmental public structures. And, of course, a lot in this world will depend on the position of the new "power centers" that are now looking for a role for themselves in the new world order.

Once more, I would like to repeat my major point in assessment of Russo-American relations, and international relations as a whole, including the North Pacific region. The end of the Cold War removed many threats and concerns, but at the same time produced a set of new challenges. It also created new opportunities for cooperation, which until even now remain far from being used effectively.

This is true also for the North Pacific.

Current Russian perceptions of security in the

Pacific now that the "American danger" has gone are shaped largely by three principal considerations. First, there is a growing belief that a threat from Western countries does not exist. As confrontation in the Asia-Pacific region was merely a projection of global confrontation, the danger of a Russian-American nuclear clash in the region can be viewed as improbable. Second, there is an awareness of the necessity to redefine adequately the old Russian strategy in the Pacific. This implies a new set of goals, including a reasonable correlation between moderate activism and self-restraint, as well as between political and military tools for maintaining regional security. Equally necessary is the formulation of a new approach to allies and partners in the Asia-Pacific region. Third, there is a view that any revision of strategy in the Pacific should not result in an uncontrolled decline of Russian ability to deter unforeseeable external threats other than global ones. The latter view is typical for new military establishments and for civilian advocates of a "strong presidential power".

Russian militarists are perhaps especially sensitive to a radical redefinition of Pacific strategy. The reasons are obvious: It will bring further reductions of military spending and result in social and personnel difficulties. This places the "guarantees issue" at the center of public attention. "Social guarantees" are expected from the government, and "international guarantees" are wanted from other regional powers. Resistance on the part of the military establishment and by military-industrial factions in the Parliament and Government slows down redefinition of Moscow's strategy in the Pacific. However, one gets a feeling this faction would be more flexible if it felt more secure economically. But thus far it does not, and so remains a source of powerful political support for ongoing public and professional debates about what should be perceived as an "external threat" and "security".

In my view, national security, as well as security in the Pacific region in the 21st century, mean for Russia not only national defense, but also a level of economic well-being sufficient at least to preclude domestic explosion. In other words, the economic component of national security is not less important than the military one.

Security in the Asia-Pacific region means, in particular, maintenance of regional stability. We understand stability as an even and predictable development on the basis of economic, political, cultural, and social progress of the Pacific nations. Stability is incompatible with attempts by any nation to gain dominance over a certain part of the region. These kind of attempts would create suspicions and upset the regional balance.

Regional stability in the years to come can be assured on the basis of existing alliances and traditional partnerships. Alongside them, we need effective international negotiation structures that can exclude misinterpretations of intentions. Russia recognizes the U.S. alliances with Japan and the Republic of Korea and is searching for a new cooperation framework with South Korea. We seek further development of relations with China (which should include informal ties with Taiwan), as well as a just and reasonable rapprochement with Japan.

Progress in arms control can enhance regional stability as well as stimulate political dialogue. A common approach could be based on the following:

1) a combination of unilateral efforts by Russia, the U.S.A., China, and other nations to reduce their military potential with internationally concerted measures;

2) a shared understanding of the necessity of a stage-by-stage approach to disarmament;

3) a broad accord on arms and military-related technology sales by major regional states;

4) freezing of large-scale military modernization programs, including Chinese navy modernization, and

5) an enhanced nuclear non-proliferation regime.

While Russia and the U.S.A. are absorbed in a search for mutually acceptable decisions on the global level, some regional powers are getting militarily stronger. This can become a serious challenge to international stability. It's time to form an international research team to prepare a special report on the present military balance among the nations of the Asia-Pacific region. The issue should be discussed in the U.N. agencies and recommendations should be prepared.

Regrettably, there are no reasons yet to expect early success in large-scale arms reductions in the region. This, I think, makes an agreement on confidence-building measures even more important. Such measures can promote a better international environment for future negotiations, and even promote unilateral (and, if possible, coordinated) decisions on arms control. What makes confidence-building measures important is that although they do not arrest military activities, they regulate them and make them more predictable. Confidence-building measures restrict the freedom of action of the militaries and help to remove baseless suspicions and concerns. All of that enhances military stability.

The following items, I think, could be discussed by the Pacific nations in this respect.

1) Mutual notification about maneuvers and military exercises by the U.S.A. and Russia, if the number of troops taking part in these exercises exceeds an agreed level;

2) Invitation of foreign military observers;

3) Occasonal joint analysis of practices regarding the use of civilian and military air lanes;

4) Agreements (between Russia and the ROK, Russia and Japan) on avoidance of incidents at sea, similar to the agreement concluded with America;

5) Bilateral (Russo-American) or multilateral military-to-military discussions about their respective military doctrines for the Asia-Pacific region;

6) Exchange of information on deployments of military forces of each country in the Pacific;

7) Establishment of a hot-line between the military leaders of the districts close to national frontiers in order to exclude mistakes and misperceptions, as well as unmanageable situations.

Maybe also the time will soon become ripe for mutual inspections on challenge.

It is understandable that the U.S.A., Japan, and South Korea have certain anxieties. But the Americans, together with their allies, should at least start a search for reasonable alternatives to the existing form of American military deployments in the region. They should do so not only because the Cold War has come to an end, but also because no matter who wins the election, Washington cannot resist for too long the increasing budgetary pressures. It looks sometimes as if Washington has yet to decide what it wants of post-communist Russia in the Pacific. Maybe this is the reason for the obvious absence of interest in cooperation with Russia in this region.

For Russia—and this should not be forgotten—Northeast Asia is one of the key regions of vital, national interest. There is a point of view expressed by some foreign experts that Russia is marginal to other Northeast Asia nations. There are several reasons why such is not the case, some of which were mentioned above.

I would add here that bilateral interdependence between Russia and the nations of the region has always been very significant. Even when this interdependence was based on confrontation, it nevertheless tightly connected Russia with corresponding countries and contributed to the "old" world order in the region. Today, when Russia maintains normal or even friendly relations with all countries of Northeast Asia, this interdependence can become constructive and cooperational, and could provide additional opportunities for development of a new system of international relations in the region.

What can be the role of Russia in the region? One can envisage several directions and dimensions of its influence and activities.

One of them is the development of the Russian Far East. Russia will inevitably reduce its military presence in the region. Already, now, a considerable part of it is open to the outside world (of course, the opening of Vladivostok was a landmark here). By developing its Far Eastern regions, Russia will enforce its own integration into the Pacific, the region which has proved the priority of economic sources of power in the contemporary world.

Secondly, Russia may develop bilateral relations with all Northeast Asian nations. The principle of Russian foreign policy in this region should be the following: nobody will be regarded as an outcast, and nobody will be regarded as the sole important partner in the region. It goes without saying that certain problems exist in Russia's relations with some nations here. Territorial disputes with Japan and relations with North Korea seem to be the major problems in the field. But they should not become obstacles to such development.

Third, Russia can, and will, play an important role in ensuring stability in the region. This function of Russia could be called natural, for objective dimensions make Russia one of the major centers of power of Northeast Asia. A stable and strong Russia will positively influence the political environment. The geopolitical role of Russia may become even more evident during and after the reunification of Korea. Russia, as a friend of Korea, will permit the reunified nation to integrate into the world community in a new quality.

I would like to turn my attention now to our relations with Korea, to our Korean policy.

The most critical consequence of the decommunization of Russia was the downgrading of proletarian solidarity dogma, which for six and a half decades dominated, or at least strongly influenced, international politics in Moscow. Facing the mid-1990s, Russia is rearticulating its national goals in terms of traditional geopolitics, political expediency, and sober pragmatism, which requires, first of all, a realistic assessment of national interests. What are Russia's aspiratons in Korea?

As before, Moscow is interested in an international environment that would exclude armed conflict at its borders. With due understanding of the fact that the danger of a full-scale military clash between the

South and the North in Korea has been reduced after radical improvement of our relations with the Republic of Korea and the signing of an Agreement on Reconciliation, Nonaggression, and Exchanges and Cooperaion between the South and the North on February 19, 1992, Moscow favors a broader, international cooperation to make these positive shifts irreversible. The normalization of political ties between China and the ROK is assessed in Moscow as an important and absolutely indispensable step toward future reunification. What is happening now seems to prove there is no other way for reunification except through a stage of full international recognition of both parts of a divided nation.

Russian diplomacy considers it important to contribute to evolutionary shifts in the strategic picture of the Korean peninsula. Reduction of tension in Korea is an indispensable element of an emerging regional structure that should be more secure and stable. To insure regional stability, we are ready to do what we can to promote the integration of equal and sovereign Korean states (like the two Germanys in the pre-reunification period of the '70s and '80s), and, when that is achieved, promote the integration of a united Korea into the international community.

We also consider it an important goal to facilitate inter-Korean dialogue. Koreans should search for their own responses to the historical challenge they are facing. The role of foreign powers is not to intervene into inter-Korean relations, but to exert their influence in order to preclude clashes and to help both Koreas to go along the way of reunification, exercising tolerance, loyalty, and readiness for reasonable, mutual concessions.

A deeper understanding among major powers—the

U.S.A., Russia, and China—can generate momentum for the process of Korean settlement. Crucial points of trilateral understanding, in my opinion, could be summarized as follows:

1. Peace and stability in Korea is the only satisfactory state of affairs for these powers.

2. None of the three will seek to attain unilateral, strategic advantages in Korea for itself and its respective ally—Pyongyang or Seoul.

3. For the cause of stability, the PRC, Russia, and the U.S.A., should exercise self-restraint and, in case of need, sustain dialogue on North and South Korean military policies and activities.

4. American withdrawal from the South must be synchronized with integration of both Koreas into international structures. A too-rapid American withdrawal, as well as abrupt estrangement between Russia and the DPRK, could be counterproductive.

5. Nuclear proliferation in Korea would endanger peace in Korea and world peace, and is, therefore, unacceptable. International safeguards and regular control over the use of nuclear materials in Korea is a cornerstone of Russo-American understanding on this issue.

It is especially important that Beijing no longer be regarded as a source of political and moral support for North Korean isolationism and hardline policies.

Japan's participation, though not as vitally important, may be connected with future international cooperation in the Korean adjustment. Economically mighty Japan can be of considerable support to North Korea should the latter turn to pragmatic reformism in foreign and domestic politics. However, the problem still remains that an active Japanese participation could breed negative emotional reactions from various social strata in both parts of Korea.

In recent years, the Republic of Korea has had a succession of diplomatic victories. Economic success and the diplomatic success that followed strengthened the national pride of South Koreans and boosted their self-confidence.

South Korea also influenced North Korean policy. The DPRK worries about being "late for the train" of cooperation with the West, and with Seoul as well, and is trying to reactivate its diplomacy.

At the same time, South Korea's higher international profile could deepen the inferiority feeling of the North and tempt the DPRK to demonstrate its own power and independence. This could impede the peace process. Whether we like it or not, Pyongyang needs a certain degree of external support that can reduce its suspicions and prevent its turn to a more defensive stand. The international integration of Korea, in practical terms, is a problem for the North, not for the South, but it is a matter of concern for the international community, too, because a more isolated regime in the North will be less predictable.

The 1961 Treaty on Friendship, Cooperation, and Mutual Assistance between the USSR and the DPRK was more than once criticized in Russia. Liberal critics underline the vagueness of the formulations in this document and the absence of reference to Constitutional procedures for bringing the treaty onto effect in case of emergency. A serious incentive for revision of Russia's commitments to the DPRK is the new political situation in Russia. It is difficult to predict, but one can hardly imagine a situation when this treaty will be put into effect automatically. The treaty and its related agreements are at the same time a very important lever of Russian influence on North Korean policy.

Russian diplomacy faces no easy task searching for alternative ways to build relations with the DPRK through development of political, economic, and cultural ties. Canceling sales of armaments to Pyongyang is not enough to guarantee stability. The DPRK has already received sufficient weapons from other sources.

The human side of relations between the DPRK and the external world should not be underestimated. One cannot be indifferent to present difficulties and the future of the people of Korea, a future which inevitably will soon be ushered in by a period of serious changes.

There is yet one last and very important change that was initiated by the end of the Cold War. In all countries—big and small, rich and poor, industrialized and developing—top priority is being given to domestic economic issues. In this sense, even with all the differences in the character and acuteness of problems, all countries—Russia, the Ukraine, the U.S., Western Europe, China, and Korea—are in one and the same boat. Therefore, a major foreign policy objective now is to create the most favorable external conditions for tackling domestic problems, for the economic, social, and cultural progress of one's own country. That means that the age of empires is past and gone. That means that rivalry, as well as imperial ambitions, are not just useless, but harmful. Finally, that means that mutually beneficial political, economic, scientific, technological, and cultural cooperation among countries becomes an urgent imperative.

CHAPTER 8

BEIJING'S POLICY TOWARD KOREA AND PRC-ROK NORMALIZATION OF RELATIONS

Parris H. Chang

The establishment of full diplomatic relations between the People's Republic of China (PRC) and the Republic of Korea (ROK) in August 1992 took most observers by surprise. True, on numerous occasions, ranking government officials in Seoul, including President Roh Tae-woo, expressed the desire to forget such ties as soon as possible and repeatedly urged the PRC to do so. On the other hand, however, Beijing had been quite reserved about such a relationship due to domestic and external considerations. The conventional wisdom was: the PRC-ROK normalization of relations would occur only after Japan and/or the U.S. recognized North Korea. What caused the PRC to go ahead? This essay will suggest the considerations that informed Beijing's calculus of decision.

Moreover, this essay will also address the following broader issues: Where does Korea fit into Beijing's global strategic picture? How does the PRC see its relations with the ROK? What is Beijing's policy toward the Democratic People's Republic of Korea (DPRK, or North Korea) and its nuclear program? How will the diplomatic recognition of the ROK affect Beijing's relations with the DPRK? What's Beijing's attitude toward Korean unification?

China's Policy Objectives

China's foreign policy toward East Asia has been shaped by four major strategic objectives. In the 1970s and 1980s, Beijing's most important goal was the deterrence of Soviet military attack and the containment of Soviet influence in Asia.[1] The Chinese carried out their own military modernization drive to close the gap with Soviet military capabilities. Moreover, the PRC allied with the United States, skillfully playing the "American card," and sought to enlist Japan and some members of NATO in a global united front against the USSR.[2] With the improvement of Sino-Soviet relations in the late 1980s and drastic changes in the former Soviet Union, the PRC has reoriented its priorities and the relationship with Russia has lost much strategic salience.

A second major strategic objective is to use foreign capital, machinery, technology, and expertise to aid China's "Four modernizations" program to develop agriculture, industry, science and technology, and

1. *Deng Xiaoping: Selected Works, 1975-82* (in Chinese) (Beijing People's Publishing House, 1983), pp. 203-204.
2. See Parris H. Chang, "U.S.-China Relations: From Hostility to Euphoria to Realism," *The Annals of the Academy of Political and Social Science*, Vol. 476 (November 1984), pp. 158-159.

national defense. Since the 1980s, this has become Beijing's topmost priority. China has been forging close economic ties with the U.S., Japan, the Western European nations and, more recently, the ROK and Taiwan. China's expanding economic ties with the ROK have greatly changed the equation on the Korean peninsula.

China's third strategic objective is to promote peace and stability on the Korean peninsula. Although China is bound by a treaty to the defense of North Korea and has given Pyongyang verbal support to its commitment of reunification, in reality China has held back North Korea from using military means to that end, for fear of provoking large-scale, armed conflict that could involve China in direct military confrontation with the U.S., which is tied to South Korea's defense by a treaty.

A fourth Chinese strategic objective lies in China's reunification, the recovery of Hongkong, Taiwan, and other "lost territories." By the mid-1980s, the PRC had concluded agreements with the British and Portugal on the return of Hongkong and Macao in 1997 and 1999, respectively. With regard to the unification of Taiwan, Beijing has launched a peace offensive aimed at pressuring Taiwan to enter into a negotiated settlement. On several occasions, Deng Xiaoping and other Chinese spokesmen have offered to permit Taiwan to maintain its present economic, political, and social systems and armed forces, on the condition that the government of the Republic of China (ROC) on Taiwan abandon its claim to sovereignty over the island. On the other hand, Beijing has refused to renounce the use of force to settle the Taiwan problem; to do so, Deng argued, would assure that the authorities on Taiwan would never agree to negotiate.[3]

Having set forth the Chinese foreign policy objectives in broad terms, now we can proceed to examine China's policy toward Korea.

No Permanent Friends or Enemies

Chairman Mao Tse-tung once wrote: "Who are our enemies? Who are our friends? This is a question of the first importance for the revolution."[4] He went on to stress the great importance of distinguishing real friends from real enemies so as to unite with the former to attack the latter. To the Chinese communists, the PRC has neither eternal allies nor perpetual enemies, only its national interests are permanent. During the more than four decades since the establishment of the communist regime, PRC foreign policy has undergone several major shifts, and Beijing's enemies and friends have changed accordingly.

From 1949 onward and until the late 1960s, the PRC leaders were vehemently anti-American. They perceived the U.S. as China's archenemy; they accused the U.S. of "occupying" Taiwan and "colluding" with the Chinese Nationalist (Kuomintang, or KMT) government to invade the mainland, attacked the U.S. for "reviving Japanese militarism" and for occupying Korea. In October 1950, the Chinese communist troops crossed the Yalu to stop "U.S.

---

3. See Deng's interview with U.S. TV commentators, *Beijing Review*, 22: 7 (Feb. 16, 1979), pp. 19-22.

4. Mao Tse-tung, "Analysis of the Classes in Chinese Society" (March 1926), *Selected Works of Mao Tse-tung*, Vol. I (Beijing: Foreign Language Press, 1967), p. 13.

aggression."[5]

Likewise, for almost three decades, Beijing pursued a very antagonistic policy toward South Korea. The Korean War and China's intervention and alliance with North Korea set the tone. The legency of the War, i.e. Sino-U.S. enmity, the Cold War, and the regional alignment of forces also served to color Chinese perception of international reality and shape Chinese policy toward Korea.

Thus, until recently, the PRC leaders saw the ROK as an American puppet regime and a U.S. base from which the U.S. imperialists could launch an invasion against China and North Korea. Moreover, the ROK used to maintain close political and military ties with Taiwan, which Beijing claims is a part of China. Although Seoul, pursuant to its "Northern policy," sought to distance itself from Taipei ever since the early 1980s,[6] the ROK was the only country in Asia that maintained official diplomatic ties with the ROC, the rival to the PRC. That has been changed since August 1992.

However, the time and the circumstances have changed, and so has Beijing's policy. As a result of the normalization of relations between the PRC and the U.S. in 1979 and Beijing's earnest quest for economic modernization at home, a shift in Beijing's policy toward Korea has become discernible in the past decade.

Inasmuch as the PRC leaders see a peaceful inter-

---

5. See Allen S. Whiting, *China Crosses the Yalu* (Stanford: Stanford University Press, 1968), especially chapters 1 and 2.

6. In their numerous state visits to various Asian countries since the early 1980s, Presidents Chun Doo-hwan and Roh Tae-woo intentionally skipped Taipei. Furthermore, they also repeatedly expressed the hope to normalize relations with the PRC.

national environment as crucial for China's modernization efforts, Beijing has moderated its military and
economic support for the DPRK, encouraged the
DPRK to hold dialogue with the South, and supported measures to lower tension on the Korean peninsula. Ever since the late 1970s, Beijing's perception
of the ROK has also undergone significant modifica-
tion. As the PRC improved its relations with the U.S.
and Japan, Beijing's hostility toward the ROK also
decreased. Not only did the Chinese cease to see the
ROK as an enemy, but also they began to recognize
the advantages of economic ties with South Korea—
as a valuable trading partner and as a source of capital and high technology.

The first official PRC-ROK contact occurred in May
1983, ironically as a result of the hijacking of a Chinese jetliner, which landed in an airport near Seoul.
PRC officials went to Seoul to negotiate the return of
the plane, its crew, and passengers (minus the six
hijackers, who were jailed for several years in Korea
and then sent to Taiwan). Thereafter, contacts
between the two sides, especially through athletic
and economic exchanges, were expanded. In 1986,
the PRC sent the largest delegation (more than 350
athletes) to Seoul for the Asian Games, and took
away most of the gold medals. In September 1988,
the PRC took part in the Seoul Olympics, notwithstanding the boycott by the DPRK.

But the most impressive development in the PRC-
ROK relationship has been in the economic sphere.
Trade, which was virtually non-existent in the 1970s,
increased steadily in the 1980s, reaching $3 billion
in 1988 and over $6 billion in 1991, making the ROK
China's fourth or fifth largest trading partner. Out of
concern for Pyongyang, the Chinese maintained, until

recently, the fiction that trade with the ROK was "indirect", but it has been an open secret in the international business community that direct trade between the PRC and ROK began in the early 1980s. Furthermore, a large number of Korean multinational corporations have established joint ventures in China.

Sino-Soviet Rivalry on the Korean Peninsula

In October 1950, the so-called Chinese People's Volunteers (CPV) crossed the Yalu to save North Korea from the liberation of the U.N. forces. Historically, Korea was the route used by foreign powers to invade China; so Mao and the PRC leaders dispatched the CPV into Korea to protect the "Chinese lips" ("When the lips are gone, the teeth will be cold," according to the Chinese communists) and secure the *Cordon Sanitaire*.[7] While the PRC-DPRK ties were forged in "blood" in the early 1950s, with the CPV suffering more than half a million casualties during the Korean War, their relationship since has seen many ups and downs.

The Sino-Soviet conflict that originated in the 1950s and intensified in the 1960s had an enormous impact. It enabled DPRK leader Kim Il-sung to steer a neutral course in the dispute and assert his independence. Furthermore, Kim took advantage of the situation to play one communist power against the

---

7. See Hong Xuezhi, *Recollections of the War to Resist U.S. Aggression and Aid Korea* (Beijing: People's Liberation Army Literary Publishing House, 1991). The author, a PLA general, played a leading role in directing the CPV operation in Korea.

other in seeking favors for his regime.

The ousting of Khrushchev, in October 1964, allowed Moscow and Pyongyang to patch up their relations somewhat. The new Soviet premier, Alexei Kosygin, visited Pyongyang in February 1965 and, in the following years, economic, technical, and military aid again flowed. Meanwhile, Chinese-North Korean relations deteriorated during the Cultural Revolution as Chinese Red Guards attacked Kim Il-sung and labeled him a "fat revisionist" in 1967-68. Subsequently, it took the considerable efforts of Premier Zhou Enlai, including the master diplomat's personal visit to Pyongyang, in April 1970, to repair the damage to PRC-DPRK relations caused by the Red Guards and their radical sponsors in the Beijing leadership. Especially in the wake of large-scale, armed clashes along the Sino-Soviet borders in Manchuria in March 1969, it became imperative for the PRC to maintain good relations with North Korea as Beijing perceived an attempt by the Soviets to invade or encircle China.

Ever since the late 1960s, the DPRK has placed enormous emphasis on Kim's *Juche* ideology and asserted North Korea's independence in foreign affairs. Kim realizes that his country must be on good terms with both the PRC and the USSR and that he needs their political and material support— hence he has tried to maintain equidistance from Pyongyang's relations to Beijing and Moscow. This is not to say that Pyongyang has been pleased with its two big neighbors; as a matter of fact, Pyongyang has had considerable grievances, because Moscow and Beijing have not, in the eyes of the North Korean leadership, provided sufficient support to Pyongyang's national objectives.

For example, Moscow's flirtation with South Korea was quite irritating to North Korea. In the 1970s, Moscow permitted South Korean citizens and diplomats to visit the USSR, and allowed Soviet officials to visit Seoul. Moscow's endorsement of North Korea's proposal for Korean reunification was lukewarm at best. Moreover, whereas Moscow periodically denounced South Korea as a dangerous American puppet, it refused to provide North Korea with advanced weapons.

Likewise, North Korea was alarmed by Beijing's reconciliation with the U.S. and Japan in the 1970s. True, Kim Il-sung sought to capitalize on China's opening with the U.S. and Japan by having a dialogue with South Korea, in July 1972, and concluding an agreement on the principle of unification. The more concrete benefits that Kim sought—improved relations with Washington and Tokyo—failed to materialize, however. Kim must have been very disappointed and bitter when he rushed to Wuhan in central China in April 1975, in the wake of the U.S. pullout from Indochina, to urge Chairman Mao on joint actions to expel the U.S. forces from the Korean peninsula and Taiwan, but found Mao unresponsive.[8] Kim's anger and frustration were vividly displayed in the suspension of talk with the South and the brutal axe murder of two U.S. servicemen at Panmunjom in 1976.

Pyongyang's relations with Moscow improved enormously in the mid-1980s. The dramatic rapprochement between North Korea and the Soviet Union began in May 1984 when President Kim Il-sung

---

8. Interview with a PRC official familiar with relations with the DPRK.

returned to Moscow for a state visit after a hiatus of 23 years. Military and economic cooperation between the two countries were stepped up.

In the military sphere, the DPRK obtained 36 MiG 23 fighters, 30 SAM-3 missiles, 47 M-2 helicopter gunships and dozens of MiG 29s from the Soviets. Moreover, the two countries held joint military exercises in the Sea of Japan, based on their Treaty of Material Aid and Friendly Cooperation. For a few years after 1985, Soviet military planes acquired the right to fly through North Korean airspace in their missions to and from Vietnam, thus changing previous routes over the Sea of Japan. Soviet warships of the Pacific Fleet called on Wonsan and conducted joint exercises with North Korean naval forces.

In this context, President Kim's trip to Beijing in May 1987 was significant. It was one of his clever balancing acts, designed to reassert the independence of the DPRK, reassure Chinese leaders of Pyongyang's everlasting friendship, and restore the delicate equilibrium. For Kim, the DPRK needs both China and the Soviet Union to underwrite its security, to furnish economic and military aid and support unification, and cannot afford to be seen as tilting to Moscow at Beijing's expense. Thus, Kim maneuvered adroitly between them and played one off against the other to secure support and assistance from the two big neighbors.

Kim's talks with Deng Xiaoping and other ranking Chinese cadres served other purposes as well. In the wake of the forced departure of Party General Secretary Hu Yaobang and the campaign against bourgeois liberalization in early 1987, the North Koreans wanted to know of any change in the Chinese leadership, of any shift in China's domestic and foreign policy, and the attending implications for the DPRK.[9]

Likewise, the Chinese used the summit to clarify their policy toward the Korean peninsula and allay Pyongyang's misgivings and grievance, which resulted from the recent port call in Qingdao by the U.S. Seventh Fleet and the ever-growing economic ties and contacts between China and South Korea. The Chinese felt compelled to display solidarity with North Korea—they reiterated China's support of Pyongyang's proposal for tripartite talks among North Korea, South Korea, and the United States, and of Pyongyang's opposition to cross-recognition of the two Koreas by the major powers and their simultaneous admission to the United Nations—proposals that had been advanced by South Korea and the United States. In private conversations, Chinese cadres pointed fingers at U.S. intransigence and efforts by Seoul and Washington to isolate North Korea as reason for Pyongyang's tilt toward Moscow.

As the DPRK launched its third seven-year economic plan, in April 1987, in the hope of accelerating technological modernization of its industries and speeding up overall economic development, President Kim also sought more economic aid from China when he met with his host. Reportedly, Deng Xiaoping invited President Kim to visit and inspect the Shenzben special economic zone—the showcase of his reform program. Deng seemed to have hinted to Kim that North Korea should institute similar reforms, but to no avail.

---

9. Parris H. Chang, "North Korea's Balancing Act," *Far Eastern Economic Review*, 30: 44 (November 5, 1987), pp. 25-26.

Constraints on Beijing's Korean Policy

In spite of Gorbachev's failure in Soviet domestic reforms, he displayed a new thinking in world affairs and took bold initiatives toward Korea. His important moves were to establish full Soviet-ROK relations in 1990 and support Seoul's admission into the United Nations in September 1991.

Moscow's bold measures put the PRC on the defensive, insofar as its policy toward the Korean peninsula was concerned. True, the PRC reversed its earlier stand and urged the DPRK to accept a package deal—the simultaneous admission of the two Koreas to the U.N. However, it was obvious that Beijing could not block Seoul's admission to the U.N. any longer, because there was a strong consensus in the world body that the ROK was an active and valuable member of the international community and should not be left out of the U.N. Hence the PRC had no choice but to go along with the overwhelming majority of U.N. members.

Whereas the PRC acquiesced in Seoul's membership in the U.N., there was no agreement yet among the top Chinese leaders, in the fall of 1991, to consummate the full Beijing-Seoul diplomatic ties. China remained the most staunch supporter of the DPRK. In the wake of collapse of the communist regimes in East Europe, Mongolia, and the USSR, the survival of the North Korean regime has both significant ideological and geopolitical implications for China. The new Beijing-Pyongyang solidarity found expression in Kim Il-sung's visits to Beijing in November 1989 and October 1991. There is no question that Kim did have powerful friends inside the PRC leadership.

To bolster the DPRK regime, the Chinese leaders have politely but unmistakably urged the North Koreans to institute economic reforms and adopt open-door policies to attract foreign investment and technology. That President Kim's itinerary during his 1991 trip included a tour of Chinese foreign joint venture enterprises is highly indicative of such thinking.

At least some top Chinese officials were reluctant to recognize the ROK, due to the following considerations. First, China's reunification has been one of the topmost leadership priorities—they do not wish to initiate a "two Koreas" policy by recognizing the ROK officially, lest other nations would use it to justify a "two Chinas" policy by restoring diplomatic ties with Taiwan. When Grenada, Liberia, Niger, and other states established formal ties with the ROC in recent years, Beijing terminated diplomatic relations with them immediately.

Secondly, conservative, senior PRC leaders still attach great importance to the DPRK. Some of them see the normalization of PRC-ROK relations as China's betrayal of the North Koreans. What worries the PRC leadership most is that such a diplomatic move could deepen Pyongyang's sense of isolation and vulnerability and may contribute to, if not precipitate, the collapse of the North Korean regime.

Some of the Chinese leaders argued that for now Beijing had no need to establish full diplomatic ties with the ROK. As a Chinese think tank analyst put it, "We already have an affair going on, a relationship could be a burden." Because the "trade offices" in both Beijing and Seoul could and did function as embassies, some Chinese did not see the urgency in establishing full diplomatic relations.

Normalization of PRC-ROK Relations

On August 24, 1992, Beijing and Seoul announced their agreement to establish formal diplomatic ties. What induced the PRC leadership to make such a move?

It should be pointed out that, rightly or wrongly, the PRC leaders saw Beijing to be in the driver's seat insofar as the establishment of full diplomatic relations with the ROK was concerned. Many ROK officials had called for it. It is not a secret that President Roh Tae-woo was eager to complete the normalization of Seoul-Beijing ties during his term of office, which formally ended in February 1993. During the Korean Foreign Minister's visit to Beijing in April 1992 in connection with a U.N. gathering, he did meet with his Chinese counterpart, Qian Qishen, and make another pitch for full diplomatic ties. So, the ball was in Beijing's court.

Moscow's recognition of the ROK and active support for ROK admission into the U.N. presented a new challenge for the Chinese. Whereas Moscow-Pyongyang relations were strained and worsened as the Soviet communist system collapsed and the USSR disintegrated, and Beijing-Pyongyang ties were correspondingly reinforced. Chinese officials in charge of foreign affairs and national security viewed Moscow's growing influence in South Korea with grave concern and felt compelled to urge the PRC leadership for action.

Among their arguments were: (1) the PRC must have a strong diplomatic presence in South Korea; if it waits much longer, Chinese influence in the Korean peninsula could be severely diminished; (2) China need not and cannot wait for Japan and/or the U.S.

to normalize relations with the DPRK, because both
the Japanese-DPRK and the U.S.-DPRK talks were
getting nowhere; (3) The DPRK could not accuse
China of betraying an old friend, because the PRC
remains highly supportive of its North Korean neighbor—besides, Beijing was only following a precedent,
as Moscow already opened the diplomatic relation
with Seoul.

These arguments, by themselves, may not have
been sufficient to convince the PRC leadership to
accept Seoul's offer. However, in retrospect, two
other factors seem decisive. One was the establishment of diplomatic relations between Niger and
Taiwan in early summer, 1992. This African state had
maintained diplomatic relations with the PRC for
years, but as a result of Taipei's checkbook diplomacy, agreed to also recognize the ROC. Beijing
demurred and promised to offer economic aid to keep
Niger from setting up diplomatic ties with Taipei.
Apparently Taipei outbid Beijing, and induced Niger
to hold firm on its commitment with an initial grant
of U.S. $50 million. Unable to keep Niger in line, the
PRC cut off ties with Niger to forestall the creation of
"two Chinas."

The setback was an embarrassment to Premier Li
Peng, who had played an active role in China's foreign affairs in recent years, and he decided to retali-
ate and teach Taipei a lesson for bragging the success of its "flexible diplomacy." One option available
to the PRC was to grab Seoul's offer of establishing
full diplomatic ties and demand Seoul sever ties with
Taipei.

The second, and probably more important, factor
was a change of mind on the part of Deng Xiaoping,
China's senior leader. Since early 1992, Deng has

been actively campaigning in the southern provinces and other parts of China to revive his open door and reform programs, most of which had been halted or even reversed in the wake of the Tiananmen Square massacre in 1989. As the 14th National Congress of the Chinese Communist Party (CCP), which was scheduled for October 1992, would set national priorities and concrete policies for the next five years, Deng tried to mobilize all the support he could to gain ascendancy at the Congress so that the CCP convention would formally approve and legitimate his reform and open door policies. Apparently Deng saw the value of the "Korean connection" in his crusade to step up China's modernization; rightly or wrongly, Deng believes that the ROK government and Korean business community would be willing and able to provide capital and technology. Hence, instead of siding with many of the conservatives who remained opposed to the normalization of PRC-ROK relations, Deng switched his position and supported the opening to Seoul. With Deng's blessing, the PRC government moved quickly, in late July, to negotiate and formalize the establishment of full diplomatic relations, which was made public on August 24, 1992.[10] The negotiation proceeded with utmost secrecy at Beijing's behest, and even many ROK officials in the Foreign Ministry and other government agencies were kept in the dark. To the chagrin of the Korean government, one week before the PRC and the ROK were to announce their official agreement, Taipei broke the news to the world and severely criticized the unprofessional way the Roh Tae-woo gov-

---

10. "Beijing Establishes Ties with Seoul," *Beijing Review*, 35: 35 (August 31-September 6, 1992), p. 12.

ernment handled the whole thing.

Like Taipei, Pyongyang was severely distressed. Although there was no open outburst from the North Koreans, they did close down the Sino-Korean borders for several months in silent protest. Apparently DPRK-PRC relations were so strained that Beijing announced, on December 29 1992, a punitive decision to end barter trade with the DPRK and insist on cash payments for crude oil and other exchanges thereafter.[11]

China harbors a strong reservation about the North Korean nuclear program; it supports IAEA inspection of the North Korean nuclear facilities and seeks to dissuade Pyongyang from further development of nuclear weapons. Whereas Beijing has become more businesslike in its relations with Pyongyang, it will continue to provide political and modest economic support in order to reassure Pyongyang and retain a measure of leverage. China favors peace and stability in Korea and has urged North Korea toward further dialogue with the ROK and relaxation of tensions on the Korean peninsula,[12] as a peaceful international environment in East Asia is crucial for China's economic modernization efforts.

How does the PRC leadership see the future of the Korean peninsula? PRC leaders' lip service notwithstanding, they don't really desire Korean unification under whatever circumstances. Although the PRC has improved relations with the ROK and tries to capitalize on South Korea's vibrant economy to accelerate its own modernization drive, for at least two

11. Nicholas Kristof, "Cash Only, No Bartering, China Tells North Koreans," *The New York Times*, December 30, 1992, p. A2.

12. "Sino-ROK Ties Praised," *Beijing Review*, 35: 41 (October 12-18, 1982), p. 7.

reasons it would strongly oppose the unification of the two Koreas under a non-communist regime. For geopolitical reasons, the PRC is concerned with any potential threat to its 800-mile-long Sino-Korean border and resource-rich Manchuria. In economic terms, the PRC does not favor Korean unification, because the enormous costs, as suggested by the German example, could greatly reduce Korea's contribution to China's economic development.

Likewise, Beijing is not enthusiastic about Korean unification under the DPRK. A unified communist Korea, like Vietnam, would be too tough to cope with. Besides, if the Korean peninsula comes under communist control, international tensions in East Asia would inevitably mount, and could adversely affect China's relations with Japan and the U.S., and that, in turn, could harm Chinese economic modernization.

Thus, two divided Korean states would seem to serve Beijing's interest better, as the PRC would be able to play one against the other. In the years to come, the PRC will strive at one and the same time to expand economic ties with South Korea and keep North Korea in line by providing political support and modest economic assistance. Beijing's goals are both to enhance Chinese influence in the Korean peninsula and to reduce/neutralize the influence of other major powers over Korea. To attain these objectives, in the near future we can expect the PRC to press for the withdrawal of American troops from South Korea.

CHAPTER 9

JAPAN'S DEFENSE ROLE: A CHANGE IN DEFENSE POLICY?

Hideshi Takesada

Introduction

The Cold War is over. The world is entering a period of historic change. When the strategic confrontation between the U.S. and the USSR ended, the two countries reached a basic agreement based on the Strategic Arms Reduction Talks (START). As a result, a nuclear war and a large-scale military conflict between East and West will be unlikely in the future.

In Europe, various military negotiations for arms control and disarmament have made steady progress. The Conventional Armed Forces in Europe (CFE) Treaty, which is the most comprehensive arms-reduction agreement, has been signed. East-West relations have been drastically changed, and an era of dialogue and cooperation has begun.

It was believed that this would bring order and stability to the world. But many people predicted the emergence of an era of economic competition and negotiation after the collapse of the USSR. Instead, we are now witnessing the emergence of dispute, confrontation, and conflict all over the world: chaos in Yugoslavia; internal dispute in the CIS; continued strain in the Middle East; the proliferation of nuclear weapons, and an arms race throughout the world.

Both the U.S. and Russia, due to their domestic and economic difficulties, can no longer afford to intervene in conflicts in other parts of the world. Accordingly, the power vacuum created by the relative decline of the U.S. and Russia has greatly contributed to the emergence of an era of dispute and confrontation.

The situation in Asia is also unstable. Asia is a region of complex geography and cultural diversity. The lack of common ground among nations doesn't allow Asian countries to easily formulate a multilateral cooperation system. Thus, alliance in this region is mostly bilateral, as, for example, between the U.S. and Japan, the U.S. and the Philippines, and the U.S. and the Republic of Korea.

With the dissipation of the Cold War atmosphere, ironically, disputes are increasing in Asia. Tension between the PRC and Taiwan was heightened when the U.S. decided to export F-16 fighters to Taiwan. The dispute over the Spratly Islands also heightened friction between China and some Southeast Asian countries. In Northeast Asia, tension between North and South Korea still exists. In addition, the unresolved conflict between Japan and Russia over the Northern Territory issue has made the region fraught with tension. In South Asia. Indian naval expansion has also been cause for worry.

The region has grown increasingly unstable with its

numerous, threatening flashpoints. This instability also helps to generate a tendency to believe that Japan will increase its military might in order to fill the power vacuum left behind by the U.S. and the CIS.[1]

The Myth of Japan's Military Expansion

There are five reasons why Asian countries tend to believe that Japan has been increasing its military power.

1. Japan dispatched peacekeeping operation forces to Cambodia after the passing of the PKO bill. North Koreans, and even some people in the ROK and PRC, see this as a possible springboard of Japanese military expansionism.[2]
2. The Japanese Government has been collecting spent nuclear fuel. Countries are suspicious of any possibility of Japanese nuclearization. The shipping of plutonium made from spent nuclear fuel by a Japanese vessel from France to Japan has generated much concern in other Asian countries.
3. There has been no visible decrease in the Japanese defense budget, even after the USSR's collapse, which fuels the belief that Japan is still interested in expanding its military capabilities.
4. Conservatism in Japanese politics is on the increase. Some Koreans see the recent increase

---

1. On the recent security situation, see Hideshi Takesada, "East Asia in the Post-War Era," *Gaiko Jiho*, May 1992, pp. 50-59.

2. A typical criticism by a Korean newspaper appears in "The dispatch of the troops must be given up," *Chung-ang Daily News*, June 20, 1992.

in visits to Shinto shrines by the Prime Minister and other ministers as a return to reactionary conservatism by Japanese leaders. Also, the Ozawa Report, presented in May 1992 by Congressman Ichiro Ozawa, which insists on increasing Japan's role in international security issues, reflects the current mood of domestic conservatism in Japan.

5. Japan is continuously purchasing hi-tech military weapons. For example, the new Patriot SAM system was purchased to replace the obsolete Nike-J, an escort ship with the AEGIS system was purchased, and the next-generation support fighter(FS-X) replaced the F-1.

In regard to Japanese defense budget increases and some foreign policy changes, some Koreans expressed concern that Japan may turn into a military superpower in Asia. They gave the following three reasons.[3]

First, if the trade friction between the U.S. and Japan escalates, the U.S. may threaten Japan with withdrawal of some of its forces, or force Japan to increase its burden-sharing. This may lead Japan to pursue a self-reliance defense capability. Second, a recent official dispute between Japan and Russia over the Northern Territories and the cancellation of Yeltsin's visit to Japan in November 1992 may increase tension between Japan and Russia. Should that occur, the Japanese people may be propelled in the direction of increasing military strength in order to protect the country against Russia. Lastly, a change in Korea's military situation will directly influence the Japanese defense consciousness. If North Korea is successful in building its own nuclear capa-

3. *Chosun-Ilbo*, July 5, 1992.

bility and continues to build up its military, Japan may be forced to develop its own nuclear capability.

The Rise of Japanese Militarism?

This myth may be dispelled by the following five very realistic points.

1. International Peace Cooperation

It was the Japanese Cabinet that decided to dispatch peacekeeping forces to Cambodia. At the U.N.'s request, the Foreign Ministry, not the Defense Agency, played the major role in the decision to dispatch PKO forces.[4] Thus it was primarily a foreign policy decision, not a military one.

In the process of deciding to dispatch peacekeeping forces, political control over the military was maintained. Japan has systems of civilian control that are entirely different from those under the old Constitution. The Diet makes legislative and budgetary decisions on such important matters as the authorized number of SDF personnel and its main organization. The Prime Minister, as the representative of the Cabinet, holds the right of supreme command and controls the SDF. A civilian minister of state is appointed as director general of the Defense Agency (See

---

4. On the decision process of PKO dispatchs, see "UN's collective security system and PKO," *Boei-Nenkan*, 1992, pp. 70-82.

Furthermore, Prime Minister Miyazawa, who promoted the PKO bill, is known for his economic concerns rather than his military ambition. Prime Minister Miyazawa is an adherent to the philosophy of the late Prime Minister Yoshida Shigeru, who believed in promoting diplomacy through economic means.

Appendix 1).

In addition, the activities of the peacekeeping operations conducted under the International Peace Cooperation Law are not intended to restore peace by forceful means, but to secure a cease-fire through the authority and persuasion of the U.N., from a neutral and non-compulsory standpoint, on the precondition that an agreement on the cease-fire has been reached among the parties to a conflict and that they have agreed on the activities of the peacekeeping operations.[5]

Before deciding to accept the U.N.'s request to dispatch JSDF forces to Cambodia, Japan thought at length about its national security and about sustaining its national image of a peace-loving country. Needless to say, Japan has also considered the possibility that the PKO decision may damage its relationships with the international community. [6]

---

5. *Boei Hakusho (Defense White Paper, Defense Agency)* 1992, p. 159.

The Law was worked out in line with strict basic guidelines. See Appendix 2.

6. In the beginning of 1992, the Japanese Foreign Ministry took a public opinion poll in ASEAN countries, the results of which were made public in July 1992.

Q. Will Japan be a military superpower?

YES	D/N	NO	NO (%)
Indonesia	23	10	68
Malaysia	35	24	40
Phillipines	32	25	43
Singapore	34	28	37
Thailand	24	24	53

(Fractions were rounded off to the nearest whole number)
[From *Disputed Points of Japan* (Bungei shunju sha, 1992) p. 77].

Table 1. Share of the Expenses of the U.N.
(1992-94)

U.S.	25%
Japan	12.4%
Russia	9.41%
Germany	8.93%
France	6%
U.K.	5.02%

Budget of U.N. from 1990-91: 1.975 billion U.S. dollars

Source: *Disputed Points of Japan (Bungei shunju sha, 1992)* p.89.

After WWII, Japan set three principles for its foreign policy: to associate itself with the U.N., to promote friendship with Asian countries, and to emphasize economic assistance to developing countries. Japan bears a big share of the expenses of the U.N. Between 1992-94, its share will be 12.5 percent, which is the second largest share, as Table 1 shows.

But because Japan did not contribute manpower to the U.N., Japan's international role has not been as esteemed as Japan had hoped. Therefore, the dispatch of Japanese PKO forces to Cambodia is nothing but a faithful fulfillment of responsibility as a U.N. member.

2. Non-nuclear Principles

Japan's three non-nuclear principles are no possession, no production, and no carrying-in of nuclear weapons. These principles are extensively supported among the Japanese people. Instead of possessing nuclear weapons, Japan has been relying upon the American nuclear umbrella for protection from any nuclear attack.

The Atomic Energy Law also prohibits Japan from manufacturing or possessing nuclear weapons. Furthermore, Japan ratified the Treaty on the Non-proliferation of Nuclear Weapons in June 1976, and placed itself under an obligation, as a non-nuclear weapons state, not to produce or acquire nuclear weapons.[7]

Atomic power generators are indispensable for the production of non-polluting energy. Because Japan lacks natural resources, it is Japanese policy to reprocess spent nuclear material and use enriched uranium and plutonium. Since Japan does not have sufficient reprocessing capabilities, it asked for some assistance from French and British companies. It is for this reason alone that Japan is shipping in plutonium.[8]

3. Is Japan's Defense Expenditure High?

Japan has three principles on arms exports, which were first enunciated on April 21, 1967, by then-Prime Minister Eisaku Sato. The principles provide that arms exports shall not be permitted to:

(1) communist bloc countries;
(2) countries to which the export of arms is prohibited under United Nations resolutions, and
(3) countries that are actually involved, or likely to become involved, in international conflicts.

In addition, exports of arms require licensing by

---

7. *Boei Hakusho*, 1992, p. 67.
8. *Sankei Shinbun*, October 7, 1992.

the Minister of International Trade and Industry pursuant to the Foreign Exchange and Foreign Trade Control Law and the Export Trade Control Law. As a result, Japan's weapons production occupied only 0.54 percent of its total industrial product in 1990.[9] Since the quantity of produced weapons is very limited, per unit cost for each weapon is inevitably very high. This is one of the major reasons why Japan is constantly increasing its defense budget.

A glance at the dollar exchange rate in recent years reveals that the value of the yen against the dollar is higher than that of the currencies of the United Kingdom, France, and Germany. Thus Japan's defense expenditure, identified by the dollar value, appears higher than the actual figure. For example, Japan's defense expenditure has increased 2.3-fold over the past 5 years (FY1985-FY1989) in dollar value, while it has increased only 1.3-fold in yen value.

In addition, Japan has taken into consideration domestic pressure to cut the defense budget. Japan's 1992 defense budget is 4,580 billion yen. In fact, the increase in defense expenditures is the lowest in 32 years. It was reduced from 5.45 percent for fiscal year 1991-92 to 3.6 percent for 1992-93, with an emphasis on improving logistic support fields rather than front-line equipment, such as ground equipment, ships, and aircraft. The ratio of front-line expenses to defense-related expenditures for FY1992 is down 3.7 percent, down about 20 percent from FY1990.[10]

---

9. See *Boei Handbook 1992 (Asagumo Shinbun)*, p. 252, and Appendix 3.

10. *Boei Hakusho*, 1992, p. 139.

On December 25, 1992, the Miyazawa cabinet decided to increase the defense-related budget for the fiscal year 1993-94 by 1.95 percent.

One of the characteristics of Japan's defense-related expenditures by use is that personnel and provisions expenses for FY1992 occupy a large portion, 41.3 percent (See Appendix 4).

4. Japanese Interest in Edo Culture

The drastic changes in international society since the mid-1990s taught the Japanese that nations with a huge territory and army—such as the CIS, PRC, India, and Brazil—faced internal turmoil and economic difficulties. On the other hand, Japan succeeded in becoming an economic superpower by following an exclusively defense-oriented defense policy.

Recently, Japanese people have become more interested in Edo culture.[11] The Edo era, under the Tokugawa Government, lasted from 1603 to 1867. During this period, various cultural aspects such as Kabuki, Noh, and Rakugo were very enriched. For a period of 260 years, the country was without a modern army, there was no threat from abroad, and people enjoyed prosperity. The current Japanese interest in Edo culture may suggest their choice of a national goal for the 21st century.

Some scholars see the recent Japanese return to 'conservatism' as an attempt to regain the pride that they lost during the post-war era.[12] In Japan, books

---

11. For the recent Japanese interest in Edo culture, see Takanori Irie, *New Civilization Made by Japanese* (Kodansha, 1992).

The Edo era was started by Tokugawa Ieyasu with a small military force and a policy of isolationism after Toyotomi Hideyoshi failed in his attempt to invade the Korean peninsula. See Sakaiya Taichi, *What is Japan?* (Kodansha, 1991).

12. Shoichi Watanabe, "Japanese who lost pride," *Seiron*, October 1992, pp. 52-61.

about seeking cooperation with the international community have become very popular. This indicates that what Japanese are most interested in is coexistence and co-prosperity, which is called *kyosei* in Japanese.[13]

In 1992, the Ozawa Report was issued. The Report appealed to Japan to tackle international issues more positively and, if it could not do so, to give thought to revising Article 9 in order to fulfill international duties.[14] In other words, the Japanese are not moving toward isolationism or egoistic conservatism, but moving away from them. Within the foreseeable future, at least, Japan will maintain this national policy.

5. Japan's Defense-Oriented Policy

In Article 9 of the Japanese Constitution, the renunciation of war, nonpossession of war potential, and the denial of the state's right to belligerency were set forth. The Japanese government, however, believes that the Constitution does not prohibit a sovereign nation from possessing the minimum level of self-defense capabilities.

Japan's defense policy is based on the Basic National Defense Policy adopted by the National

---

13. On "Kyosei" see "Kyosei could change how people live, work and compete," *Far Eastern Economic Review*, August 6, 1992, pp. 52-56.

14. Congressman Ozawa denied the Japanese old-type nationalism of the 1920s and 1930s.

See "Interview with Ichiro Ozawa," *Seiron*, September 1992, pp. 80-90. On the Ozawa Report and the PKO issue, see "Argument concerning Japan's contribution to the world community: An analysis of the Ozawa Report," *Shin Boei Ronshu (The Journal of National Defense)*, Vol. 20, no. 2, (September 1992) pp. 68-81.

Defense Council and approved by the Cabinet in May
1957. The objective of national defense is to prevent
direct and indirect aggression, but once invaded, it
repels such aggression, thereby preserving the independence and peace of Japan.[15]

For that purpose, Japan maintains an appropriate
level of its own defense capability and firmly maintains the Japan-U.S. security arrangement, the two
pillars of Japan's defense policy. By following this
policy, Japan has made efforts to maintain a moderate defense capability level sufficient for its exclusively defense-oriented defense policy, but one that
does not pose a threat to other countries. Japan's
moderate defense capability means a level of defense
force that does not allow the creation of a power vacuum in and around Japan. Japan has a very important geo-strategic location. Therefore, if Japan leaves
room for a power vacuum, it might invite aggression
and cause regional instability.

Japan's exclusively defense-oriented policy does
not allow Japan to exercise any military force unless
an armed attack is initiated. Thus, the scope and
level of defense are maintained only for the purpose
of self-defense, which is consistent with the fundamental spirit of the constitution.[16]

The Situations Surrounding Japan

One of the reasons why Japan sustains its present
defense policy is that the situations surrounding

---

15. See Appendix 5.

16. On the function of air defense to secure the safety of maritime traffic and counter airborne and seaborne invasions based on
the exclusively defense-oriented policy, see *Defense of Japan 1992*,
pp. 86-94.

Japan are still unstable and volatile. In Southeast Asia, India has built up its naval forces and is planning to expand its presence in the Indian Ocean. India suggested joint naval exercises to ASEAN countries and allowed the use of Indian ports to the PRC.[17] The Middle East, Africa, and Southwest Asia are indispensable suppliers of oil and other raw materials to Japan. The Indian Ocean also constitutes a vital maritime traffic route for Japan. Situations in the Indian Ocean have a direct impact on the stability and prosperity of Japan.

After the end of the Cold War, China began making concerted efforts to modernize its military equipment and facilities by purchasing SU-27s from Russia. It also increased its arms exports to Third World countries. The Chinese Navy is pushing forward with its modernization, including the construction of destroyers carrying helicopters and new-type guided missiles. Newspaper reports have hinted that China has asked the Ukraine to sell it aircraft carriers.[18] The Chinese Navy also demonstrates a strong interest in expanding its scope of operation in this region. China has been strengthening its military presence in the Spratly Islands and Paracel Islands while improving the bases for operation in these islands.

The seeds for conflict also exist in South East Asia. Several countries, including the PRC, Malaysia, and Vietnam, are claiming sovereignty over some territories. Confrontation over the Spratly Islands heightened after the PRC adopted its new territorial law on the islands in February 1992. The South China Sea is of vital importance to transportation linking the

17. *Sankei Shinbun*, October 2, 1992 and October 4, 1992.
18. *Sankei Shinbun*, September 11, 1992.

Pacific Ocean and the Indian Ocean. Any disputes in this area may have an impact on Japanese supply lines.

Considering the cool relations between the U.S. and China since the Tiananmen Incident in June 1989 and the deterioration in relationships between China and major Western countries, the Chinese military will be a factor of instability in this region.

Compared with past years, it is not as likely that Russia will initiate any offensive actions against other countries, due to its domestic conflicts and the decline of its international influence. Nevertheless, Russia still maintains about 320,000 ground forces in 36 divisions.

The Pacific Fleet eliminated about 75 main surface combatants and submarines between 1991 and 1992. But 15 new-type naval vessels have been commissioned to the Pacific Fleet. Russia keeps 1860 aircraft in this region. The total number of combat aircraft was cut down by 200 within a year. Although about 240 old, second-generation fighters and other old-type aircraft were removed, at the same time, about 40 fourth-generation fighters were purchased.[19]

On the Korean peninsula, the South-North Prime Ministers Talks and joint committees are still in session. But in spite of the emergence of a seemingly cooperative mood between North and South Korea, basic issues, such as simultaneous inspections of nuclear facilities in both Koreas and cultural exchanges, have stalled. Furthermore, military tension prevails, with a total of 1.5 million ground forces confronting each other across the DMZ.

---

19. See *Boei Hakusho*, 1992, pp. 54-56.

U.S.-Japan Defense Cooperation

By following Japan's exclusively defense-oriented policy, Japan and the U.S. have different functional roles in their security relations. This role division is complementary, but not interchangeable. According to the Guide Lines for U.S.-Japan Defense Cooperation agreed upon in 1978, should Japan be attacked, the Japanese Self-Defense Forces would carry out defensive operations mainly in Japanese territory and in the surrounding air and seas. U.S. forces, in turn, would support the operations of the JSDF, and carry out operations only if Japanese forces were unable to handle things alone. Japan expects the U.S. to provide not only a credible nuclear umbrella, but also offensive striking power, if necessary, especially with its Seventh Fleet.

As of the end of 1991, a total of about 39,300 U.S. troops were stationed in Japan. Of this, about 2,200 are ground forces, about 5,500 are naval forces, about 21,300 are marine corps, and the rest are air forces. Even the new East Asia Strategy Initative (EASI) doesn't show any fundamental change in U.S. security policy for the Asia-Pacific region.

Japan makes the utmost effort to maintain the effectiveness of U.S. forward-deployment policy because it is most suitable for Japan's self defense as well as for regional security. Accordingly, there is no reason why Japan would seek to change its security policy unilaterally or to become a military superpower.

The Mid-Term Defense Program

With regard to its defense build-up, Japan started

the new Mid-Term Defense Program in 1991, and it will run through to 1995. This program reflected the achievements of the 1976 National Defense Program Outline, which ended in 1990. Actually, the new mid-term plan will contribute to the overall improvement of the security environment for the following reasons. First, the defense budget's annual growth rate over the period will decrease to less than 3 percent. This is lower by far than the 5.4 percent of the previous five-year period. The Japanese defense budget is not likely to exceed one percent of the GNP until 1995. Second, the new program puts a priority on quality improvement of equipment rather than quantity, along with improvements in the living standards and welfare of JSDF members. Without a visible improvement of living standards, recruitment would not be easy. Finally, this new defense program also includes an increase of host-nation support for U.S. troops in Japan. About 10 percent of Japan's overall defense expenditures will cover this area.

The current Mid-Term Defense Program was revised at the end of 1992 to reflect the new post-Cold War climate, and the total amount of defense-related expenditures for the Mid-Term Defense Program was cut by 580 billion yen.[20]

Conclusion

The international military atmosphere surrounding Japan is uncertain. The fundamental conditions of Japan's defense policy have not changed. Japan is eager to show its interest in being cooperative on

---

20. See *Boei Hakusho,* 1992, p. 131, and *Sankei Shinbun,* December 25, 1992.

international issues, which is neither a result nor a reflection of any defense policy change.

Japan is seeking ways to cooperate with the rest of the world. South Korea is also seeking a way to make military exchanges with Japan in the post-Cold War era.[21] But there is a gap in understanding about Japan's defense between Japan and Asian countries, particularly Korea. This may become an obstacle for creating multinational cooperation in the future.

In the autumn of 1991, the United Nations requested that several countries, including Japan, the ROK, and China, consider participation in peace-keeping operations. But these three nations considered their participation individually. ROK journalists criticized intensely Japan's participation in PKO in Cambodia. The ROK decided not to participate there. In a broad sense, PKO may be a good avenue for multilateral cooperation in international security issues. But in Asia, there was no forum to address this issue because of the caution put on Japan's increasing of its defense role in Asia.

How can we deal with these misunderstandings and misperceptions? The most important way is to promote the exchange of experts on defense issues between Japan and other Asian nations, including the ROK.

There may be a negative view in relation to the promotion of military exchanges between Japan and the ROK. Due to past history, it is natural for Koreans to be suspicious of Japan's defense efforts. Among

---

21. According to the ROK's Defense White Papaer, the ROK will seek to promote military exchanges with Japan in consideration of Japan's increasing regional role and the development of U.S.-Japan security relations. See *Defense White Paper of 1992* (ROK: Defense Ministry), p. 23.

Koreans, feelings about the Japanese are complicated and contradictory. Some dislike the Japanese and feel threatened. Others are willing to cooperate with Japan. As an indicator of this sentiment, a recent poll carried out by the Choong-ang Daily revealed that 49.9 percent of South Koreans think Korea must learn from Japan.[22] At the same time, ironically enough, 53.4 percent claimed they disliked Japan.

For Japanese, it may be difficult to understand this mixed and complicated sentiment expressed by Koreans. But this may suggest that South Korea won't always refuse to communicate with Japan. Japanese should notice this mixed sentiment and should make efforts to explain to Koreans, the background of Japan's defense policy.

---

22. The second nation was Germany, at 9.4 percent. Only 15.3 percent said they disliked North Korea. *Chung-ang Daily News*, August 27, 1992.

Appendix 1. Outline of Organization of Defense Agency and SDF

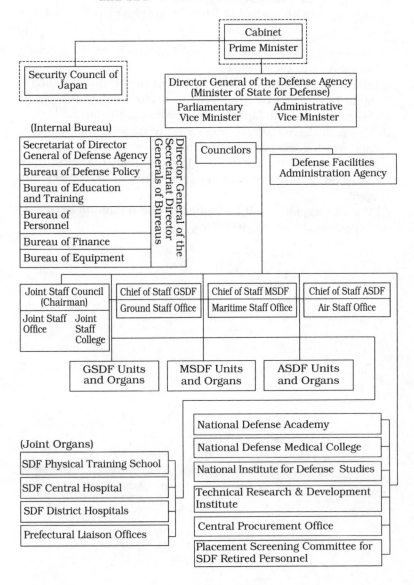

Appendix 2. Basic Guidelines for Japan's Participation
in Peacekeeping Forces
(The so-called Five Principles)

I.   Agreement on a cease-fire shall have been reached among the parties to the conflict.

II. The parties to the conflict, including the territorial state(s), shall have given their consent to deployment of the peacekeeping force and Japan's participation in the force.

III. The peacekeeping force shall strictly maintain impartiality, not favoring any party to the conflict.

IV. Should any of the above guideline requirements cease to be satisfied, the Government of Japan may withdraw its contingent.

V.   Use of weapons shall be limited to the minimum necessary to protect the personnel's lives, etc.

Appendix 3. Changes in Amount of Japan's Defense Production

(Unit: ¥1 million)

Fiscal Year	Amount of Production Directed to the Defense Agency (A)	Special Procurements (B)	Total Amount of Defense Production (C=A+B)	Industrial Production (D)	Ratio (C/D) (%)
1982	1,049,509	2,117	1,051,626	230,883,431	0.46
1983	1,165,211	3,378	1,168,589	235,834,726	0.50
1984	1,210,133	3,796	1,213,929	254,495,738	0.48
1985	1,349,249	3,135	1,352,384	266,322,142	0.51
1986	1,392,529	3,266	1,395,795	253,972,797	0.55
1987	1,458,506	4,406	1,462,912	253,080,614	0.58
1988	1,477,833	2,174	1,480,007	275,840,682	0.54
1989	1,631,235	1,831	1,633,066	300,533,693	0.54
1990 (Preliminary Report)	1,757,680	1,738	1,759,418	324,959,179	0.54

Notes: 1. "Amount of Production Directed to the Defense Agency" is based on figures obtained as a result of a "Survey on Procurement Contracts of Equipment, etc.," carried out each fiscal year. As regards "aircraft," and "weapons and ammunition" procurements, they are based on figures available in the calendar year of the "Year Book of Machinery Statistics" complied by the Research and Statistics Department of the Minister's Secretariat of the Ministry of International Trade and Industry.
2. "Special Procurements" are based on figures of the "Special Procurements" available in the calendar year of the "Year Book of Statistics" compiled by the Research and Statistics Department, Minister's Secretariat, Ministry of International Trade and Industry.
3. "Industrial Production" is based on figures available in the calendar year of the "Census of Manufacturers" compiled by the Research and Statistics Department, Minister's Secretariat, MITI. As regards "aircraft," and "weapon and ammunition" procurements, and "coal" procurements, however, they are based on figures available in the calendar years of the "Year Book of Machinery Statistics" and the "Mining Year Book of Japan" respectively, both compiled by the Research and Statistics Department, Minister's Secretariat, MITI.
4. Figures for FY 1990 were estimated on the basis of the value from preliminary report.

Appendix 4. Defense-Related Expenditure Classified by Use

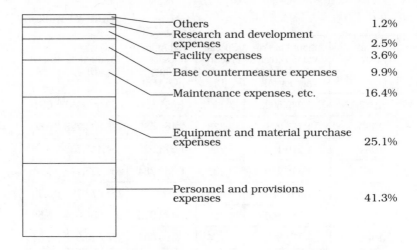

Others	1.2%
Research and development expenses	2.5%
Facility expenses	3.6%
Base countermeasure expenses	9.9%
Maintenance expenses, etc.	16.4%
Equipment and material purchase expenses	25.1%
Personnel and provisions expenses	41.3%

Appendix 5. Basic Policy for National Defense

The objective of national defense is to prevent direct and indirect aggression, but once invaded, to repel such action, thereby preserving the independence and peace of Japan founded upon democratic principles.

To achieve this objective, the government of Japan hereby establishes the following principles:

1. To support the activities of the United Nations and promote international cooperation, thereby contributing to the realization of world peace.
2. To promote public welfare and enhance the people's love for the country, thereby establishing the sound basis essential to Japan's security.
3. To develop progressively the effective defense capabilities necessary for self-defense, with regard to the nation's resources and the prevailing domestic situation.
4. To deal with external aggression on the basis of the Japan-U.S. security arrangements, pending the effective functioning of the United Nations in the future in deterring and repelling such aggression.

CHAPTER 10

JAPAN-NORTH KOREAN NEGOTIATIONS FOR NORMALIZATION: AN OVERVIEW

Masao Okonogi

Since the conclusion of the INF Treaty in December 1987, conflict between the U.S. and the Soviet Union has been greatly reduced. In the two years following, the political changes in Eastern Europe brought about a de facto ending to the Cold War. The bipolar world order has become a thing of the past, and new regional orders are being searched for in each part of the world. The new regional orders will be more or less combinations of U.S. leadership and situations in each area, but in East Asia, the influence of the Soviets (Russia), China, and Japan cannot be over-looked.

The establishment of diplomatic relations between South Korea (ROK) and the Soviet Union in September 1990 showed that the process of terminating the Cold War in East Asia, which had stagnated since the "Tiananmen" incident, had been resumed. It is

noteworthy that since then, North Korea (DPRK) proposed to Japan a normalization of relations and, at
the same time, initiated high level North-South talks.
President Kim Il-sung even suggested the form of
unification as "one nation, one state, two governments, two systems" to Premier Kang Young-hoon of
South Korea, who visited Pyongyang in October. It is
apparent that North Korean policy toward Japan is
closely related to the country's survival strategy.

North Korea's Sudden Initiatives Toward Japan

The political changes that took place in Eastern
Europe in the fall of 1989 convinced North Korea of
the real significance of the "repression of a counter-
revolutionary disturbance" at Tiananmen. The sup-
pression by force at Tiananmen and the cooperative
actions of China and North Korea, which were later
confirmed, minimized the shock of the collapse of the
socialist camp, as symbolized by the fall of the Berlin
Wall. In the beginning of November, when Erich
Honecker fell from power and the situation in East
Germany seemed to have reached the point of no
return, Kim Il-sung payed a visit to Beijing where the
top-level leaders of China and North Korea exchanged words on towing the party line in leadership
and on following the way of socialism.[1]

The collapse of the socialist camp, however, had an
even more serious influence on a divided country like
North Korea than on China. The series of events not
only posed a question as to the future of socialism,
but also seemed to urge Eastern European countries

---

1. *Renmin Ribao*, November 13, 1989.

to recognize South Korea, which would, as a result, build up an international consensus for "two Koreas." This was why a Chinese spokesman for the Ministry of Foreign Affairs dared to state the following after Kim Il-sung left Beijing: "South Korea's joining the United Nations will create a difficult situation for reunifying Korea." He even suggested the possibility of exercising China's veto power at the U.N. Security Council.

Moreover, the recognition of South Korea by the former Soviet Union, in September 1990, trapped North Korea into an even more difficult situation. In fact, North Korea criticized this Soviet action by saying that it was an act of "joining a conspiracy designed by the U.S. and South Korea to overthrow North Korea's socialist system by building a triple alliance." Behind this statement was the perception that "South Korea will use the Soviet's position as an excuse to reunify Korea by absorbing North Korea, as in Germany."[2]

On the other hand, the collapse of the socialist camp also dealt a severe blow to the North Korean economy and made the long depression even worse. The depression was, in the long term, due to a number of reasons, including the deterioration of production facilities and technologies, unaffordably high military expenditures and a generally inefficient economic system, a policy of giving the highest priority to politics, and a foreign policy based on exclusion. Actually, however, a series of actions taken against the Seoul Olympics induced a new financial crisis. It took 4.7 billion dollars to launch the the 13th World Festival of Youth and Students in Pyongyang in July

---

2. *Rodong Shinmun*, October 8, 1990.

1989, an amount that had not been budgeted for in the existing "third seven-year plan."

Furthermore, a shift in the Soviet and the East European countries from planned economies to market economies gave an additional blow to the already troubled North Korean economy. It made it impossible for North Korea to continue its barter trade, depriving it of the base for external economic relations. Edward Schevardnadze, the Soviet foreign minister at that time, visited North Korea in September 1990 and notified the North Korean side that the Soviets would establish diplomatic relations with South Korea and would also begin using international currencies in its trade and selling Soviet products, including petroleum, at international prices. This inevitably meant a sharp decrease in North Korea's trade with the Soviets, which had accounted for about 60 percent of the total amount up until that time.

Given these circumstances, it was most reasonable for North Korea to suddenly suggest the establishment of diplomatic relations with Japan at a time when the former Soviet Union was establishing diplomatic relations with South Korea. As the secretary of the Korean Workers' Party Kim Young-sun frankly indicated, North Korea decided to open the way through Japan for adjusting itself to the drastic changes in the international situation and resolving its severe economic difficulties. North Korea also knew that a large amount of "reparations" would accompany the establishment of diplomatic relations with Japan (but not with the U.S.), and thus it was a case of killing two birds with one stone. They had no other choice if they wanted to avoid international isolation and escape from their economic difficulties.

Looking at the development of these events, it can be said that North Korea's need to establish diplomatic relations with Japan, rather than simply make an improvement in their relations, was closely tied to the circumstances existing between the Soviets and South Korea. With those two countries having established diplomatic relations, the aims of North Korean foreign policy toward Japan had to change accordingly. Otherwise, North Korea would not have been able to settle the unrest within the country. The point is that Japan was beginning to be recognized by North Korea as a friendly nation to replace the Soviet Union. The following statement of Kim Il-sung explains it: "Problems within Asia must be solved by Asians."[3]

Informal Contact Between Japan and North Korea

Looking back over the past few decades, one can see that it was the change in South Korean foreign policy toward North Korea that the Japanese government had been waiting for all the time. In reality, at the time of the conclusion of the Japan-South Korean treaty in 1965, the Japanese government limited South Korean jurisdiction to the southern half of the peninsula, despite the strong opposition of South Korea. Prime Minister Sato Eisaku and Foreign Minister Shiina Etsusaburo stuck to their positions, saying that relations between Japan and North Korea are "blank." The Japanese government later explained its foreign policy toward North Korea as

---

3. *Asahi Shimbun*, September 27, 1990.

"intending to extend contact gradually" during the period of detante in the '70s.[4]

Of course, it did not mean immediate political contact with North Korea. As Foreign Minister Kimura plainly pointed out, the Japanese government was expecting the situation to change either by both North and South Korea joining the United Nations at the same time or by an international recognition of both Koreas making it possible for Japan to negotiate diplomatically with North Korea.[5]

However, progress in South Korea's Northern Policy coincided with the "new-thinking diplomacy" pushed by Soviet Secretary-General Gorbachev, especially the "July Seventh Declaration" by President Roh Tae-woo, which stated that "we are ready to cooperate with North Korea in improving their relations with our friendly nations, such as the U.S. and Japan." He also said to Prime Minister Takeshita Noboru, who was attending the opening ceremony of the Seoul Olympics in September 1988, that "Japan has a big part to play in making North Korea contribute to international society." He even proposed in his speech at the U.N. General Assembly holding a peace conference among six Northeast Asian countries.[6]

From that point onward, Japanese reactions to the new situation were quick. On the same day that President Roh announced the "July Seventh Declaration," the Japanese government showed its intention to "improve Japan-North Korea relations after closed talks with the related countries." It announced that Japan intended to discuss "all aspects of Japan and

4. *Asahi Shimbun*, January 21, 1974.
5. *Yomiuri Shimbun*, December 7, 1974.
6. *Asahi Shimbun*, September 18, 1988.

North Korea" under the conditions of a settlement of the No. 18 Fujisanmaru case. Then, on September 16, just before the opening of the Seoul Olympics, Japan decided to remove the sanctions against North Korea for the terrorist bombing of a Korean airliner.

Also, the Japanese government communicated its opinion to President Kim Il-sung through the Soviet foreign minister in December, and it even allowed a delegation of the Korean Workers' Party to come to Japan to attend a party convention of the Japan Socialist Party in January 1989. In addition to that, the Japanese government announced, on January 20, that "We ready to discuss, with no conditions, all the problems that lie between Japan and North Korea in any form."

However, what was most important were the remarks made by Prime Minister Takeshita at the budget committee of the House of Representatives on March 30. There he showed "deep reflection and regret" toward the unfortunate past with North Korea and an intention to proceed with improving relations with the "Democratic People's Republic of Korea" with new considerations. This message was carefully checked and transmitted to the ambassador of North Korea in China by the former secretary-general of the Japan Socialist Party, Tanabe Makoto, who had stopped at Beijing on his way to Pyongyang on the same day. It was also interesting that Tanabe had been carrying a note from Kanemaru Shin, the former Deputy Prime Minister of Japan, to President Kim Il-sung. Since his visit to Pyongyang in May 1985, Tanabe had been keeping in close contact with the leaders of North Korea and acting as an intermediary between the Japanese Liberal Democratic Party and the Korean Workers' Party through secretary Ho

Dam.

Having talked with Tanabe twice, Ho Dam promised to solve the case of the No. 18 Fujisanmaru under the charge of the North Korean government, paying careful attention to Takeshita's apology. He also promised to accept a delegation of the members of the Diet, including Kanemaru. Kim Il-sung stated that "some Japanese authorities have been speaking positively" and that he was ready to welcome Kanemaru's visit to Pyongyang. Thus, the plan for Kanemaru and Tanabe's visit to Pyongyang, which would actually be realized a year and a half later, began to take shape through the channels of the Japan Socialist Party.[7]

However, the plan was delayed due to the domestic situations in both Japan and North Korea. As mentioned before, North Korea was in a situation where it was necessary to give highest priority to domestic unity because of the Tiananmen incident in June, the fall of the Berlin Wall in November, and the civil war in Romania in December. On the other hand, Prime Minister Takeshita resigned as a result of the Recruit Scandal, in April. Moreover, in July, the Liberal Democratic Party was severely defeated in the House of Councilors' election, and the stability of the newly-inaugurated Kaifu Cabinet was questioned. Also, while these events occurred, the so-called "pachinko suspicion" in which the Japan Socialist Party and Pro-North Korean *Chosoren* (General Association of Korean Residents in Japan) had been involved, stiffened North Korean attitudes toward Japan.

---

7. Tanabe Makoto, "Korega Kanemaru hochodan no butaiura da" [This is a Backdoor Dealing until Kanomaru Visits North Korea], *Gekkan Asahi*, December 1990.

Visit to Pyongyang by Kanemaru and Tanabe

To the surprise of the Japanese, North Korea suddenly proposed an "early establishment of diplomatic relations with Japan" to Kanemaru and Tanabe, who were visiting Pyongyang in September 1990. During the initial, informal contacts, North Korea never brought up the possibility of establishing diplomatic relations. They had also been strongly against the Soviet action of recognizing South Korea, perceiving the action as recognizing the "two Koreas." The aim of Kanemaru and Tanabe, too, was only to release the two detained crewmen and prepare the base for formal relations with North Korea.

However, North Korea had already made up its mind to "set up early diplomatic relations." In the first talks with Kanemaru and Tanabe on September 25, Kim Young-sun mentioned that "There is a fear that our negotiations might never end if we do not establish normal diplomatic relations." In the second talks, on September 27, Kim Young-sun broached the subject by saying, "We desire to begin official negotiations with Japan, starting this November." He explained that this idea was a result of a change in the former policy, for which there were the following two reasons: (1) there were drastic changes happening in the international situations surrounding North Korea and (2) there were opinions circulating in the Japanese government that it is impossible to atone for the past unless relations are normalized.[8]

Of course, it did not mean that North Korea had given up defending the idea of "two Koreas" or "cross

---

8. *Yomiuri Shimbun*, September 27, 1990.

recognition." On the contrary, the North tried to justify the idea of setting up diplomatic relations with
Japan by using another argument that could lead to
admitting parts of the above idea. For example, Foreign Minister Kim Young-nam explained at the press
conference after the first day of the Japan-North
Korea negotiation[9] that "Japan would normalize
relations with North Korea not for so-called 'cross
recognition,' but to form an independent, peaceful,
and prosperous Asia by Asians."

Thus, Kanemaru and Tanabe's visit to Pyongyang
resulted in agreements to release the two crewmen of
the No. 18 Fujisanmaru in October and to start official negotiations in November. However, the text of
the "Joint Statement" from the Japan Liberal Democratic Party, the Socialist Party, and the Korean
Workers' Party, especially the expression of apology
and promise to compensate for the "losses that the
North Korean people suffered for 45 years after the
war," was the critical point in Japan, as we all know.

Nevertheless, in spite of many defects and diplomatic crudities, Kanemaru and Tanabe's visit to
Pyongyang was obviously in line with Japanese
diplomacy since the end of the Second World War.
Their visit confirmed the role of politicians at each
historical moment, such as the normalization with
the Soviets, South Korea, and China. Also, if Japan
had refused the proposal from North Korea, it would
have internationally isolated North Korea, which now
partly admitted the "two Koreas."

However, when it came to establishing diplomatic
relations, Japan would have to organize an important part in the post-Cold War international order in

---

9. *Asahi Shimbun*, February 2, 1991.

East Asia. So, it was obvious that a series of contacts between Japan and North Korea for normalization could not remain a problem between the two countries alone. Although President Roh Tae-woo did not oppose the normalization itself, he emphasized to Kanemaru, who was visiting Seoul on October 8, the importance of connecting it with the North-South Korean dialogue and to the nuclear inspections of North Korea by IAEA.

The American government had the same opinion about this, as was shown in the talks between the American Ambassader to Japan, Michael Armacost, and Kanemaru. Since the American government had been keeping a strict watch on North Korean nuclear weapons development, they showed the Japanese authorities a satellite picture of a reprocessing plant for nuclear fuel under construction in North Korea. There was also a statement by the Secretary of State, Richard Solomon, at the end of October, which went as follows: "We view nuclear proliferation on the Korean peninsula as the number one threat to stability in East Asia."[10]

Government-Level Negotiations

The first official contact between Japan and the North Korean government took place at a preliminary meeting in Beijing between the Ministries of Foreign Affairs in the beginning of November. However, since the former contacts among the political parties were proceeded at North Korean pace, the attitude of the

---

10. Richard Solomon's Address, October 30, 1991. *Official Text*, USIS, Tokyo.

Japanese Ministry of Foreign Affairs was cautious. North Korean authorities stuck to "compensation for the past 45 years," while the director of the Asian Bureau, Tanino Sakutaro, maintained that the agreements among the political parties did not have the power to restrict negotiations between the governments. He insisted that an improvement in relations between Japan and North Korea should contribute to "the peace and the stability of the Korean peninsula," and for that we need to gain "understandings and supports from the related countries."

As a result of complications, the four following agenda items were resolved by the middle of December: "the basic problems for normalizing the relations;" "some economic problems with the normalization of the relation;" "international problems related to the normalization," and "other problems in which both countries were interested." Since Japan insisted strongly on North Korean acceptance of nuclear inspections by IAEA, and the problems dealing with compensation had been required by North Korea to open discussions even at the preliminary meeting level, the decision was made to discuss them in succession at the regular meeting. In other words, the above problems were recognized by both sides as important problems that could affect the result of the regular meeting.

Actually, at the first regular meeting held at the end of January, the chief representative of the North Korean side, Chun In-chul, demanded property claims, war reparations, and postwar compensations. However, the Japanese side only acknowledged the property claims and, on the inspection of nuclear weapons, it asked for an early acceptance. Then North Korea demanded an inspection of nuclear weapons that might be at the American military bases in South Korea, thereby making the discussion parallel. Furthermore, on the nuclear problem, North Korea tried to avoid the discussion by regarding the problem as one between the U.S. and North Korea.

These situations did not change at the second meeting held in the middle of March. Despite the postponement of the talks between South and North Korean prime ministers, due to the enforcement of Team Spirit, North Korea was still expecting an early settlement of the meetings with Japan. Secretary Kim Young-sum visited Japan in the middle of February and had a talk with Kanemaru and Tanabe. Then he not only reconfirmed the agreements among the three parties, but also invited Takeshita to North Korea and delivered a correspondence from Kim Il-sung to Prime Minister Kaifu, in person. Also, at the press conference right before leaving Japan, he said that the negotiations would be settled within the year: "We can start with the one we can settle."[11]

With that point of view, North Korean authorities introduced a new policy at the third conference in May and tried to speed up the negotiations. Chun In-chul insisted on giving priority to the "basic problems" related to the normalization of the relations, apart from other problems. According to his proposal, after reaching a certain measure of agreement, it would then be time to establish diplomatic relations. As for economic and international problems and so on, the decision was made to continue to discuss these problems and to solve them, in order, later on. Also, because that point of view was related to the "basic problems," the North Korean govern-

---

11. *Sankei Shimbun*, February 25, 1991.

ment made a small concession to the Japanese idea about the right of jurisdiction of the North Korean government.

However, besides refusing that proposal, Japanese authorities made the following three preconditions for the further progress of negotiations: (1) an inspection of North Korean atomic facilities by IAEA, (2) an early re-opening of the meeting between South and North Korean prime ministers, (3) South and North Korea join the U.N. at the same time. In reference to the problem of nuclear inspections, Nakahira Noboru, the chief representative of the Japanese delegation, emphasized that "It is impossible to gain the support of the public in Japan if we try to make progress without solving this problem."

Also, Nakahira referred to "Lee Un-hae," who had been in charge of teaching Japanese to Kim Hyun-hui (the criminal responsible for the Korean Air disaster who was identified by the police just before the third meeting) and who demanded North Korea confirm her information. It goes without saying that North Korea was strongly opposed to that demand. Chun In-chul said it was an "unbearable humiliation" and stated that North Korea would not accept the fourth meeting unless the Japanese side retracted that demand and apologized.[12]

The upshot was the North Korean side proposed a new plan giving top priority to establishing diplomatic relations while the Japanese government proposed "three conditions" and tried to put the brakes on the North Korean proposal. And as for the "economic problem," North Korea decided to expect the negotia-

---

12. *Asahi Shimbun*, May 21, 1991; *Yomiuri Shimbun*, May 22, 1991; *Sankei Shimbun*, May 23, 1991.

tions would take place among the political parties after the establishment of diplomatic relations, rather than be established at the level of the foreign offices. And these policies might reflect North Korea's strategy to proceed with the talks with South Korea by establishing an early settlement of the negotiations with Japan, which would, in effect, be applying diplomatic pressure to South Korea.

In any case, the opinions of both Japan and North Korea collided head-on, and the third meeting ended without setting the next meeting. Thus, the North Korean strategy to try to put pressure on South Korea by refusing nuclear inspections, settling the negotiations with Japan early, and getting as much compensation as possible, ended up a failure, and long-range negotiations between Japan and North Korea became inevitable.

The Nuclear Inspection Problem

After an informal agreement was made on the "Lee Un-hae" problem, the fourth Japan-North Korea talks were held in late August. Although there were no substantial changes in North Korean attitudes, international pressure continued to increase before the opening of the IAEA Council in September. Also, simultaneous U.N. membership of the two Koreas became definite, and the reopening of the North-South Prime Ministers' Conference was agreed upon. Furthermore, the coup d'etat in the Soviet Union failed, and the dismantlement of the Communist Party was declared. For this reason, the fourth North-South Prime Ministers' Conference, once agreed upon, was delayed until the latter half of

October.

From the start, the talks became complicated. At the working-level consultations held before the main conference, North Korea refused to accept investigations on 'Lee Un-hae,' which was a violation of a previous informal agreement. Afterwards, on the first and second agenda, the Japanese side explained its position in more detail than during the previous talks. Also, the Japanese side again strongly demanded the acceptance of nuclear inspections by North Korea, and urged the reopening of the North-South Prime Ministers' Conference. There was no change in North Korea's stance, but there was greater significance in the holding of the talks themselves than in the content of the discussions.

However, at the fifth round of talks held in November, some changes in North Korea's attitude were seen. Although the opinions of both sides regarding nuclear inspections and the 'Lee Un-hae' problem were still on par with each other, concerning the second agenda, Chun In-chul demanded "compensations for the enormous human and material damages, misfortunes, and sufferings incurred by the Korean people by the forcing of colonial rule," without mentioning "reparations between belligerents" or "postwar compensations." Also, the gap between the claims of both countries narrowed partially, even with respect to the first agenda.[13]

The sixth talks, in late January 1992, were held in a favorable climate due to the North-South Joint Declaration of Denuclearization of the Korean Peninsula and North Korea's signing of the nuclear inspec-

---

13. *Asahi Shimbun*, November 20, 1991; *Sankei Shimbun*, November 21, 1991.

tions agreement with the IAEA. However, despite these measures, there were no substantive movements. Meanwhile, Chun In-chul claimed that, "The problem of concluding the nuclear inspections agreement is completely solved." Nakahira still demanded that North Korea faithfully implement the agreement with IAEA and the joint declaration between the North and South and clear the suspicion about nuclear weapons development completely. Also, Nakahira demanded the abandonment of the nuclear fuel reprocessing plant under construction. On the other hand, the North Korean side brought up anew the comfort women problem, and criticized Japan's reserving of plutonium for the generation of electricity.

The seventh round of talks were delayed until May due to the death of Chun In-chul, whose place as the chief representative was taken by Lee Sam-roh. However, the demands of both sides were already fully enunciated by the time of the sixth talks, and no new development in the discussions could be seen. But, reflecting the fact that even after the Joint Declaration on Denuclearization the North-South mutual inspections had not been implemented, the conflict between Japan and North Korea was increasing. Also, on other problems, points of disagreement between both sides had been made clear by the sixth talks.

It is clear that the nuclear inspections problem was the largest obstacle in Japan-North Korea negotiations. From the beginning, instead of specific measures, the Japanese side demanded a "clearance of suspicion" from North Korea that would make the settlement of negotiations possible. For that purpose, even after the conclusion of the inspections agreement with IAEA, which was demanded from the beginning, Japan continued to call for the abandonment of the reprocessing plant, and, furthermore, after the denuclearization declaration was adopted, it called for the North-South mutual inspections. In fact, what the Japanese side demanded of North Korea was nothing more than faithful implementation of international treaties and the North-South joint declaration. To settle the talks without that was impossible.

The North Korean side, on the other hand, avoided discussion on the nuclear inspections problem as much as possible and tried for early normalization of relations. While the Japanese side called for a blanket solution of all agendas, the North Korean side claimed, as enunciated in the third talks, that first, agreement on the first agenda be made and relations normalized, and, afterwards, move to the second agenda. To induce that formula, they showed a rather flexible stance on the first and second agenda. In fact, after the fifth round of talks, the North Korean side did not mention "reparations between belligerents" and "postwar compensations."

Future Prospects

Two years are about to pass since the start of the Japan-North Korea negotiations. However, as indicated earlier, if North Korea approached Japan in order to overcome its international isolation and economic difficulties, the situation has not improved at all. Rather, the China-South Korea normalization in August 1992 made the Japan-North Korea normalization more important for North Korea. In fact, if North Korea had solved the nuclear inspections problem promptly and made progress in North-South talks and Japan-North Korea negotiations, the shock of the China-South Korea normalization would not have been so great. This is clearly North Korea's diplomatic failure.

Although it is just my own impression, North Korea seems to have promoted nuclear weapons development and endeavoured to use it as a diplomatic means. For this purpose, the North ventured to show its own nuclear development ability to be larger than it actually is. This tactic was effective in making the U.S. forces in Korea remove their nuclear weapons and terminate the Team Spirit exercise. However, it also resulted in maximizing international suspicion about the North's nuclear development. The rappoachement between China and South Korea since last October reflected China's mistrust toward North Korea's stance. In other words, North Korea has lost much to gain little.

Moreover, as a result of the IAEA ad hoc inspections, North Korea's nuclear development ability is not in question. But, as seen in the statements of U.S. Deputy Assistant Secretary of State Richard Solomon, President Roh Tae-woo, and U.S. Ambassador to Korea Donald Greegg, its value as a diplomatic means is rapidly decreasing. In other words, a situation is emerging that is meaningless for North Korea to adhere to. On the other hand, if North Korea continues to refuse North-South mutual inspection, Team Spirit will be reinitiated, and North-South talks and Japan-North Korea negotiations will be significantly delayed.

However, we need not interpret the present situation in only a pessimistic way. As can be seen in the proposal for Japan-North Korean normalization, simultaneous North-South U.N. membership, the Joint Declaration for Denuclearization, and the signing and ratification of the nuclear inspections agreement, North Korea has, at the last moment, after resisting new situations and obtaining the maximum returns, chosen to respond to the realities of international politics instead of international isolation. The possibility always exists that these behavior patterns may be repeated again and that new phases may be opened in North-South talks and Japan-North Korea negotiations as a result of acceptance of mutual inspections.

If those kinds of decisions were to be made again and, as a result, the North-South talks progress, the biggest obstacle in promoting Japan-North Korea negotiations will have been removed. The focus of negotiations would rapidly move on to the second agenda, i.e., economic problems, and discussions about "property claims and economic cooperation" would become active. As mentioned earlier, the Japanese government is not intentionally trying to prolong the negotiations. Also, criticisms of Japan concerning such issues as comfort women and plutonium reserves should be seen as "expressions of courtship" to promote negotiations.

However, apart from such situations, it must be noted that another difficulty is emerging, but this time within Japan, in the form of disturbances in leadership due to political scandals. As Kanemaru, who was the most eminent promoter of the Japan-North Korea negotiations, resigned as parliamentary representative, and Takeshita has fallen into a troubled situation, a big doubt remains as to how much aspiration the Miyazawa regime can bring to the settlement of Japan-North Korea negotiations. Also, I cannot imagine that the passive attitude of the economic circles, mass media, and the people will easily change.

CHAPTER 11

THE END OF THE COLD WAR AND KOREA-JAPAN RELATIONS: OLD PERCEPTIONS AND NEW ISSUES

Hosup Kim

Korea and Japan are fundamentally liberal democratic countries with traditional, friendly relations in the area of security. In the case of a threat of communist attack, they both assert the existence of cooperative relations. However, the Cold War, which displayed its symptoms in Sino-American conflict, and the ideological conflict and arms race that attended it have ended. There are some pessimistic outlooks on whether the friendly relations between the two countries can be maintained, in the post-Cold War period, on the same ground.[1] The future for maintaining a strong relationship on the basis of mutual security interests seems gloomy. According

---

1. Katsumi Sato et al., "Taiketsu: nikkan keizai masatsu," [Confrontation: Japan-Korea economic friction] *Bungeishunju* (July 1992), p. 280.

to the pessimists, the cement that bonded relations between the two countries, even under the pressure of nationalism, was a shared anti-communism. In this post-Cold War period, however, such means of alleviating nationalistic conflict are no longer available. The talk of Japan's colonial past, the discussion of a proper apology in Korea, and Japan's "Kenkan" (Dislike Korea) phenomenon are sometimes interpreted as the results of the disappearance of the common security interest that bonded the two countries.[2] In this paper, it will be argued that because Korea and Japan share many common interests other than security, the relation will not culminate just because the Cold War has ended.

Major Issues in Korea-Japan Relations

There are at least four critical issues in current Korea-Japan relations. First, regarding the settlement of past colonial domination and the question of proper apology, Koreans feel that the pains of the past have not been appeased on an emotional level, while efforts to deal honestly with colonial transgressions have been conspicuously lacking on the part of the Japanese. The ghost of the colonial past has been the thorn in the side of Japan-Korea relations from time to time. Koreans are disturbed by the distorted account of the war in Japanese history text books and the discriminatory treatment of Korean-Japanese in Japan, which requires mandatory finger printing and the demeaning, obligatory possession of a "foreigners" registration card, and the dubious legal sta-

---

2. Chikara Nishioka, "Ianpumondai towa nandattanoka," [What is the problem of comfort girls?] *Bungeishunju* (April 1992), p. 300.

tus this treatment implies. Another thorn is the choice of terminology used in the official apology during the Korean President's visit to Japan and the Japanese Prime Minister's visit to Korea. In 1991, during President Roh's visit to Japan, the Emperor said, "Japan deeply regrets the pain Koreans suffered by Japan." The Prime Minister went a little further, actually using the word 'apology,' for the first time, in his official statement. He said he "feels remorse and apologizes for Japan's actions."

In 1992, another compensation and apology dispute reared its head. During the Pacific War, many Korean women were forcibly mobilized by the Japanese government to various military camps as "comfort girls." The vast majority of Koreans are of the opinion that the survivors should be compensated and there should be an official apology from the Japanese government. The Japanese government argues that all compensations were paid during the normalization of diplomatic relations in 1965, in accordance with the Property and Claims Fund. Therefore, compensation for the surviving "comfort girls", on a government-to-government level, is impossible. Currently, the surviving women are proceeding with litigation against the Japanese government in a Japanese court. Korea specialists in Japan are expressing their dismay. They argue that despite the fact the Emperor and the Prime Minister have apologized to the President of Korea, every time the 'past' is discussed apology becomes an issue and the Koreans demand an apology each time.[3]

---

3. Akira Tanaka and Katsumi Sato, "Shazaisuru hodo warukunaru nikkankankei," [The more we apologize, the worse the Japanese-Korean relationship becomes] *Bungeishunju* (March 1992), pp. 134-142.

Second is the issue of the negotiation between North Korea and Japan on the normalization of diplomatic relations. In September 1990, the vice president of the Liberal Democratic Party, Kanemaru Shin, and the vice chairman of the Socialist Party, Tanabe Makato, visited North Korea. During a meeting with Chairman Kim Il-sung, they agreed to hold a conference on opening diplomatic relations between the two countries. Between then and November 1992, a preliminary meeting and eight conferences have been held. In these conferences, they have negotiated issues concerning the normalization of diplomatic relations. The following are the four major conference agenda in normalization negotiations between North Korea and Japan.

1. Basic issues, such as range of jurisdiction and the effectiveness of the Annexation of Korea Treaty.

2. Economic issues, such as the format and the amount of compensation for the colonization of Korea.

3. International issues, such as the development of nuclear weapons in North Korea and the North-South Dialogue.

4. Other issues, such as home-visits for Japanese spouses residing in North Korea.

A North Korea-Japan normalization of relations would influence not only the relations between the two countries involved, but also those between Korea and Japan. In 1990, the Korean government proposed five principles as conditions to the improvement of relations between North Korea and Japan.

1. Close prior consultation between Japan and Korea.

2. Opposition to economic cooperation with North Korea before the normalization of relations.

3. Meaningful progress in North-South Korea

relations.

4. Urge North Korea to sign the Nuclear Security Agreement.

5. Prevent appropriation of the economic coopera- tion fund for military build-up.

The Korean government has pressed for the con- sideration of the above five principles during various ministerial-level meetings and during the Japanese Prime Minister's visit to Korea. The Japanese reac- tion has been positive.

Japan has proposed three conditions that North Korea must accept in order for the normalization negotiations to progress.

1. North Korea must clear all suspicion of develop- ing nuclear weapons.

2. The North-South Korea Dialogue must be ad- vanced.

3. North and South Korea must obtain simultane- ous membership in the United Nations.

North Korea's membership in the United Nations has, in fact, been seen as heavily influenced by Japan's pressure.

The normalization negotiation does not seem, at the moment, to have much chance of making progress until the nuclear issue has been resolved. Although Japan's primary condition regarding the nuclear question has not been met, North Korea is no longer expressing its traditional hardline position that the nuclear issue is not a North Korea-Japan issue and that it should not be Japan's concern. Recently, North Korea seems to be responding more positively toward the nuclear issue. The IAEA have inspected North Korea and currently the North- South Nuclear Regulations Committee is negotiating reciprocal inspection. On the other agenda, such as the range of jurisdiction of North Korea, it has taken a much softer approach, since North Korea's jurisdiction is limited to above the 38th parallel. Furthermore, although the amount of the compensation has not been decided, North Korea relented that the format of compensation can be similar to the Property and Claims Fund formula used in 1965 during the negotiation of diplomatic relations between Korea and Japan.

The third issue in Korea-Japan relations is the possibility of Japan's once again turning to militarism. This apprehension was revived by the dispatching of Japan's Self Defence Forces (SDF) to Cambodia as part of the United Nations Peace Keeping Operations (PKO). This is not a government-level issue but, rather, an anxiety expressed within the Korean mass media. In June 1992, the Japanese Diet passed the legislation allowing the deployment of SDF as part of the U.N.'s PKO forces and, in September, the current SDF draft forces arrived in Cambodia. The PKO legislation received pressures from the international community. The United States, in particular, wished Japan to participate not only with monetary support, but also with Japanese forces, in such conflicts as the Gulf War. The dispatching of Japanese SDF in PKO can be seen as an extension of Japan's effort to search for a more active foreign policy and to take on more responsibility in the international arena. Since its maturation into an economic giant after 1970, such has been Japan's goal, which also means that there has been a change in the previous Japanese foreign policy line. In the past, Japan relied only on economic means to ensure world peace and security; now it is no longer limiting the scope of such means to the economic field, but is expanding its range to include military means.

In the post-Cold War period, Japan seeks to play a major political role in establishing the New World Order based on the changing international environment and its own mighty, economic strength. The PKO legislation is an expression of Japan's will and desire to be actively involved in the establishment of the New World Order. It also points to the likelihood that Japan's participation in the Asia-Pacific region is imminent.

There is a high degree of concern within Korea about the SDF overseas deployment. Japan has an enormous trade surplus, particularly since the late 1980s when Japan achieved about 100 billion U.S. dollars in trade surplus, which enabled Japan to improve its economy. In the late 1980s, Japan matured into an economic giant that was responsible for almost 15 percent of world GNP. Economic power can easily transfer into military might, and Japan has the benefit of advanced technology, which can directly and indirectly supply the means for a military build-up. Japan has the potential for formidable military strength; it is possible for Japan to become a military superpower. This is the main concern in the Korean peninsula. If Japan becomes a military power, Korea may once again suffer the brunt of its military ambitions.

Japan argues that it has no national will to use military power against another state to threaten or to attack. It is natural, however, for Korea, which has suffered under the mighty sword of the late 19th century Japanese invasion, to express apprehension and mistrust. The profound distrust of Japan's potential for expansionist militarism has not faded with time. If

Japan truly wishes to rid itself of such distrust, it must convince neighboring states that it has no national will to attack, by exorcising the ghost of past military history. Japan must confront its history head on, through a more rigorous self-examination.

The fourth issue between Japan and Korea is bilateral industrial-technology cooperation and the trade imbalance. The Korean trade deficit with Japan in 1989 was 3.6 billion dollars. The Korean government is demanding that the Japanese government transfer industrial technology to improve the trade imbalance between the two countries.

The Korean trade deficit with Japan has continued since the normalization of diplomatic relations. Although Korea experienced a brief period of trade surplus from 1986-1989, the trade deficit phenomenon returned and has since become a serious issue in the relations between the two countries. For the last 27 years since the normalization of diplomatic relations, the Korean trade deficit with Japan has totaled 66.1 billion dollars, which surpasses Korea's total trade deficit of 33.3 billion dollars in the same period.[4] Korea is hungry to receive Japanese high technology in order to improve the quality of products, enhance the industrial structure, and thus increase exports in high-value, technology-oriented products. In 1990, the Japanese technology-transfer share of the total Korean technology import was 50.9 percent (sum after 1961), and the cost of import was 31.2 percent of the total cost, thus surpassing other countries by far. However, Japan is avoiding transfer

4. Bank of Korea, "Choekunoe daeilmuyukjukja hwakdae yoinkwa hwanghukwaje," [Causes of recent expansion of trade deficit toward Japan and Future Tasks] Chosayunkujaryo, 92-9 (May 1992), p. 1.

of technology, and after the high point of 1988, which saw 354 transfers, in 1989, there were 343 cases, in 1990, 333 cases, and still the numbers are decreasing rapidly.[5]

Korea claims that the source of the trade deficit is Japan. The origin of the claim is the argument that the Japanese economic structure is very closed, so it is very difficult to penetrate the Japanese market. Furthermore, Japan is evading the technology transfer that would make the export of high technology products possible for Korea.[6] On the other hand, Japan argues that the trade imbalance is the result of the difference between the industrial structures of the two countries.[7] Moreover, Japan claims that Korea has increased its exports by importing capital and parts, and thus the trade deficit with Japan should not be seen as an economic barrier but as an economic contributor. As for technology transfer, Japanese industries are hedging because they fear the boomerang effect due to the large corporation-oriented industrial structure in Korea. The small- and medium-sized industries are unstable, and they possess low levels of basic technology, weaknesses that limit the degree of technology absorption. Recent developments, such as labor disputes, decreases in

---

5. Seung-Hoon Lee, "Kisulhyubryukoe ilbansanghwang," [General Situation of Technology Cooperation] Byung-Jik Ahn and Jong-Yoon Lee, eds., *Ilbonoe sanubkisu* [Japan's Industrial Technology] (Seoul: Seoul National University Economic Research Institute, 1991), pp. 269-270.

6. Bank of Korea, *Op. cit.*, p. 32.

7. Koji Matsumoto, *Nikkan keizai masatsu* [Japan-Korea Economic Friction] (Tokyo: Toyokeizaishinposha, 1986); Koji Matsumoto, "Tainichi boeki gyakucho wa nihon no sekinin dewanai," [Japan is not responsible for Korean trade deficit toward Japan] *Gendai Korea* (January 1992), pp. 16-19.

profit opportunity, a rise in the value of the won, lack of aspiration in industry, and a sharp drop in exports, are the current troubles confronting Korean industry. In the midst of such harsh conditions, Japanese industries are cutting back on their direct investment (see *Table 1*).

Table 1. Japanese Direct Foreign Investment toward S. Korea

	1988	1989	1990	Sum (1951-90)
No. of cases	153	81	54	1,847
Amount (US$ million)	483	606	284	4,138

Source: Sekai keizai joho sabis. ed.. *The World 1992: Sekai kakkoku keizai joho fairu* [Information files on the economy of each country] (Tokyo. 1992). p. 9.

The End of the Cold War and Korea-Japan Relations

There are two external developments that may change Korea-Japan relations in the 21st century. First, with the end of the Cold War, there will be less chance of military or ideological conflict between democratic and communist camps than there was after World War II in Northeast Asia. The tension between North and South Korea will decrease and relations will improve. The United States, which is the back-bone of security and order in Southeast Asia, will eventually decrease its direct military involvement in this region. Second, Japan's economy will continue to improve, and Japan will play a more active role in world political and economic arenas, especially in the Asia-Pacific region.

In Korea, there is much discussion about how Korea should prepare for Japan's increased international role based on military might and economic power in the post-Cold War period. There are six main perceptions in Korea about Japan, and each has a corresponding possible response scenario. They are, 1) Japan as role model; 2) Japan as partner sharing security interests; 3) Japan as economic partner; 4) Japan as competitor; 5) Japan as exploiter, and 6) Japan as a threat.

Japan as Role Model

Some perceive Japan as the guide, the role model for Korea's progress and development. Although there are still painful emotional remnants from the past, for Korea's further progress, it must learn from Japanese society, in many respects. Such opinions were expressed in a documentary series aired on both KBS and MBC on the theme of 'learning from Japan,' as well as in economic newspapers that write about Japan's business administrative methods and prepare special reports.[8]

The premise of such programs is that Japan, being comparatively developed relative to Korea, has wisely overcome many internal and external problems. Thus, Korea can learn important lessons from Japan's experience, which can help solve today's problems, Furthermore, because Korea and Japan share similarities in culture, language, environment, and ethnicity, if Japan can achieve such success, Korea can do it too.

---

8. Maeil kyungje shinmunsa, *Ilbonul tasi bonda* [Look at Japan Again] (Seoul: Maeil kyungje shinmunsa, 1991).

The proponents of this model claim that, economically, Korea succeeded by following the export-oriented Japanese economic policy. Socially, individual Japanese are hard-working and harmonious in nature, so that labor-corporate relations are amicably maintained. A hard-working labor force, active investment from industry, a supportive government that successfully led Japan to the international market—all are good lessons for Korea.[9]

Politically, those who see Japan as the role model assume that Japan is engaged in democratic politics and has achieved political stability. The claim that to achieve political stability such as in Japan, the Korean government should adopt the cabinet system of government or implement the medium electorate system could be a manifestation of the desire to hold Japan as a political role model. Such claims can easily turn into a Japanese ethnic and cultural superiority complex.

Japan as Partner Sharing Security Interests

"Japan shares common security interests with Korea," is another perception in Korea. The argument is that Korea and Japan are fundamentally liberal democratic countries with traditional friendly relations in security aspects. In the case of a threat of communist attack, they both assert the existence of cooperative relations.[10]

The Korea-Japan common security interest was

---

9. Bong-Jin Lee, *Ilbonsik kyungyung* [Business Administration in Japanese Style] (Seoul: Hankuk kyungje shinmunsa, 1992).

10. Ralph N. Clough, *East Asia and U.S. Security* (Washington, D.C.: Brookings Institution, 1975), pp. 170-172; Franklin B. Weinstein and Fuji Kamiya, eds., *Security of Korea* (Boulder: Westview Press, 1980), pp. 41-49.

first officially confirmed in 1969 in the Nixon-Sato Communique between the United States and Japan. Since then, it has been reconfirmed many times, at various official and unofficial U.S.-Japan, Korea-U.S. and Korea-Japan events and functions. For example, in various communiques signed at Korea-Japan ministerial conferences between 1968 and 1970, Korea-Japan security is described as 'closely' or, in 1969, 'very closely' connected. However, recently, in Japan and on official documents, the choice of words has changed from 'ROK's security' to the 'security of the Korean peninsula.' Still, the pursuit of East Asian security is the basic policy in Japan. There also does not seem to be any change in the line of thought that to achieve success in East Asian security, Korea is a very important variable.

Some experts on Korea-Japan security relations insist it is the American security interest in East Asia, rather than Japan's direct security interest in 'Korea' or the 'Korean peninsula', that prompts Japan to share the official Development Assistance.[11] Some argue that because Korea is an important factor in East Asian security and because Japanese domestic conditions would prevent a radical expansion of military capability or direct military aid to Korea, Japan should exercise its second option of sharing the burden of U.S. defence expenditure. The argument claims that Japan's fundamental diplomatic policy faithfully reflects American East Asian security policy. Such a theory of sharing responsibility has been used often. Since 1945, when there were

---

11. Edward A. Olsen, *U.S.-Japan Strategic ·Reciprocity: A Neo-Internationalist View* (Stanford: Hoover Institute Press, 1985), pp. 114-142.

important issues in Korea-Japan relations, the U.S. has used the theory to try and convince Japan to accept Korean demands. For example, the arguments were employed during the normalization of diplomatic relations between Korea and Japan, in 1981-82, at a four billion dollar economic cooperation negotiation, the U.S. used it to convince Japan to cooperate with Korea. The Korean government applied this theory, in 1982, in justifying demands for economic cooperation with Japan. The Korean government argued that because Japan was receiving direct benefits from the Korean defence capability, Japan should comply with economic cooperation with Korea.

However, the Cold War and the ideological conflict and arms race that attended it have ended. It is as yet uncertain whether the friendly relations between the two countries during the Cold War period can be maintained on the same ground. The future of maintaining a strong relationship on the basis of mutual security interests seems gloomy. The cement that bonded the relations between the two countries, even under the pressure of conflicts of nationalism, was the common interest of anti-communism. In this post-Cold War period, however, such means of alleviating conflict is no longer available.

Japan as Economic Partner

The image of Japan as an economic benefactor to Korea is based on an understanding of Korea-Japan relations in terms of economic utility from a liberal economic perspective. Korea and Japan have pursued a successful cooperative relationship in the economic area. In 1965, during the normalization of diplomatic relations, trade between the two countries was only 2.4 million dollars. By 1992, the amount had grown to 30 billion dollars, and Japan had become Korea's second largest trade partner after the U.S. The two countries must put more effort into medium-to-long-term cooperation, despite the current trade imbalance and other problems.

This perspective assumes that first, because Korea and Japan are economically interdependent, if Japan and Korea continue to have economic exchanges, it is mutually beneficial. To assist the development of a less-developed country, the scarce resources, in other words the capital, technology, and administrative techniques, must be imported from the developed countries for economic growth. For Korea to develop, it must import capital and technology from a developed neighboring country, and such economic relations between Japan and Korea will be beneficial to both countries. Korea will receive the resources necessary for development, while Japan can benefit from accelerated exports and expanding investment.

Second, recently the 'flying geese' model is gaining popularity. According to this model, if Japan transfers technology to Korea, Korea in turn will modify the technology to a level that other neighboring countries can import, thus enhancing the effectiveness of cooperation.[12] All of the Asian countries can develop in harmony and achieve economic progress. This claim argues that horizontal specialization can be achieved by Japan's actively transferring technology to Korea, even though vertical specialization may be inevitable in the short run.[13]

---

12. Takashi Inoguchi, *Gendai kokusai seiji to nihon* [Modern world politics and Japan] (Tokyo: Tsukumashobo, 1991), p. 196.

13. Toshio Watanabe, *Gendai kankoku keizai bunseki* [An analysis of the current Korean economy] (Tokyo: Keisoshobo, 1982), pp. 187-194.

According to this opinion, the future of Korea-Japan relations requires bilateral cooperation to settle issues between the two countries, as well as international cooperation for larger issues. First, Korea and Japan have prospered from the free trade system, and both countries can cooperate in sustaining that system because it is of common interest. Second, they share an interest in alleviating trade conflict with the U.S. Korea and Japan can strengthen the APEC through close cooperation with other countries, and cooperate in preventing the EC and the NAFTA from becoming exclusive economic blocs. Third, Japan has much to gain from opening the market. It is estimated this year that Japan's trade surplus will be one hundred billion dollars. If trade surpluses continue to grow, the result will be accelerated economic bloc formation and a worsening of trade conflicts. Thus it is in Japan's interest to open the market now, which will also benefit Korea. Fourth, if Japan's capital, Korea's development experience and medium-level technology, Russia's resources, and China's labor and resources can be effectively combined, Northeast Asia can be one of the most active economic growth areas. This region's economic progress can be achieved, which will benefit everyone involved.

In Korea-Japan economic cooperation, the most important issues are improving the trade imbalance and speeding up technology transfers. To solve the trade imbalance, Korea must first achieve stable wage rates, enhance productivity, and develop technology; but, with Japan's help (both government and private sector), such improvements can be achieved much faster.

Japan as Competitor

Another major perception in Korea is that Korea and Japan are in a competitive relationship. Japan and Korea are competing in export commodities as well as in the export market. In Europe and the U.S., the two countries are competing for a larger share of the market in automobiles, home appliances, steel products, semiconductors, and other export products. It is also believed the two countries are competing for investment in Russia, China, and North Korea.

A similar theory of competition was suggested in Japan as well. In the late 1980's when Korea achieved an economic growth rate greater than 10 percent, successfully hosted the Olympics, and displayed remarkable overall growth, there were some concerns in Japan that Korea may surpass Japan. Japan's reason for seeing Korea as a competitor seems to be influenced by the mirror-image effect. Japan was helped by U.S. capital and technology in the post-World War II rebuilding period, but today it has surpassed the U.S. in many areas. According to the argument, if Japan transfers technology to Korea, it may surpass Japan.

In reality, Pohang Steel company has grown enough to compete with the Japanese steel companies, and Japan also must deal with increasing competition in semiconductor technology, home appliances, and Korea's challenge in the U.S. automobile market. The small-car market that was dominated by Japan was successfully challenged by Korean exports. Such concerns, however, disappeared with the economic depression created by trade deficits and Korea's low exports in the 1990s. If Korea wants to be considered

Japan's competitor, the Korean economy must show growth once again.

Politically, the partisans of Korea-Japan competitor theories contend that Japan does not want the reunification of Korea. If the North and South are reunited, it will be much harder for Japan to deal with Korea. To Japan, as competitor, having the two Koreas separated and competing with one another is much more useful than having them united. Thus, Japan does not desire the two sides to be reunited. There is a large portion of the Korean population that believes this theory to be true. If Japan wishes to convince Korea that it does not oppose reunification, it would require a more active involvement from Japan.

Japan as Exploiter

There are those who perceive Japan to be dominating Korea economically. Domination is defined as an economic relationship between a developed and an underdeveloped country where the developed country dominates the underdeveloped country in economic, political, and cultural areas. Students of this view are critical of Korea-Japan relations. They insist that Korea-Japan economic cooperation, in reality, is Japan's monopolization of Korean markets, and Japanese domination of Korea is in the process of deepening. These students are critical of three areas of Korea-Japan economic relations. First, in Korea-Japan relations, political and economic collusion is emphasized.[14] Second, Japanese imperialism is seen

---

14. Chosen toitsu mondai kenkyukai, *Keizai yuchaku* [Economic Collusion] (Tokyo: Banseisha, 1978), 25-53.

as part of the U.S. imperialistic world strategy.[15] Third, just like before the Pacific War, Japan is attempting a Neo-Great-East-Asia Co-Prosperity Zone to promote the expansion of Japan's economy. The problem is that Korea will likely be the first target for inclusion in the Zone.[16]

The assumption is that the Korean industrial structure has been distorted by Japanese influence. The resulting trade imbalance evolved from that distortion and is abnormal. Even if the capital imported from Japan contributed to the increase of Korean exports, it is still responsible for creating a Japan-dependent industrial structure. Korea has unnaturally specialized in consumer goods and a processing-oriented industrial structure that induces imports. Thus, if the Korea-Japan economic exchange continues, Korean economic dependency on Japan will also increase. This point of view argues that it is in Korea's long-term national interest to gradually decrease the economic exchange as well as other exchanges.

This point of view teaches the important lesson that Korea should not be dominated. But blaming all the problems in Korea-Japan relations on imperialistic exploitation by Japan is open to criticism.

Japan as a Threat

Koreans, understandably, perceive Japan as a threat when it comes to the security of the Korean peninsula. This apprehension is influenced by the

---

15. Jon Halliday and Gavan McCormack, *Japanese Imperialism Today* (New York: Monthly Review Press, 1973), pp. 135-164.

16. Yong-Ha Shin, "Iloe shindaedongagongyongkwon yashim," [Japanese ambition for neo-greater-East Asia co-prosperity zone] *Dong-A Ilbo*, Oct. 3, 1992.

past experience of numerous Japanese attacks and invasions. Adherents to this line of thought mistrust Japan and tend to connect all of Japan's behavior to the intent of invasion of Korea. Although the threat is economic, cultural, and military, most of the time the threat means military threat. The main argument of the Japan-as-threat theory is that Japan's economic power will inevitably turn to militarism and Japan will spread its wings of ambition by expanding its influence and eventually invading Asia. Korea will probably be the first to be attacked. This argument is clearly visible in the National Defence White Paper published by the Korean Ministry of Defence in 1991. In the Paper, a radical observation was made. Since the "Japanese forces have been evaluated as being in the 'offensive' position,"[17] some have interpreted that it is necessary for Korea to respond and prepare for the future and imminent attack. However, if the majority of Koreans were to agree with this theory, the existing anti-Japan sentiment coupled with such concerns would be detrimental to the relations between the two countries.

The partisans of the Japan-as-threat theory currently monitor and will continue in the future to follow Japan's behavior. First, Japan's increase of its defence expenditure, in absolute terms, shows that it may once again turn to militarism. As the U.S. military role in Asia is decreasing, Japan's share of defence spending demands is increasing. In Asia, if Japan's military capability is strengthened, Korea will be threatened in economic and security terms,

---

17. Ministry of Defense, ROK, *Kukbangbaksu 1991-1992* [Defense White Paper 1991-1992], p. 71.

according to the history of past invasions by Japan. It is also argued that after the end of the Cold War, Japan's increasing investment in defense goes against international political trends. According to this opinion, Japan's dispatch of Self Defence Forces for Peace Keeping Operations is the beginning of Japanese military expansionism.

Second, recently, Japan's nuclear capability and nuclear threat are being refocused. In August 1992, a Japanese ship left Yokohama for France. This ship is scheduled to return to Japan soon with about one ton of plutonium as its cargo. This is the first time Japan has independently transported plutonium, and it raises the question whether Japan intends to strengthen its nuclear capability. As an economic and political superpower, apprehensions are rising about Japan's plans to import and reserve large amounts of plutonium. Already, North Korea has questioned whether Japan's plutonium is all for peaceful usage.

There are other less radical responses to the Japan-as-threat theory. First, some in the Korean media argue for the Japan encirclement theory. A cooperative affiliation can be formed between Korea-China or Korea-Russia in East Asia to isolate Japan. It is doubtful whether executing such an encirclement theory will be beneficial to Korean national interests. It is likely that more harm will be done to the Korean national interest, not to mention the negative effect on the long-maintained friendly relations between Japan and Korea. In terms of economic interest, Russia or China's importance fades in comparison to the economic benefits that could be gained from maintaining a good relationship with Japan. (see *Table 2*)

Table 2. Major Economic Indices of 1991 (US$ billion)

	USA	Japan	China	CIS
Trade	910	551	135	209 (1990)
Trade with S.Korea	37.5	32.4	5.8*	1.2
GNP	5,681	3,363	368	2,660
GNP per capita	22,512	27,093	320	9,140

Source: Sekai keizai joho sabis, ed., *The World 1992: Sekai kakkoku
        keizai joho firu* (Information files on the economy of each
        country) (Tokyo, 1992).
*Amount including trade by way of Hong Kong. KOTRA, *Bukbang
tongsang jungbo* [Information about northern trade].

Also, the approach of isolating Japan by using
China or Russia has a high probability of backfiring,
since such an approach may conflict with America's
world strategy. It is true that the U.S. economy has
been relatively weakened since the end of the Cold
War, but America is still a superpower. It is highly
probable that America will form the basis of the
world order for a considerable time in the future. In
the Asia-Pacific region, the U.S. wishes to have
Japan as its partner in forming and executing its foreign policy. Thus, to agitate or disturb the existing
order of North East Asia, which is formed by Japan
and the U.S., we must feel very confident that Korean national interest will benefit from it. Otherwise, it
will be dangerous and unwise.

Another response to the Japan-as-threat theory is
the Asian CSCE (Conference on Security and Cooperation in Europe) concept. Instead of competing with
Japan in economic and military aspects, Japan and
other Asian countries should cooperate with each

other for political stability and economic growth. For the Northeast Asian region to avoid regional escalation of military competition, many argue the necessity of cooperation and suggest the concept of cooperative security.

For the perception of Japan as a threat to actually translate into the reality of Japanese independent military strategic action as a military superpower will only be feasible when and if there is a breakdown in U.S.-Japan relations. There is a remote possibility that Japan would attack Korea while under the cooperative security system. Considering the increasingly conflictive U.S.-Japan economic relations, however, there is some apprehension about the future of relations between the countries. A serious international political change is needed to break U.S.-Japan cooperative relations, and thus it is unlikely that there will be a radical change in the relations between the U.S. and Japan in the near future.

Conclusion

In this paper, various important issues in Korea-Japan relations were discussed. Also, some of the major perceptions and corresponding responses of Korea on the issue of Japan's taking a more active role in the international arena were analyzed. The issues between the two countries are complex, with roots in historical, psychological, cultural, and political aspects, which also describes the complexity of Japan-Korea relations themselves. Korea's possible responses are also very complex. Thus, it is difficult to visualize the relations being broken by one or two special variables.

The end of the Cold War is an important factor, but it is not the most critical variable in the future of Korea-Japan relations. In other words, the end of the Cold War does not automatically mean that Korea-Japan relations will be negatively influenced. It is true that there are fewer incentives for both countries to maintain security cooperation. There are, however, other less conspicuous but important common interests between the two countries that will prevent the relationship from being radically terminated. Even when the common security interest has been very clear, there have been issues between the two countries, such as history texts, appeasement for past military crimes, and apologies and other various conflicts, which still exist today.

Korea-Japan relations have historical, economic, political, and psychological aspects. For Korea-Japan relations to be truly friendly would take a very long time, and as new issues arise, both countries must truly cooperate to solve problems.

CHAPTER 12

SOCIAL CHANGES IN NORTH KOREA AND PROSPECTS FOR UNIFICATION

Jae Jean Suh

Introduction

Is unification possible on the Korean peninsula? Existing studies assume that North Korea will collapse soon and that the issue now is simply the cost of unification. Arguments differ on whether or not unification should be phased in gradually to reduce costs. But will the North Korean system inevitably collapse? Or will its collapse automatically mean unification? We must distinguish our hopes for unification and the actual preconditions that are required for unification to occur.

Factors that are influencing the prospects of unification are first, the international environment surrounding the two Koreas; second, South Korea's northern policy, and third, changes in North Korea itself. The external environment favors South Korea —the end of the Cold War, the collapse of the former

socialist countries, and the resulting deepening of
North Korea's isolation. At the moment, the United
States, Japan, China, and the Soviet Union have
their own interests in the Korean peninsula, but it
seems unlikely that any of them will seriously block
the current trend of unification; furthermore, it is
also questionable whether these countries have the
actual power to resist the trend. In the unification of
Germany, the interests of the major powers were
important at the beginning, but when the end of the
Cold War was confirmed with the perestroika of the
Soviet Union, external obstacles to German unification were gone.

The continuous pursuit of South Korea's "Northern
Policy", coupled with the changes in the international system, have greatly enhanced South Korea's
negotiational leverage vis-a-vis North Korea. When
we consider such circumstances, the major variable
concerning the unification of Korea is the direction of
change North Korea will take. Therefore, the question
is, will North Korea's change have positive consequences for the unification of the two Koreas?

The aim of this paper is to foresee the changes North
Korea will take as it faces increasing internal and
external pressures for change, and to examine how
these changes will affect the prospects for unification.

A Critical Review of Existing Studies of Unification

The mainstream studies on Korean unification
assume the following. First, North Korea's collapse is
inevitable and coming soon. Second, the collapse of
North Korea means the immediate unification of

South and North. Thus, our northern policy must be aimed at reducing the cost of unification as much as possible, and we must give massive economic support in order for North Korea to improve its economy.

However, such reasoning rests on the assumption that North Korea will follow the same faith as other former communist countries. It is true that North Korea is facing external and economic crises, a burden of transition of leadership, and social uncertainties due to its economic problems. In the long run, North Korea will collapse as the capitalist world system completes its hegemony. But why has not North Korea collapsed yet? Will it collapse at all?

An accurate analysis of North Korean society is thus required here. The reason it has not collapsed and has been able to maintain its system can be found in the unique political and social factors of North Korea.

Political Factors

How do we explain the puzzling fact that North Korea's system has not collapsed when others have? In the former Soviet Union, China, and other socialist countries, factionalism among ruling elites was prevalent as much as multiple parties are prevalent in democracies. The Soviet Union and China could pursue reforms and changes because of the development of factionalism among the ruling elites and debate about different or alternative policies. In contrast, North Korea shows a remarkable unity at the ruling elite level, and the sole leadership system of Kim Il-sung and Kim Jong-il is well established. Why didn't North Korea develop factionalism?

First, transition of power from the first generation

244 Jae Jean Suh

revolutionaries to the next has not yet occurred in North Korea, unlike in China or the Soviet Union. This is probably the biggest reason for the absence of factionalism in North Korea.

Second, preparations for the transition of leadership to the first son have been going on for twenty years. In addition, the possibility of downgrading the previous leadership or adopting an alternative line do not exist. Already, the existing elite structure has espoused Kim Jong-il as the next leader and, thus, factionalism after Kim Il-sung's death will probably not exist for a while.

Third, North Korea does not have the kind of political environment that allows for the competition of different ideas, such as the disparaging of Stalinist leadership by Khrushchev and the rise of elite pluralism in the Soviet Union, or Mao Tse-tung's principles of conflict resolution in China. Only one ideology, one system, one line is allowed; such a political climate cannot foster competitive factions or policies in North Korea.

Fourth, there have been changes in the nature of bureaucrats, such as an increase in the number of technocrats, but these changes have been minimal in North Korea.

Due to the above reasons, the sole leadership system of Kim and Kim is well established, and despite the many problems North Korea faces, struggle for power or policy lines over solutions is not occurring.

Nevertheless, changes are occurring in North Korea. The most important factor in its political crisis is the leadership change when Kim Il-sung eventually dies. While Kim is alive, unity among the elites is possible; but after his death, it cannot be assured. The transition of power from Kim Il-sung to Kim

Jong-il represents not only the change of an individual's rule, but also a change from the generation of revolutionaries to non-revolutionaries.[1] With the emergence of Kim Jong-il, there is a change among the elites as well.

The Political Bureau, the central organ of power in the party, holds 10 economic technocrats among the 15 members at present (since December 1990), and the 9 candidate-members of the Political Bureau, with the exception of Kim Chul-man, a first generation revolutionary, are all economic technocrats.

In addition, the party's Secretary Bureau comprises 12 members, all of whom are technocrats. In the Supreme People's Assembly, the ratio of doctors, professors, scientists, and technicians is on the rise. When comparing the educational backgrounds of the 7th class of the Supreme People's Assembly of April 1982 and that of the 9th class of 1990, the ratio of the intelligentsia has increased from 49.4 percent to 64.5 percent, and the ratio of university graduates increased from 50.4 percent in 1982 to 68.2 percent in 1990. The members of the 10 secretariats of the KWP Central Committee have all either studied abroad or traveled abroad.

Despite these changes, "redness" rather than "expertise" is required of elites in North Korea. Even if new lines are suggested by the new elites, they will come about as a unified policy after going through the top leadership level; development of factionalism is highly unlikely.

---

1. See Robert Scalapino, "Inter-Korean Relations: Prospects for the Future," paper presented at the Conference, "Korea: Its Political and Economic Future," sponsored by The Asian Studies Center, Michigan State University and the Asia Society, New York, 1992.

Social Factors

Another factor that can explain the systemic unity found in North Korea is the presence of a unique "subjectional personality" in the society. Ionescu believed that every individual is a subject or a captive client in a Stalinist society.[2] In North Korea, a combination of paternalistic tradition, the legacy of Japanese colonial rule, a command economy, and totalitarianism under Kim Il-sung has led to the development of a "subjectional personality".

In North Korea, every individual is a loyal servant to the absolute leader, Kim Il-sung. Citizens are educated to think and act according to Kim's will, and they do so in reality.[3] This is because of the belief that every individual's problem is solved thanks to the beneficial care of Kim, and all one need do is obey the leader faithfully. Such belief is reflected and supported in the system of state ownership of property and in the rationing system of food and everyday necessities.

How does this subject personality affect change in North Korea? This subject personality is passive and subservient, very useful for social integration, and thus effective in maintaining the system against internal and external threats. This can explain the apparent strength of the North Korean regime when other socialist countries have experienced resistance from below, such as China's Tiananmen incident.

However, it needs to be pointed out that the North

---

2. Ghita Ionescu, "Patronage Under Communism," in Ernest Gellner and John Waterbury, eds., *Patrons and Clients* (London: Duckworth, 1977), p. 98.

3. *Ingan-gaejo-yron* (Theory of Human Transformation) (Pyungyang: Sahoegwahak Publisher, 1985), p. 173.

Korean people's subject personality is not totally internalized. Beneath the official ruling ideology lie beliefs in individualism and freedom. This duality carries the potential for resistance, although it may not take organized forms. The social engineering pursued in North Korea has not been completely absorbed by the ruled. In any society where there are weapons of the ruler, weapons of the ruled exist as well. In a democracy where civil society is developed, many grass roots organizations can develop to resist the leadership. But in societies where a repressive absolute leader exists, open defiance is pointless. Thus, everyday forms of resistance or passive resistance develop. James Scott points out that these kinds of resistances are the weapons of the weak.[4]

Everyday forms of resistance mean that the subjects pretend to be passive and working hard for the ruler, but in reality they are resisting. Such resistance is found to exist in North Korea. In societies where open resistance is prohibited, these everyday forms of resistance are bound to develop. Of course, when loopholes in the control of the repressive system occur, the duality behind the subject personality may erupt and may develop into open resistance.

If the changes in the former Soviet Union and Eastern Europe can be seen as due to the evolution of the subject personality toward a civil-society personality, then the potential for such change in North Korea does exist, although small. The main reasons why this change is not occurring quickly are due to the absence of factions, the leadership's control over

---

4. James Scott, *Weapons of the Weak: Everyday Forms of Resistance* (New Haven: Yale University Press, 1985); Vaclav Havel et al., *The Power of the Powerless: Citizens Against the State in Central-Eastern Europe* (London: Hutchinson, 1985).

information, and the unique subject personality of the people. Therefore, conflict in the leadership, resistance from below, or mass revolt are unlikely in North Korea.

Policy Measures Toward the Imperatives of System Changes

Thanks to the unbroken leadership, the subject personality, and absolute isolation from the outside world North Korea has not yet experienced the changes the former socialist countries are going through. But the changes in the external environment, economic crises, eventual leadership change, change in the social structure, and accumulation of social discontent all point to the potential for system change. What kind of response is North Korea making to the imperatives of changes?

It seems as if North Korea is pursuing two different policies at the same time. Politically, it is emphasizing "our way of socialism" and increasing its ideological education of the people by introducing the theory of socio-political organic life and consolidating the society to maintain the system.[5] But, economically, it seems to have definitely changed from a self-sufficiency orientation to outward liberalization policies. The North is actively pursuing normalization of ties with Japan, with the aim of getting reparation loans and technology, introducing the Najin-Sunbong special economic zones, Tumen River development pro-

---

5. Jae Jean Suh, "Social Change and Ideology Change in North Korea," paper presented at the Annual Conference of the Korean Sociological Association, Dec. 1991.

ject to foreign investors, and entering the U.N. and adopting officially the South-North agreements. These movements are clear signs that North Korea is moving away from its previous isolation from the world capitalist economy and adopting elements of capitalism in order to revive its economy. In a word, what may be called a gradual and limited reform liberalization is taking place.

The following is a detailed examination of the policy measures taken to consolidate the political regime. Amidst the crisis environment of the 1980s, North Korea reinforced control over ideology and idolization of Kim and Kim to prevent the possible occurrence of mass revolt. North Korea believes that if economic development takes priority over political consolidation, the "old and corrupt ideas will recur in the minds of workers and destructive bourgeois ideology will creep in, and our socialist system cannot be maintained."[6] Let us look at some of the methods North Korea has taken to strengthen the regime.

First, it insists upon the superiority of socialism. North Korea has been telling the North Korean people that the collapse of the socialist countries is only temporary and incidental, and that socialism's eventual victory is an unchangeable law, that the people must be wary of the invasion of bourgeois ideas and rely on the *Juche* ideology and the two Kims to live "according to our own way."

The ideas expressed in the May 5th communique—"Our Own Way of People-Centered Socialism Cannot Fail"—and the January 3rd 1992 communique—"The Historical Lessons of Socialist Building and Our Party's Central Line"—are repeatedly

---

6. *Rodong Daily*, May 26, 1992.

emphasized in many radio, newspaper, and other mediums. Let's look at an editorial from *Rodong Daily*, for example:

> The imperialists are arguing that socialism has collapsed and capitalism has triumphed, and talking as if the end of socialism has arrived. It is well known that capitalism crushes the independence of people. Capitalism has left a legacy of human killing, class subjugation, corruption and exploitation in history. The only way to live freely and without constraints — the people's world-wide desire — is the way of socialism. There cannot be a third way for humanity.[7]

Second, North Korea is tightly controlling the flow of information. This isolation policy has been especially reinforced since the failure of the Soviet Union's ultra-rightist leaders' coup. North Korea is completely blocking the winds of freedom that caused the collapse of communism in Eastern Europe and the Soviet Union. To block this "external wind", Kim Jong-il has instructed the removal of existing materials on the Soviet Union and Eastern Europe. The measure can be divided into 4 parts: 1) the publication department is to remove all the speeches of heads of states of the former socialist countries and the written works of Gorbachev; 2) the Central Party Education Department is to remove the history of these countries from the school curriculum and change the content as necessary; 3) each regional Party Committee is to remove works of and about Lenin from all the libraries, and 4) the Central Broadcasting Committee will stop all showings of films and programs from these countries in question.

In addition, people who have traveled or studied

---

7. *Rodong Daily*, July 20, 1992.

abroad are under special surveillance. They are catagorized as "Surveillance category 710," and they include students, fishermen, visitors to China, bureaucrats stationed overseas, lumber workers in Siberia etc. Foreign students in North Korea are very closely monitored. Not only that, the examination of the personal belongings of Korean-Japanese is being intensified. These people are not allowed to carry video tapes, magazines, or books and are prohibited to talk about the changes in the former socialist countries with the North Korean people.[8]

Third, North Korea has changed the content of *Juche* ideology to adapt to the changing political circumstances. Previously, *Juche* ideology was used to exhort the workers' productivity with the aim of stimulating economic growth. But since the late 1980s, *Juche* ideology has been emphasizing socio-political integration. As the contradiction of reality becomes greater, ideological strengthening becomes absolutely necessary. Two significant changes can be found in *Juche* ideology: first, the introduction of the socio-political organic-life theory, and second, the emphasis on "our way of socialism".

On July 15th, Kim Jong-il presented a communique under the title, "On Some Issues Raised with Respect to Inculcating *Juche* Ideology."[9] The core ideas of the socio-political, organic-life theory is well summarized here:

> Nothing is more important to an individual than human life. Of all forms of life, socio-political life is more important than physical life, and social group

---

8. *Weekly Naewoe Press*, Vol. 771, Nov. 22, 1991.

9. Kim Jong-Il, "Some Issues Related to Juche Thought," *Kulloja*, July, 1987.

life is more important than individual life. Only by relying on social group life can individual life be possible. Thus, when an individual is loyal to his Leader-party-people, the origin of his own life, he is doing it out of the intrinsic need required of his socio-political life, not because someone is asking him to do so. This is because being loyal is not for others, but for himself.[10]

The socio-political life theory justifying why people must be loyal to their Leader is reinforced by adopting a biological, organic-life theory. As the Leader is the center of the socio-political group, revolutionary camaraderie and loyalty must center on the Leader as well. Loyalty to the Leader, who is the center of the group's life, must be absolute and unconditional; disloyalty is strongly prohibited by using arguments such as the following:

A child loves his parents not because they are better than others or they have given him many benefits; a child loves his parents because he owes his life to them. Whoever is faithful to the revolutionary faith places his destiny with that of the Leader-party-people in good times as well as bad. If someone abandons his country, which has nurtured him in the past, just because it is in danger, he cannot be called a man of conscience.[11]

Since the introduction of this socio-political organic life theme by Kim Jong-il, it has been repeatedly used in all forms of media in North Korea.

Another change in *Juche* ideology is the theme of "our way of socialism," which was published in the communique, "Our People-Centered Way of Social-

---

10. *Kulloja*, July 1987, p. 16.
11. *Kulloja*, July 1987, p. 17.

ism," by Kim Jong-il, on May 5th 1991. The same theme can be found in another article, "The Historical Lessons of Socialist Building and Our Party's Main Line," reported on January 3rd 1992. North Korea is worried that the collapse of the former socialist countries will be repeated in North Korea as well. This 37-page article analyzes the causes of the collapse of Eastern Europe and the Soviet Union, and argues that for North Korea to escape that fate, it must continuously emphasize social engineering, the development of the Three Great Revolutions, and the removal of bureaucratic corruption, and stress the worker's class principles and revolutionary principles. It stresses that only socialism can get rid of all forms of domination and subjugation, remove social inequalities, and give true freedom, equality, and happiness to the people.[12]

Through these theoretical restructurings, North Korea is placing primary emphasis on the concept of "our way of socialism" and trying its utmost to prevent any possible ideological breakdown.

Prospect for Change in North Korea

As noted above, North Korea is pursing dual policy measures. On the one hand, it is pursuing ideological strengthening and blocking outside information; on the other hand, it is pursuing the opening of its economy to the external world. How will these measures influence the North Korean system?

---

12. Il-Chul Shin, "North Korea's View on Socialist Collapse," in Jin-Young Suh, ed., *Socialist Reforms and North Korea* (Korea University: Asia Affairs Institute, 1992).

Two scenarios can be envisioned. First, North Korea's strategy of gradual opening fails; second, the current measures of opening will succeed and help overcome North Korea's economic impasse. Let's look at the two scenarios in detail.

Scenario 1: The Gradual Opening Strategy Fails

Can a strategy to increase political isolation and increase economic exposure to the outside world succeed? The possibility of North Korea's maintaining "our way of socialism" seems low, and the reasons are the following.

First, although North Korea might succeed in normalization with Japan, it may be a while before it can receive reparation payments. Thus, the Najin-Sunbong project or the Tumen River project may be delayed, impeding economic recovery.

Second, South-North economic cooperation may not bring the immediate fruits North Korea is expecting. North Korea seems to want South Korean capital through joint ventures, but not the social interactions that come with them. Like the dual policy of separating politics and economics, North Korea may want to avoid human interaction and focus on economic interaction in relations with the South. Even if it agrees to the exchange of people, it might limit them, such as in the "guided visits" Korean-Americans are allowed. As long as the North is unwilling to allow South Koreans to visit North Korea freely, South-North relations will be severely limited. On the part of South Korea, it will refuse to provide just technology and capital to the North, which is what North Korea really wants.

Third, even though Japanese and South Korean

industrialists are eager to invest in North Korea, there is a limit to what the North can absorb, and focused economic development may not bring the expected great results. Due to the underdevelopment of the North's infrastructure, Japanese and American investors are reluctant to invest. Even if North Korea opts to invest in constructing its infrastructure, other sectors will have to be sacrificed, resulting in more hardship for the North Korean people's livelihood.

Fourth, the current opening strategy will end up in failure, as did the joint management laws of the 1980s, due to the reluctance of foreign capital to invest in North Korea. The Najin-Sunbong FEZ project, or the Tumen River project, are still in the inception stage, and the North is still at the stage of promoting the ideas to the West. In addition, in pursuing these projects, many political and judicial problems still remain.

Fifth, North Korea must face systemic risks with the introduction of foreign companies in their economy.[13] But North Korea faces a dilemma in turning toward reform and liberalization: It knows from the historical lessons from the former socialist countries that ideology, polities, economics, and social factors are invariably linked, as in a chain, in a socialist system; any change in one of them will cause the collapse of the entire system.

Sixth, unless an internal reform is conducted, economic benefits from the liberalization policies can

---

13. Dongwon Kim, "Socialist Reforms and Changes of North Korean Foreign Economic Policies," in Jin-Young Suh, ed., *Socialist Reforms and North Korea* (Korea University: Asia Affairs Institute, 1992).

only be limited.[14] When we look at the reforms taken
by the socialist countries, we see that political democracy, the introduction of a market economy, and liberalization accompanied them. Even in China, where
no political democratization occurred, major internal
reform took place corresponding to the level of economic liberalization. China's economic reform can be
said to have started at the beginning of Deng Xiaoping's rule, with the dissolution of the collectivization
of agriculture, in December 1978. By dissolving collectivization, China's agricultural economy was revi-
talized, and agricultural production increased enormously. China's liberalization policies were implemented starting in 1979 with the establishment of
four Free Economic Zones. These zones are open to
foreign investment and technology, and even Chinese
companies have independence ranging from procur-
ing their own sources of capital to disposing of products in order to be competitive with foreign companies. China experienced success with the adoption of
a free market economy in the four zones and has
announced plans to expand to up to 14 zones from
1980.

China, emboldened with the success of the initial
economic reforms, announced in 1984 the decision
made by the Twelfth Party Conference that China
would turn from a planned, command economy to a
market economy. The leadership concluded that the
success of the reform lay in giving individuals material incentives and setting up markets in the coun-
trysides. It decided to set up a similar market economy in urban areas as well. The initial success of the
reforms was owing to Deng Xiao-ping's "liberalization

---

14. Dongwon Kim, *op. cit.*, p. 227.

ideology." China adopted a policy of eliminating mass rallies, and liberalized the flow of ideas, thus giving a well-needed stimulus to people tired of political inculcation.

Unlike China, North Korea has no intention of liberalizing other parts of society; in fact, ideological strengthening and control is maintained to buttress their systems. Thus, the major characteristic of North Korea's liberalization policy is that it extends to only the base, through the absorption of capital and technology, and not to the superstructure where "our way of socialism" will be staunchly maintained. This fusion of "our way of socialism" and liberalization policy is bound to fail.

The failure of economic recovery will cause great discontent among the North Korean people. Any mass discontent against the leadership will come across as a shock to the ruling elites. This may, in turn, result in conflicts between conservatives and reform-minded power elites over policies for overcoming the economic crisis. Thus, limited reform to maintain the system may give way to voices for more reform and liberalization.

Scenario 2: Gradual Liberalization Succeeds

The second scenario on change in North Korea is one in which liberalization succeeds. The most important factor for the North's success would probably be early normalization with Japan and the importing of commercial capital and technology worth about $5 billion. In addition, to prevent the Japanese domination of the North Korean economy, South Korea and its industrialists will engage in active economic contact with North Korea. The result would be a plentiful supply of foreign capital and technology and, thus, improved economic performance for North Korea. The current economic projects of Tumen River development and Najin-Sunbong FEZ will proceed on plan and the people's livelihood will improve.

As economic conditions improve, the political domination of Kim Jong-il will continue and political factionalism will be repressed, as is currently the case. In turn, the subject personality in society will continue, and loyalty to Kim's leadership will not falter, despite the inflow of outside information. The result could then be a reform not unlike that of China where economic growth and system stability is maintained.

Prospects for Unification on the Korean Peninsula

We can predict two scenarios for unification based on the directions North Korea takes.

If Gradual Liberalization Reform Fails: Some Possibility for Unification.

If North Korea fails to recover its economy under the dual policy of system maintenance and gradual liberalization, it will probably take the path of making policy changes similar to those of China. The reasons Deng Xiao-ping argued for reform and liberalization after his visit to the Southern FEZ in January 1992 were based on his conclusions that the collapse of the former socialist countries was due to economic reasons, not political ones. He argued that by introducing elements of capitalism and increasing the people's livelihood, socialism can be maintained.

In North Korea, this kind of logic of economic primacy will be adopted not to recover the failing economy per se, but for a combination of other reasons. The biggest reason is that it will be difficult to persuade the North Korean people to tolerate limited and ineffective reform; thus the only way to persuade the people would be to follow Deng's ideas on economic primacy.

Another reason for this kind of policy change would be Kim Il-sung's death. With his death, the once-repressed technocrats will raise their voices over economic policies and a wide-scale reform to overcome the failures of past policies under Kim may take place. North Korea will experience a new phase with the adoption of major reforms following Kim's death, and political reform as well as economic reform might take place, for North Korea has already learned that economic reforms cannot be successful without political reforms. Along with these changing policies, there will be conflict between the conservatives and the reform-minded, factionalism will be on the rise, and people's attitudes will rapidly change. Consequently, Kim Jong-il may be ousted in a coup d'etat by an alternative force.

However, the collapse of Kim's rule does not mean immediate unification. An alternative force may take control over North Korea and may pursue coexistence with the South by distinguishing itself from the previous leadership. This just means that conditions for unification will have improved; no immediate unification will occur.

But, if a pro-South regime takes over, the mutual needs of South Korea's economy and North Korea's social needs may quicken the prospects for unification. In all probability, outside powers will not interfere. The unification of the peninsula might follow the German precedent.

If Gradual Liberalization Reform Succeeds:
Extended South-North Coexistence.

If North Korea succeeds in economic recovery, unification may become impossible. Most researchers on North Korea say that reforms will bring on winds of freedom and mass revolt will lead to the collapse of the regime. But if the North is successful in recovering the economy, it may become like China, touting its economic success as due to the superiority of its socialist system, and remove any anti-regime elements. Even though the North Korean people may become aware of the external world, North Korea will be able to crush any mass revolt or protest, as China did in the Tiananmen incident. In this case, with the North Korean economy strengthened, the two Koreas may simply coexist for a substantially long period, probably until China becomes a complete capitalist state.

Conclusions

Existing studies on North Korea have tended to assume that the collapse of North Korea is inevitable and will lead to unification. This paper has challenged such hopeful views. From what has been discussed, it becomes clear that North Korea may not necessarily collapse. If North Korea fails to recover its economy, conditions for unification may become favorable. But if North Korea succeeds, the current socialist system may become strengthened. North Korea has a unique, elite power structure based on the subject personality of the society, and has been successful at blocking outside information to control the people; thus, mass revolt arising from economic difficulties or isolation is unlikely.

Therefore, current discussions on the minimization of the cost of unification based on a specious assumption that North Korea's collapse is imminent should be seriously questioned. We must reexamine whether resuscitating the North Korean economy to decrease unification costs or isolating it to the point of system collapse are desirable options.

The northern policy created conditions favorable for unification, but they are only partial conditions. Also, the current strategy of economic recovery taken by North Korea may or may not fail. Thus, at this point, detailed and realistic policy options to safely secure unification must be searched for.

CHAPTER 13

NORTH KOREA'S FOREIGN
RELATIONS AFTER THE COLD WAR

Byung-joon Ahn

Faced with the post-Cold War world, how North Korea is going to conduct its foreign relations is attracting serious attention, especially with respect to the nuclear issue. It is important, therefore, to examine North Korea's relations with Russia, China, Japan, and the U.S. in the post-Cold War context.

We can raise a number of crucial questions about these relations. What are the overall goals of North Korean foreign policy? In the post-Cold War world, how are North Korea's relations with the major powers changing? For what purpose has North Korea developed its nuclear programs, and what problems are these causing? What specific approach is North Korea taking, and what dilemmas is it encountering? Can the economic imperatives prevail over the political imperatives in North Korean foreign relations? These are the questions this paper will address.

By the post-Cold War period, I mean the years following the fall of the Berlin Wall at the end of 1989. For the sake of better understanding, I include North Korea's policy toward South Korea as part of its foreign relations.

Regime Survival and National Interests in North Korean Foreign Relations

In the post-Cold War world, communism and the Soviet Union are in a state of collapse. North Korea has been engaged in a struggle for regime survival for Kim Il-sung, and for national interests like security and economic cooperation. Ever since the former Soviet Union normalized diplomatic relations with South Korea in September 1990,[1] and China did likewise in August 1992, North Korea has been diplomatically isolated; this is a serious challenge to its foreign policy, mainly because the two countries had been not only its allies, but also its ideological reference groups.

Moreover, Russia and China had been the main sources of North Korea's military and economic cooperation. Ever since they began to regard their economic partnership with South Korea as more important, their cooperation with North Korea had to decline. As a result, North Korea is facing an acute economic crisis in energy, food, and foreign exchange. For example, the former Soviet Union almost suspended its oil supply to North Korea in 1991 by asking the latter to pay in hard currency; China deliv-

---

1. Byung-joon Ahn, "South Korean-Soviet Relations: Contemporary Issues and Prospects," *Asian Survey* 31:9 (September 1991), pp. 816-825.

ered only about one million tons of oil in 1991 and also asked North Korea to pay in hard currency from that time on. Now that Sino-Russian relations have warmed up, North Korea can no longer capitalize on their conflicts by playing one against the other.[2]

Thrust into this hostile international environment, North Korea is determined to survive as a "socialist" regime, as Kim Il-sung has defined it, and as a "normal" state like any other. To survive the sweeping external changes as a revolutionary regime, North Korea has to continue justifying the legitimacy of Kim Il-sung's *Juche* thought and policy of "one Korea" at home; to survive them as a state, it has to maximize its security and its economic and political interests in the rapidly changing outside world.

It is the central theme of this paper that North Korea is on the defensive in seeking these two goals — i.e., regime survival and national interests — simultaneously in its foreign relations, and that the general trend is a gradual shift from the former to the latter, as has happened in other socialist countries such as China and Vietnam.

With this overview in mind, we can make five broad observations about the state of North Korean foreign relations after the end of the Cold War. First, it is important to note that North Korean foreign policy reflects both the very nature of the North Korean regime and the constantly changing situations of the post-Cold War world. There is no other regime in this world where the founding father of the regime has been ruling the country since September 1948. As

---

2. Byung-joon Ahn, "Prospects for Sino-South Korean Relations: A Korean Perspective," *The Journal of East Asian Affairs* 6:1 (Winter/Spring 1992), pp. 51-65.

long as Kim Il-sung is alive, it will be extremely difficult to change the very raison d'etre of the political
regime, and, hence, this fact has been the most
important constraint on North Korean foreign relations.

Second, ever since Russia and China sought to
normalize their relations with South Korea, North
Korea's relations with these former allies have become
strained, even though they have yet to change their
treaty obligations and diplomatic relations with
North Korea.

Third, since 1990, North Korea has actively sought
to normalize diplomatic relations with Japan and the
U.S. in order to obtain not only political recognition
but also economic cooperation. To accomplish these
foreign policy goals, it has also carried out high-level
talks and signed the basic accord and other protocols with South Korea.

Fourth, North Korea's reluctance to accommodate
transparent inspections of its nuclear facilities with
IAEA and South Korea is blocking substantive
progress in the quest for diplomatic recognition and
economic cooperation. Initially, the North appeared
to have developed its nuclear programs as a means
for survival, but, later on, it began to use them with
considerable success as a bargaining chip for exact-
ing concessions from Japan, the U.S., and South
Korea.

Fifth, North Korea is taking the dual approach of
guarding its old political and revolutionary stand
toward South Korea by sticking to the theory of "one
Korea" and, simultaneously, seeking a two-Korea
policy in practice by requesting political recognition
and economic cooperation from Japan and the U.S.
The North has yet to resolve this dilemma between

its unification policy toward the South and its foreign policy toward the other major powers.

Sixth, only when the economic imperatives prevail over the political imperatives will the North be able to resolve this dilemma. But such significant change may not be feasible without a structural transformation in the North Korean regime and political system, at least to the extent that they can follow the Chinese model of reform and an open-door policy.

North Korea's Relations with Russia and China: From Revolutionary Ally to Normal Relations

After the communist systems in East Europe collapsed in 1989-1990 and the Soviet Union itself collapsed in 1991, and especially after the former Soviet Union normalized diplomatic relations with South Korea in September 1990 and with China in August 1992, North Korea's relations with Russia and China began to shift from revolutionary ally to normal state-to-state relations. In comparative terms, its relations with Russia have deteriorated substantially and its relations with China have steadily cooled.

Relations with Russia: Strained

Ever since the establishment of diplomatic relations between Moscow and Seoul, North Korea's relations with Russia have been strained. The role of Moscow as the center of the world communist movement and as the supplier of military and economic assistance is gone. This has forced Pyongyang to reorient its foreign and economic policy toward such Western countries as Japan and the U.S. since 1990.

That no top Soviet or Russian leader has visited Pyongyang as yet attests to the strained relationship between North Korea and Russia. Although Moscow is still supplying military spare parts to Pyongyang, its oil supply almost halted in 1991 and, as a result, it is no longer Pyongyang's largest trading partner. Over 60 percent of North Korea's trade until 1991 was with the Soviet Union. Even though Pyongyang still maintains its embassy in Moscow, the growing differences between Russia, under Boris Yeltsin, and North Korea, under Kim Il-sung, are bound to create more stresses and strains in their bilateral relations. For example, Moscow has lent its official support for Seoul's stand on the need for mutual inspections of nuclear facilities in the North and South.

Relations with China: Cooling

Officially, North Korea's relations with China remain friendly as North Korean leaders have tried to maintain them intact as much as they can for their own interests. But since Beijing's normalization with Seoul, these relations have become cooler. Unlike Russia, Beijing provided about one million tons of oil and some amount of food to Pyongyang in 1991. As a result, China has become the most important friend for North Korea.

Now that Beijing has established diplomatic relations with Seoul by pledging the so-called "five principles of peaceful coexistence," the alliance relationship has to undergo some change. Especially when South Korea's trade with China reaches $10 billion and its investment about $300 million, which will happen in 1992, the South will become much more important than the North for the success of China's reform and open-door policy.

Because North Korea shares a long border and remains a "socialist" partner, China is committed to continuing its friendly relations with North Korea. Yet the differences in domestic and foreign policy between China and North Korea make it difficult for them to sustain their traditional "lips to the teeth" relationship. Beijing signaled its support for a simultaneous admission of both Koreas to the U.N. in 1991 and is signaling now its objection to any nuclear weapons on the Korean peninsula. Thus, even after Kim Il-sung carries out a state visit to China in November 1992, the state of coolness in North Korea's relations with China will not disappear, especially when Sino-South Korean rapprochement will yield subtantial results in many fields.

The Quest for Political Recognition and Economic Cooperation from Japan, the U.S., and South Korea

The quest for political recognition and economic cooperation from Japan, the U.S., and South Korea marks a significant departure in North Korean foreign relations, which used to be skewed toward Russia and China until 1991 and 1992. The changes in Europe, the former Soviet Union, and China, and the spectacular sucesses of the South's *Nordpolitik*, have prompted the North to redirect its foreign policy from the basic tilt toward the Soviet Union, China, and the Third World to Japan and the U.S. The normalization of South Korean-Soviet relations on September 30, 1990 and the advent of German reunification on October 3, 1990 made Pyongyang's objection to "cross-recognition" less persuasive and realistic. Had it stuck to the old thinking that such cross-recognition would perpetuate the Korean division, the South only would have entered the U.N.; therefore, the North did choose the simultaneous entry in September 1991, albeit reluctantly, for Beijing had discreetly made it clear that it could not veto the South's separate admission into the U.N. at the Security Council.

Against this background, from September 1990 on, North Korea launched its diplomatic campaigns for normalizing relations with Japan, the U.S., and South Korea, using all the available means at its disposal.

Normalization with Japan

The first sign in Pyongyang's policy to accommodate the idea of cross-recognition was shown by its demand for establishing diplomatic relations with Japan in September 1990. During the visit of former Deputy Prime Minister Shin Kanemaru to Pyongyang from September 24 through 28, Kim Il-sung volunteered to negotiate diplomatic normalization with Japan. Evidently, Kim seized upon Kanemaru's trip, which was designed to seek the release of two Japanese sailors, as a good opportunity to make a breakthrough in North Korean-Japanese relations.

In the Beijing normalization talks, which began in January 1991, the North Korean side has been eager to establish diplomatic relations even before resolving other pending issues. But the Japanese side has made it clear that unless Pyongyang accepts both IAEA and mutual inspections with South Korea on its nuclear facilities, Tokyo is not going to normalize relations.

Beginning in January 1992, Pyongyang shifted its focus of diplomacy to Washington on the grounds that the U.S. had been dictating Japanese policy toward North Korea.

Efforts to Upgrade Contacts with the U.S.

Pyongyang began to have counselor-level diplomatic contacts with Washington in Beijing in October 1988. Since early 1990, Pyongyang has tried to upgrade its contacts with Washington to higher levels and to even normalize relations as soon as it can by showing reconciliatory gestures toward the U.S. It is Pyongyang's perception that once Washington recognizes the Democratic People's Republic of Korea, it will be easier for Japan and other Western powers to follow suit.

There have been several signs indicating that Pyongyang is serious about improving its official relations with Washington. For example, it returned the remains of five American soldiers to the American side at Panmunjom in May 1990, 11 in June 1991, and another 15 in May 1992. In addition, it has invited American scholars, reporters, and former high officials to Pyongyang and told them that it is interested in having high-level talks with Washington. Since 1984, Pyongyang has been consistently calling for tripartite talks with Washington and Seoul to discuss the withdrawal of American troops from the South and to conclude a peace agreement directly with Washington.

On the other hand, North Korea has sent a number of its representatives to academic meetings held in the U.S. in recent years. Pyongyang reportedly established the Institute of Peace and Disarmament in

October 1988. "Scholars" from this new institute have participated in various gatherings in the U.S. to present Pyongyang's views on arms control and confidence-building measures.

These endeavors led to the contact between Kim Young-sun, Director of the International Department of the North Korean Labor Party, and Arnold Kanter, Under Secretary of State, on January 22, 1992 in New York. It was at this meeting that Mr. Kantor made it clear to Mr. Kim that should Pyongyang accept both international inspections with IAEA and mutual inspections with Seoul, Washington is willing to upgrade its contacts with Pyongyang to an ambassadorial or assistant secretary level, which can be held on a regular basis either in Beijing or New York. In the contacts in Beijing, too, the American side has told the North Korean side that as soon as Pyongyang begins mutual inspections, Washington is prepared to improve official relations with Pyongyang by lifting the trade embargo and by taking other constructive steps.

High-level Talks with South Korea

Parallel with the attempts to improve relations with Tokyo and Washington, Pyongyang also carried out high-level talks with Seoul from September 1990 until it concluded the Agreement on Reconciliation, Nonaggression, Exchange and Cooperation, and the Declaration on Denuclearization of the Korean Peninsula in December 1991. From Pyongyang's point of view, these talks were necessary to make substantive progress in its contacts with Tokyo and Washington.

North and South Korea have further agreed on protocols to launch five joint committees on nuclear control, reconciliation, military affairs, economic cooperation, and cultural and social exchange, in addition to the agreement on establishing liaison offices at Panmunjom. All that has been agreed upon, however, are matters of form, with little progress having been made in substance because Seoul has maintained the position that unless Pyongyang accepts mutual and challenge inspections on its nuclear facilities and weapons, if any, it will not provide substantive diplomatic and economic cooperation.

The Nuclear Issue as a Means for Survival and Bargaining

It should be clear that Pyongyang's refusal to have mutual nuclear inspections with Seoul has become the major obstacle to accomplishing its foreign policy goals of normalizing relations with Tokyo, Washington, and Seoul. Pyongyang has been reluctant to disavow the nuclear option in a transparent manner because it has been regarding it as a means for survival and a bargaining card to extract maximum concessions from Tokyo, Washington, and Seoul.

The Nuclear Issue as the Major Obstacle to Pyongyang's Sudpolitik

Suspicions about nuclear weapons development in North Korea, which have been heightened by the North's refusal to accommodate challenge inspections, have become the major obstacle to Pyongyang's *Sudpolitik* aimed at improving relations with Tokyo, Washington, and Seoul. Since the end of May 1992, Pyongyang has allowed IAEA to conduct ad hoc inspections of its "declared" nuclear facilities. In September 1992, it subjected two additional facilities, including one military one, to IAEA inspections. And yet, it has been resisting Seoul's calls for mutual and special inspections of not only civilian, but also military facilities to clear up suspicions about weapon development.

On the need for undertaking transparent mutual and special inspections to verify weapon possibilities, Tokyo, Washington, and Seoul have sustained a coordinated position. The G-7 summit in July 1992 endorsed this idea, and Russia also has supported it. When President Roh Tae-woo raised this issue with President Yang Shangkun in Beijing in September 1992, Yang told Roh that China also wants a nuclear-free Korean peninsula, but he stressed "persuasion, and not pressure" as the most effective way to deal with Pyongyang.[3] By normalizing diplomatic relations with Seoul, Beijing is expecting that Pyongyang can make a prompt settlement on the nuclear issue so that it can normalize relations with Tokyo and Washington as early as possible.

The Nuclear Option as a Means for Survival

There is reason to believe that Pyongyang has regarded the nuclear option in terms of regime survival and national security. Considering the possibility that the gap in the conventional military balance between the North and the South may widen in the 1990s, it is plausible that Pyongyang's strategists resorted to the nuclear option as a cheap means of guaranteeing their regime survival and state secur-

---

3. *Far Eastern Economic Review*, October 8, 1992, p. 10.

ity.[4] This school of thought makes sense, especially when North Korea is deprived of its credible alliance with either Russia or China.

The results of IAEA inspection have confirmed the observation that Pyongyang was building sizable nuclear facilities. They revealed that Pyongyang's contention that it had neither the intention nor the capability for nuclear weapons has been less than candid because Pyongyang did produce a certain amount of plutonium and was in the process of building a 180-meter-long reprocessing facility at Yongbyon. In addition, some reactors were being controlled using graphite instead of heavy water and were therefore unsafe. Despite these revelations, Pyongyang is said to be committed to continuously building these facilities, ostensibly for peaceful purposes.

The Nuclear Option as a Bargaining Card

Pyongyang has been using the nuclear option as a most effective bargaining card in negotiation with Tokyo, Washington, and Seoul. In fact, this card had enabled it to exact maximum concessions from them before 1992, for the U.S. withdrew tactical nuclear weapons from the South, South Korea abandoned any plan for uranium enrichment and reprocessing, and these allies suspended the Team Spirit exercise in 1992 to encourage Pyongyang to tackle the nuclear issue satisfactorily.

Having accomplished this much, Pyongyang seems to be equally bent on pursuing the nuclear option as

---

4. Andrew Mack, "North Korea and the Bomb," *Foreign Policy*, No. 83 (Summer 1991), pp. 90-91.

its final bargaining card for forcing Washington to establish diplomatic relations first, or to guarantee its political survival and security by some other means. As a simple card, this may sound rational; but if Pyongyang tries to overplay it by actually developing nuclear weapons surreptitiously, as did Iraq, it would run the serious risk of inviting international sanctions because a worldwide consensus is now emerging on the importance of nuclear nonproliferation.

North Korea's Dual Approaches and Dilemmas

As North Korea is adopting these dual approaches of trying to normalize relations with Japan, the U.S., and South Korea, and trying to keep the nuclear option and political line at the same time, it is encountering many dilemmas between its unification policy and foreign policy, and between the political and the economic imperatives it is pursuing.

Dual Approaches

Pyongyang's dual approaches are discernible in its efforts to normalize relations with the U.S., Japan, and South Korea without abandoning the nuclear option, and in its signing of the basic accord and other protocols with Seoul while continuing the united-front strategy of undermining the legitimacy of the South Korean regime by all means, including espionage activities. Even when it is advocating reconciliation and nonaggression at the high-level talks, its propaganda attacking the South has not relented.

Most surprising of all in this regard is the recent

discovery, in October 1992, of the spying activity involving about 400 people in the South. In this largest investigation ever made since 1948, some 62 people, including former leaders of the Masses Party, were arrested.[5] What is unusual about this incident is that the group's activities were said to have been directed by Pyongyang at the same time as the high-level talks were producing the basic accord. The duplicity of this story is bound to deepen distrust about the North's intentions.

Factional Struggles or Dual Goals

The question is, how can we interpret this seemingly contradictory attitude? Some observers are advancing the view that it reflects the factional struggles looming between "conservatives" and "reformers"; the former are dominant in the party and the military, and uphold the doctrine of a united front and self-reliance (*Juche*), whereas the latter are more dominant in the foreign and economic ministries, and advocate reforms and open policies. In order for this interpretation to hold up, there must rise a differentiation of these two factions among top leaders, as has happened in China, for example.

A contrary view is that Pyongyang's dual approaches reflect two related goals: the political goals of defending regime survival at home and the economic goals of securing recognition and cooperation abroad. As long as the top leadership remains intact, Pyongyang has no choice but to seek these two simultaneously. It may be that the same people are seeking these two goals at the same time without

---

5. *Korea Herald*, October 7, 1992.

necesarily knowing their contradictory nature, depending on the situation they are experiencing. Until the time when North Korea can formally commit itself to systemic transformation, the regime will have no other choice but to seek such dual goals.

Dilemmas between Unification and Foreign Policy

In pursuing these dual goals, however, North Korea is facing many dilemmas. Nowhere else is this more serious than between Pyongyang's unification policy and its foreign policy. In its unification policy directed at the South, the North is advocating the "one Korea" stand in the name of the "Koryo Confederal Democratic Republic of Korea." But in its foreign policy directed at Japan and the U.S., the North is actually practicing a two-Korea stand by demanding diplomatic normalization, even though these countries have recognized the South and maintained good relations with it.

After the North agreed to put the Basic Accord into force, it reverted to the old line that the principle of non-interference in the other side's domestic affairs does not apply to the unification question. As long as the North Korean regime is being legitimated by resorting to Kim Il-sung's unification policy of building one federal state on his terms, which are coterminous with a communist revolution, it will be difficult for the regime to do away with these political imperatives. Even after it was admitted into the U.N., the North is still arguing at the high-level talks that North and South Korea should join other international organizations under one seat, and that all previous treaties must be revised if they are hampering the cause of national unification!

Can Economic Imperatives Prevail over Political Imperatives in North Korean Foreign Policy?

In conclusion, we want to explore an answer to this question. The duality in North Korean foreign policy goals derives from the very nature of the political system, as analyzed above. This means that Pyongyang's choices are currently motivated by both its political and economic imperatives. In relative terms, politics still takes command in North Korea, in stark contrast to China and Vietnam. Whether political imperatives can prevail over economic ones depends on whether North Korea is able to succeed in opting for the Chinese model of reform and opening, and thereby undergoing a peaceful change. To help North Korea choose this course of action, it is necessary for the U.S., Japan, and South Korea to synchronize their North Korea policy by rewarding the economic imperatives while deterring the political imperatives.

The Chinese Model of Reform and Opening

A successful case where economic imperatives have prevailed over political imperatives is the Chinese model. Ever since Kim Il-sung made a state visit to China in November 1991, there have been some indications that North Korea is cautiously opting for the Chinese model. Among these are the Tumen River development project, the opening of Sunbong and Najin as "free trading zones", and reports on revisions of the constitution and other laws to allow privatization of ownership. At least in foreign policy, Pyongyang is clearly emulating the examples of Beijing's open and pragmatic policy toward the West.

Unlike China, North Korea has yet to adopt reforms in its domestic policy. There is no reform-minded leader like Deng who is saying, in effect, that capitalism is necessary to save socialism in China. Kim Jong-il is stressing that capitalism is imcompatible with socialism. Nor have agricultural reforms appeared in North Korea. Most important of all, the principle of "seeking truth from facts" has to be realized in North Korea before it can truly follow the Chinese example as a way out for survival and development.[6]

A Peaceful and Orderly Change

If the viability of the North Korean system is in doubt as it faces the information revolution and the post-Cold War world, it is in the interests of South Korea and its allies that the North undergo a peaceful and orderly change instead of a violent and messy collapse. A violent breakup of the North Korean system will not only be extremely costly in terms of human and material wellbeing; it may well trigger war, or destabilize the security situation on the Korean peninsula where the interests of China, Russia, Japan, and the U.S. intersect.

Yet we cannot completely rule out other possibilities, for unanticipated events can happen any time. No one is sure, for example, about exactly what will take place after Kim Il-sung passes away from the scene. Hence, South Korea and its allies must be prepared for all contingencies, including some early scenarios of reunification.

---

6. Byung-joon Ahn, "The Possibilities of Change in North Korea," *Korea and World Affairs* 16:3 (Fall 1992), pp. 406-417.

South Korean-American-Japanese Coordination for Economic Incentives and Coercive Diplomacy

To encourage the economic incentives and deter the political imperatives in North Korea, it is necessary that South Korea, the U.S., and Japan closely coordinate their policy and action in coping with the North Korean problem. In so doing, they must combine carrots of economic incentives and sticks of coercive diplomacy with common perspectives on managing peace and reunification.

Managing reunification is the primary responsibility of the two Koreas themselves, but managing peace must involve the surrounding powers.[7] It is incumbent upon South Korea, the U.S., and Japan to take the initiative both in providing economic incentives so that North Korea can choose the economic imperatives, and in applying coercive diplomacy should the North choose, instead, its political imperatives. This is easier said than done. It calls for a truly skillful diplomacy among these countries. Only when they sustain such coordinated diplomacy will Russia and China also render their assistance toward the common goal of ensuring peace and stability in Korea. The newly-elected president of the U.S., Bill Clinton, clearly reaffirmed the American commitment to security and nuclear nonproliferation in Korea when he said: "I hope that someday the Korean people will be reunited in a democratic and free society. I hope that we can continue to be a force for the security of South Korea. And I hope very much that the North

---

7. Byung-joon Ahn, "Managing Korean Reunification," a paper prepared for the 34th IISS conference, Seoul, Korea, September 9-12, 1992.

Koreans will not be successful in developing real nuclear capacity."[8]

Now that China has established diplomatic relations with South Korea and is having more influence over North Korea than any other power, the world's attention is focused on what China will do for the nuclear issue. It is our genuine hope that China will be able to persuade North Korea to abandon the nuclear weapon option for the cause of peace and development in Northeast Asia.

---

8. *International Herald Tribune*, November 13, 1992, p. 13.

CHAPTER 14

CONCLUSION

Richard W. Mansbach and Manwoo Lee

The wide-ranging essays in this volume have touched upon a variety of topics, from North Korean political intransigence to economic relations in a world marked by concern over relative gains. The authors themselves have at times taken different paths to different conclusions, while maintaining a strong sense of scholarship and reason. Although no firm conclusions were reached by the contributors, several critical themes have emerged. The world has changed dramatically and permanently and, with it, so has Northeast Asia. Above all, the specter of nuclear war no longer casts a shadow over political and economic relations in Asia. This alone is a cause for relief. The prospects of a military confrontation in Asia between the major powers are probably lower now than at any time in the last one hundred years, with China, Japan, and Russia closer to solving their long-term conflicts than ever before.

The authors remind us that the U.S. remains the pivotal actor in Northeast Asia, both as a stabilizing

military influence and also as a major economic partner. The U.S. has the potential either to encourage or
inhibit discourse in Northeast Asia. By remaining
committed to the region and to the principle of open
markets and free trade, the U.S. can help to stem the
proliferation of disputes over trade and technology.
By retaining credible military force in the region, the
U.S. may help to calm worried allies and to constrain
nervous antagonists. Nevertheless, even as a new
administration takes over in the White House, the
U.S. faces the old dilemma between isolationism and
internationalism. Although the pattern of the 1930s
is unlikely to be repeated again, the possibility of a
full-scale U.S. military withdrawal combined with the
erection of trade barriers could be shocks that would
topple the fragile détente that is emerging in Northeast Asia.

The authors have also focused on the role that an
emerging Japan can play. In particular, they have
reached something of a consensus that, although
Japan is not to be treated lightly, the current concern over rearmament and expansionism is much
exaggerated. Japan's role, particularly within the
economic sphere, is subject to much debate. Some of
the contributors argue that Japan is the engine in a
regional bloc that will propel Northeast Asian
economies into the 21st century. Others argue that
Japan is merely exploiting and abusing its Asian
neighbors by keeping trade barriers high and the
level of technology transfer low. Although no consensual prediction or interpretation was reached here,
there is consensus about the importance of the
issues to the future of the region.

The North Korean regime is widely regarded as an
anachronism in Northeast Asian politics. Had it not

been for the commotion about nuclear weapons—
generally more smoke than fire—North Korea would
have become increasingly irrelevant to Northeast
Asian politics. Aside from the nuclear issue (and
the tension created by North Korea's decision to
withdraw from the Nuclear Nonproliferation Treaty),
the principal concern about North Korea now is how
and when the South should press for unification.
The threat of a war on the peninsula remains low by
historical standards. As the North looks to Japan
and the U.S. for an expansion of diplomatic and economic contacts, it continues to hope that it can survive for an extended period into the future.

The roles of China and Russia remain unclear at
this time. Although China seems to have made a
credible commitment to introducing and sustaining a
market-oriented economic approach, politically the
regime remains highly authoritarian. Russia, on the
other hand, has introduced far-reaching economic
and political reforms. Both of these countries, traditional Great Powers, are experiencing a transitory
loss of confidence and capability. Just as surely,
however, they will be important players in Asia in the
coming years. Both China and Russia could play a
positive role by resolving their differences and opening trade and communications with each other and
other nations. Or, after a brief interregnum, they
could again become locked in a cycle of suspicion
and conflict. The overall sense of the contributors to
this volume is that both China and Russia are
strongly in step with the idea of a new, peaceful
Northeast Asian order.

Thus we finish this book as we began: with few
answers and many questions. The lack of consensus
is not entirely to be regretted. Indeed, it mirrors the

complexity of contemporary global politics and the issues that are coming to dominate the global agenda. Only now are scholars beginning to address some of these issues without the shadow of the Cold War. The essays in this volume are among the first to shed light on the place of Northeast Asia in the new world order, and they clarify the key issues that the region will face and the alternatives available to the players in the regional game.

Contributors

Manwoo Lee is Professor of Political Science at Millersville University of Pennsylvania and is currently the Director of the Institute for Far Eastern Studies, Kyungnam University, Seoul. He is widely known for his recent books, *The Odyssey of Korean Democracy: Korean Politics 1987-1990; Alliance Under Tension: The Evolution of South Korean-U.S. Relations*, co-authored with Ronald D. McLaurin and Chung-in Moon, and *Current Issues in Korea-U.S. Relations: Korean-American Dialogue*.

Richard W. Mansbach is Chairman of the Department of Political Science, Iowa State University. He is well known for two books, co-authored with Yale Ferguson: *The State: Conceptual Chaos and the Future of International Relations*, and *The Elusive Quest: Theory and International Politics*. His numerous books and articles focus on international relations and global systems.

Charles F. Doran is the Andrew W. Mellon Professor of International Relations at the Paul H. Nitze School of Advanced International Studies (SAIS), The Johns Hopkins University in Washington D.C. He is also Director of International Relations and Director of the Center of Canadian Studies at SAIS. His recent book (1991), *Systems in Crisis: New Imperatives of*

High Politics at Century's End, deals with the theory and policy implications of systems transformations.

Yung-hwan Jo is Professor Emeritus in the Department of Political Science at Arizona State University, and is currently visiting professor at Yonsei University Graduate School of International Relations, in Seoul. He is widely known as a specialist in Northeast Asian relations, particularly China, Japan and Russia.

Young-Kwan Yoon is Assistant Professor in the Department of International Relations at Seoul National University, Seoul. He has published several articles on International and Korean political eco-nomies. His specialty is in Asian political economic cooperation.

Melvin Gurtov is Director of the International Studies Program at Portland State University. He is well known for his numerous articles on China, Southeast Asia, and U.S. Foreign Policy published in *Asian Survey, China Quarterly,* and *Current History,* and for his book, *Global Politics in the Human Interest.*

Georgi A. Arbatov has served as Director of Moscow's Institute of the USA and Canada since 1967. He has published several articles on international relations and economic problems and has specialized in U.S.-Russia relations.

Parris Chang is Professor of Political Science and Director of the Center for East Asian Studies at Pennsylvania State University. His work on China has appeared in books, scholarly journals, magazines and newspapers. The third edition of his well-known book, *Power and Policy in China,* appeared in 1990.

Hideshi Takesada is Professor and Head of the research department of the Asia-Pacific Region of the National Institute for Defense Studies in Tokyo. He is the co-author of *International Relations in the Cold War Era* (1987). His current research is on Asian security, Japan-Korea relations, and Japan's defense policy. His new book, *North Korea and the Super Powers,* is forthcoming.

Masao Okonogi is Professor of Political Science, Keio University, Tokyo. He is widely known for his studies on North Korea and international relations in Northeast Asia. His most recent publication is a three volume series, co-authored with Kamia Fuji, entitled, *The Postwar Documents on Korean Affairs.*

Hosup Kim is Assistant Professor, Department of International Relations at Chung-Ang University. He has written articles on Japan-Korea relations, with particular emphasis on foreign policy in the two countries.

Jae Jean Suh has a Ph.D. in sociology. Currently, he is the Director of the North Korean Studies Division, The Research Institute for National Reunification, in Seoul. His recent research focuses on personality and social change in North Korea, and political regimes and development strategy in North Korea.

Byung-joon Ahn is Professor of Political Science and International Relations at Yonsei University in Seoul. He is widely known for his 1976 book, *Chinese Politics and the Cultural Revolution.*